1993

SOCIAL SECURITY AND MEDICARE

A POLICY PRIMER

Eric R. Kingson and Edward D. Berkowitz

Foreword by Arthur S. Flemming

AUBURN HOUSE
Westport, Connecticut · London

Library of Congress Cataloging-in-Publication Data

Kingson, Eric R.
    Social security and medicare : a policy primer / Eric R. Kingson
and Edward D. Berkowitz.
        p.   cm.
    Includes index.
    ISBN 0-86569-200-9. — ISBN 0-86569-201-7 (pbk. : alk. paper)
    1. Social security—United States.   2. Medicare.   I. Berkowitz,
Edward D.   II. Title.
    HD7125.K535   1993
    368.4'3'00973—dc20   92-43384

British Library Cataloguing in Publication Data is available.

Library of Congress Catalog Card Number: 92-43384
ISBN: 0-86569-200-9
ISBN: 0-86569-201-7 (pbk.)

First published in 1993

Auburn House, 88 Post Road West, Westport, CT 06881
An imprint of Greenwood Publishing Group, Inc.

Printed in the United States of America

The paper used in this book complies with the
Permanent Paper Standard issued by the National
Information Standards Organization (Z39.48-1984).

10 9 8 7 6 5 4 3 2 1

For Nelson Cruikshank (1902–1986) who gave labor its
voice in Social Security affairs and worked tirelessly to
improve the system. He was a gentle man with a
wonderful sense of humor, who nonetheless fought
fiercely for a better Social Security program. It was he,
more than any other single individual, who encouraged
labor leaders to overcome their traditional fear of federal
social welfare programs and it was he, more than any
other single individual, who spoke on behalf of organized
labor in Social Security policymaking councils. He did his
job exceptionally well: with humor and grace and
eloquence and perseverance. We salute his efforts, and we
commend him as a model in the art of effective political
persuasion. We would like to think that this book builds
on the traditions that Nelson Cruikshank
helped to establish.

Contents

Foreword

Social Security and Medicare is a book that the nation needs. The two authors have provided us with both a genuine "policy primer" and a "call to action."

Social insurance, the authors remind us, is a part of a package of legislation that was passed over sixty years ago under the umbrella title of "Social Security." Today this legislation stands out, according to Senator Bradley of New Jersey, as "the nation's best expression of community." We have a tremendous stake in its future.

If we are one of the 41 million citizens who receive Social Security and Medicare benefits and we want to check up at anytime on the benefits we should be receiving, we will want to use this book in order to refresh our memories on the essential facts.

But this is not just a primer of facts. It is a policy primer—a fact that will be deeply appreciated by professionals and policymakers, as well as the average citizen. A reading of the entire book will make the reader understand that, as the authors put it, "myths and misinformation are the Achilles heel of Social Security and Medicare." They are right in alleging that an "open political dialogue through which policymakers and experts help explicate choices and their implications" is essential.

This book contains valuable information as to how and when Social Security and Medicare came into existence and how they have grown over the years.

There is a clear pointing up of the issues that now confront the two systems and that will confront them in the future. There also is a frank discussion of the proposed solutions to these issues, and the arguments that have been advanced for and against them. Running throughout these discussions is a clear pointing up of the conflicts in values that these issues and proposed solutions often present. For example, the authors spend a great deal of time in making a critical analysis of the manner in which the nation has sought to deal with persons with disabilities.

The authors have certainly made their contribution to an "open political discussion" of the strengths and weaknesses of the two systems. They also have made it possible for the average citizen to participate in and influence the policy choices that will be made in the future. They have demonstrated that these policy choices do not have to be made solely by "experts" and a comparatively few "policymakers," important as they are in the decision-making process.

An informed public—informed by experts and policymakers—is certainly preferable to a public choosing up sides on the basis of myths and misinformation. Decisions made in this manner will be decisions that will adversely affect the lives of the 41 million persons who are receiving benefits and the 132 million who are making payroll contributions so that they can receive benefits in the future. A public informed by *Social Security and Medicare* will not be satisfied with the status quo but will insist on actions designed to improve the two systems.

Finally, the authors put Social Security in the setting that brought the system into existence in order to confront the "hazards and vicissitudes" of life because of inadequate income.

The Committee on Economic Security, established by President Roosevelt under Francis Perkins as chairman, argued that the only way to serve the nation as a whole is through a combination of a jobs program, unemployment insurance, social insurance, welfare, health and social services measures. That was right then as the nation confronted the worst depression in history. It is right now as we confront a serious recession and millions of persons who face an untimely death and unnecessary suffering.

As the authors of this outstanding book conclude: "Ultimately only by thinking of the national community as a whole can the vision of Social Security be realized." We must remember that the vision called for a package of programs all under the name of Social Security and all dependent on one another to ultimately lift our nation out of poverty. The authors of *Social Security and Medicare* have made a very effective contribution to the attainment of this goal by emphasizing the nation's dependency on these two programs.

Arthur S. Flemming
Secretary, Department of Health, Education and Welfare (1958–61)
Chair, U.S. Civil Rights Commission (1974–82)
Chair, Save Our Security Coalition (1981–   )

Acknowledgments

In the course of writing this book we have incurred numerous debts—to scholars and other experts who have shaped our understanding of social insurance, to those kind enough to critique various aspects of this book, to institutions and organizations who have supported our collaboration, and to family and friends who have understood our frustrations and shared the joy of completing this task. We are appreciative of all these contributions.

We would also like to mention the special contributions of a few people and organizations. Robert J. Myers, chief actuary of the Social Security Administration (SSA) from 1947 to 1970, later deputy commissioner of SSA from 1981 to 1982 and then executive director of the 1982–83 National Commission on Social Security Reform, gave generously of his time to comment carefully on each chapter. John Harney, acquisitions editor for Auburn House, also provided insightful comments and encouragement. Roberta Feinstein Havel, executive director of the Save Our Security Coalition, and Maria Steele, district manager of the Social Security office in Framingham, Massachusetts, commented on portions of the manuscript. Laurel Beedon, senior policy analyst of the American Association of Retired Persons' Public Policy Institute, Kurt Czarnowski, regional public affairs officer, Social Security Administration, Boston Region, Stephen Goss, supervisory actuary for SSA's Office of the Actuary, and Regina O'Grady-LeShane, assistant professor at the Boston College Graduate School of Social Work made themselves available for our inquiries. Together, their critiques and suggestions greatly strengthened this book. The shortcomings, we hasten to add in more than a pro forma manner, are very much our own.

We would be remiss if we did not express our appreciation to the Save Our Security Education Fund, which sponsored the Nelson Cruikshank Social Insurance Study Project and the many organizations and individuals who contributed to its success. The collaboration resulting in our book grew out of this earlier project which was designed to strengthen understanding of social insurance at the secondary education level and led to the publication in 1989 of *Social Security in the USA: A Guide to Social Security with Discussion Plans* by Eric Kingson, Edward Berkowitz, and Fran Pratt. Fran Pratt, director of special projects for the Center for Understanding Aging, developed lesson plans on social insurance for use by high school teachers and later helped to coordinate a series of training sessions throughout the United States for secondary education teachers. Roberta Feinstein Havel played an important role in facilitating this project. The project's National Advisory Committee was chaired by Arthur S. Flemming, Secretary of the Department of Health, Education, and Welfare from 1958 to 1961, chair of the United States Civil Rights Commission from 1974 to 1982, and chair of the Save Our Security Coalition and Education Fund since 1981. Dr. Flemming remains a source of inspiration—a passionate advocate for Social Security and a thoughtful, caring man. Although this new work departs substantially from the previous one in approach, content, and level of analysis, we have, with the permission of the Save our Security Education Fund, drawn passages from *Social Security in the USA.*

We also wish to acknowledge the institutional support of Boston College and George Washington University. The Boston College Graduate School of Social Work provided a special sabbatical leave to Eric Kingson, secretarial support and access to faculty computer facilities, which hastened the writing of this book. Edward Berkowitz received more than the usual level of help and support from William H. Becker, who served as department chairman and helped to make the George Washington History Department a wonderful place to work.

And finally, and most importantly, we thank our wives, Emily Frank and Joan Fernbach Kingson, for their humor, patience, and perspective, and we mention our children, Rebecca Alice Berkowitz, age 5, Sarah Elizabeth Berkowitz, age 8, Aaron Michael Fernbach Kingson, age 11, and Johanna Elise Fernbach Kingson, age 8. This book is about the world we have made for them, a world soon to be theirs.

Social Security and Medicare as Policy Problems— Recurrent Themes

Social Security reaches so many people and costs so much money that, as Senator Robert Dole once said, it overwhelms all other domestic priorities. Few people deny its importance. Henry Aaron, the Brookings economist, has called Social Security the most important social program of the century. Bill Bradley (D-NJ), the Senate's former basketball star, considers the program to be the nation's best expression of community.

A RATIONALE FOR THE INQUIRY

Social Security and Medicare may be important, but as subjects of inquiry many people regard them as dry and dull. Although most people want Social Security and Medicare to be there for them when they reach retirement age, few people want to know the details of how these programs operate. Despite the existence of a grand political debate on the subject of Social Security and Medicare, few of the participants want to take the time to gather facts about the program for fear of stumbling over its complexity. Even Robert Ball, the former Commissioner of Social Security who has done as much to rally support for the programs as anyone, expresses concern that, although political support for Social Security and Medicare remains strong, the public's understanding is thin.

Maybe it does not matter. Perhaps our Social Security program should function with the efficiency and anonymity of a Swiss bank. Just as we do not need to know all of the details of the loans made by the bank, so we might not need to follow all of the rules that govern Social Security and Medicare. In both cases, results matter far more than does our understanding of the methods used to obtain them.

We think it does matter. To be sure, not every citizen needs to be an expert in actuarial science or demography. At the same time, we believe that everyone should have a sense of the choices involved in Social Security, Medicare, and related policy. As the baby boom generation ages and as the economy fluctuates, these choices will come to have a prominent place on America's public agenda. Indeed, as we have implied, people have already started to argue about Social Security, often with only the vaguest idea of how the program operates. Beyond these societal concerns, the details of program operation have very personal implications that make it imperative for all of us to know what we can expect from Social Security and Medicare.

It does not help either public discourse or private decisions that misunderstandings about these programs abound. Medicare, a program of health insurance for people on Social Security, could serve as an example. Because the contents of Medicare are murky to so many people, a spell of illness often leads to a mystifying trail of bills and financial statements for which many people are unprepared. Nor are the limits of Medicare and how it differs from Medicaid clearly understood. Often as the painful decision is made to enter a nursing home, elders and their families are not aware until it is too late that Medicare does not provide significant long-term care protection. Prudence demands prior knowledge of how the program works.

Not just Medicare, but Social Security, too, lies shrouded in myths. Gaps in the common knowledge about Social Security include the fact that some people must pay income tax on their Social Security benefits. Many young people are dismayed to discover that Social Security payroll tax contributions do not go into accounts earmarked for them. Often liberal and conservative critics of the program ignore the fact that, as the Census Bureau reports, Social Security, by itself, does more to reduce poverty and income inequality than either the American tax system or welfare programs.[1]

Just who benefits from the program remains a mystery to many Americans. Not everyone, after all, receives the same return on his Social Security investment. A hypothetical "winner" might be someone with a low income who is married and has young children under his or her care and then, after working for a number of years, suddenly finds himself disabled, unable to work. This winner will receive far more in Social Security payments than he or she paid in Social Security taxes. A hypothetical "loser" might be a wealthy single person, in good health, who delays retirement beyond 65 and elects voluntary "supplementary" insurance from Medicare and then dies shortly after retirement without ever entering the hospital or visiting the doctor.

These outcomes do not occur by chance. As with other forms of insurance, the purpose of the program is to protect against identifiable risks, not to provide equivalent benefits to everyone regardless, for example, of whether they become disabled. Thus, the program provides more help to the first person than the second by conscious design. It makes good sense from a policy point of view for the program to help some people more than others. At the same time, society needs constantly to monitor Congress as it makes decisions about winners and losers and to guard against bias toward a race, region, age group, or some other category defined more by politics than by objective need.

We want the program to rise above politics, yet we realize that goal is impossible. Winning and losing constitute the very essence of politics and guarantee that Social Security, however much we would like it to function like a Swiss bank account, will always be a highly political program. The trick of effective public policy lies in blending scientific, impartial program administration and the imperatives of political management. Within broad boundaries, we want the right people to get benefits, and we want to keep our political options open, so that we, as citizens, get to choose our Social Security and Medicare programs.

Admitting that Social Security and Medicare are inherently political scares many people, fearful that shifts in public opinion and the nation's politics might trigger undesirable policy changes. A group of liberal defenders of Social Security has argued that politics as practiced in this country leads some conservatives to characterize Social Security as a program in crisis, mainly as a strategy to undermine the program. As they note, "If long continued, a sense of crisis in and around Social Security could undermine public confidence and political support. And that truly would be a disaster."[2] Given large federal deficits, some are concerned that the temptation to scapegoat the old (and the disabled) and to cut back on expenditures earmarked for Social Security and Medicare will be very great. Others worry that as Social Security accumulates large reserves during the next decade, Congress will be unable to avoid the political temptation to raise benefits.

Yet another view, and one held by some conservatives, is that a different type of politics is threatening Social Security and Medicare. Insiders, it is argued, have restricted the flow of information about the program and obscured the nature of the choices that needed to be made. Without the proper information and because it was easy to expand the program in the beginning, politicians have not always acted in society's interest. They have overexpanded the program and promised more to future generations than the program can reasonably deliver. Hence, they argue, there is a crisis in the program that demands redress, but whether Congress, the very agent that engineered the crisis, can reform the program remains in doubt.

As this discussion has implied, Social Security is a topic for lively political debate that belies its reputation as dull. The potential for conflict and misunderstanding exists in abundance. If, for example, everyone gets benefits under Social Security, then it is inevitable that some people who do not need the benefits will nonetheless receive them. It does not mean, however, that Social Security benefits are simply "middle class entitlements," which are poorly targeted to persons in greatest need, as some on both the right and the left argue. Giving something to everyone may be the best way to underwrite the political stability of the system and assure that the poor get something; it may also be seen as wasteful. The political system must somehow decide this matter by striking a balance between contributions and benefits. To cite another example, if African Americans live shorter lives than white Americans, then, arguably, Social Security is discriminating. Yet most people would concede that the matter is more complicated than that. If blacks are poorer than whites or more likely to receive disability benefits—as they are—then the program also rewards African Americans more than white Americans. Here again complicated judgments need to be made. Debate requires that all people be informed. In fact, limited public understanding is the Achilles' heel of sound social policy. It potentially undermines public discourse about the future of Social Security and Medicare, allowing myths and half-truths to substitute for fact and reasoned discussion. It tends to polarize debate between those who argue that Social Security and Medicare are inequitable and unsustainable and proponents who are often positioned to defend all aspects of these programs—thereby allowing flaws to remain uncorrected.

That suggests a need to augment public understanding of Social Security and Medicare, but this need must be interpreted in a cautious manner. Knowledge always contends with power on unequal terms. Knowledge, even knowledge that is in some sense "correct," will not by itself liberate the debate from its present debilitating structure. At best, it might improve the terms of the debate. And we are mindful that explaining Social Security and Medicare in ways that enhance public discussion represents a formidable challenge.

Many, many others have preceded us. As early as 1948, for example, a book of readings appeared that set down the basic principles of Social Security and provided balanced information on the leading issues in the field.[3] A second generation of effort led in 1978 to the publication of *Social Security: Today and Tomorrow*.[4] Written by Robert Ball, one of the grand masters of Social Security and Medicare, the book featured a reasoned dialogue between a hypothetical member of the public and Ball, in which the details of the programs were explained and the fears of the public about the programs' future were addressed. Together with Robert Myers' tract on program features, it provided a plethora of information about the program.[5] Conservatives followed with salvos about Social Security as a "fraud" in your future. The literature, begun as an informational aid, had gradually taken on an acrimonious tone.

Nor did that exhaust the literature. It also contained specialized academic monographs, the most influential being Martha Derthick's analysis of Social Security policymaking, and nuts-and-bolts guides to program benefits.[6] The former were often impenetrable to non-specialists and the latter dull and impossible to read as anything other than reference books.[7]

This book, then, builds on what has preceded it. We will strive to keep it accessible, informative, and interesting in the hope that college students, graduate students, policymakers, and the general public will read it and use it as a means of gaining a sound basis for assessing choices about future directions.

Before we can get into the substance of Social Security and Medicare, we need a framework from which to understand and judge them. Since Social Security and Medicare are forms of social insurance, we explain the concept of social insurance, delineate the issues to which it gives rise, and then consider the general themes that dominate policy discussions.

SOCIAL INSURANCE IN BRIEF

In the simplest sense, social insurance programs function as insurance programs that provide money should a particular problem (sickness) or condition (old age) arise. Hence, one can speak of social insurance as a contingency payment against the financial or medical risks associated with the realities of modern life. At the same time, social insurance programs operate as social benefit systems in which the government transfers money from one group, the working able-bodied, for example, to another, such as the retired. Social insurance, in other words, has some of the features of a public assistance program (often called "welfare"). It is neither exactly like private insurance, which operates on the principle that a person is getting either a monetary return or a service in direct proportion to his investment or fee, or welfare, which operates on the notion that the government should tax those with income or property to support the poor.

We believe that a real need exists for social insurance, even though social insurance programs, by their very nature, attract political opposition. We can bring little scientific evidence to support our belief. We simply posit that a certain amount of security does not fatally undermine liberty and individual initiative and may augment them. Social Security and Medicare represent the major forms of social insurance in America and, in our opinion, they form two of America's most necessary and most effective social programs.

Not everyone agrees. Hybrids of the social insurance type face opposition from right-wing purists who favor private control over the economy and want the government off the people's backs. And they are criticized by left-wing purists who want bold programs of income redistribution. Program defenders must argue for the programs on pragmatic grounds as successful mixtures of public responsibility and private initiative, or in effect, as the best that we can get out of a system in which proponents of public and private approaches to Social Security continually tug at one another.

Whether good or bad, social insurance, with its contrary characteristics, is difficult to explain. Here is where social commentators have most failed their public by not making an effort to describe the program in terms that all of us can understand. If one realizes the program's hybrid nature, its practices become easier to comprehend.

THE HISTORY IN BRIEF

As government programs, Social Security and Medicare exist at the whim of Congress, which could abolish them in an instant (if its members were willing to suffer the political consequences). As public trusts, Social Security and Medicare are the constant objects of future planning. Hence, program officials attempt to estimate future costs and to indicate ways of meeting those costs. As government programs, Social Security and Medicare benefits reflect the perceived wisdom of Congress, which is capable of legislating windfalls to groups whose political favors it seeks or of expanding protections for those at greatest risk. At the same time, as insurance programs, Social Security and Medicare strive to provide basic protections for all contributors.

Multiple objectives have led to compromises. These compromises, masked by program jargon, have never been well understood, nor have the reasons for making the compromises been well explained. By exposing these compromises and explaining them in their original contexts, we can assess first whether these compromises ever operated in society's interest and, second, if they still do.

Such an exercise requires an appreciation of the history of our social insurance programs. We cannot talk about social insurance programs in general; we must instead concentrate on the ones that we really have, ones that have developed their own traditions as a result of specific historical experiences. This book uses history as a major means of analyzing Social Security and Medicare. We need only highlight some major historical developments here.

Thirty years separated the enactment of Social Security and Medicare, and in a sense one paved the way for the other. The Social Security Act of 1935 established a program in which the federal government taxed employers and employees and promised in return to pay benefits to workers when they retired. The chosen device was something known as a payroll tax. For each worker in an industrial or commercial workplace, the government required that one percent of the worker's paycheck be withheld and sent to Washington. Before sending the worker's contribution to the federal government, the employers had to contribute an equal amount of money.

At base, then, Social Security, as this program came to be called, consisted of two sets of rules. One set governed the payroll taxes, and the other set described the benefits to which workers were entitled. Both the level of taxes and the amount and types of benefits changed over the years. In 1965, legislators raised the tax level and established a major new type of benefit. By adding hospital insurance to the array of Social Security benefits, they launched Medicare.

On the route between the Social Security Act of 1935 and the Social Security Amendments of 1965, the program passed three important milestones. The first occurred in 1939. Without raising the tax rates, Congress decided to expand the list of benefits.[8] In addition to the original retirement benefits for workers over 65, the new benefits included payments to the wives and children of retired workers and to the widows and children of workers who died before age 65. After 1939, therefore, Social Security included benefits to a worker's survivors. The second milestone occurred in 1950 when

Congress decided to raise the tax rate, and, updating benefit levels for price changes in the 1940s, to increase substantially the level of payments to retired workers and the survivors of workers.[9] The third and final milestone came in 1956 when Congress added disability coverage to the program. Workers who retired before age 65 because of an impairment that prevented them from working could now receive benefits. After 1956, therefore, Social Security came to be known as Old-Age, Survivors, and Disability Insurance.

With the enactment of Medicare in 1965, the contours of the modern program came into view. Subsequent developments involved changes in the benefit rules, usually to expand the range of the benefits or to protect beneficiaries against inflation. Importantly, Congress enacted legislation in 1972 establishing automatic cost-of-living adjustments ("COLAs"), designed to maintain the purchasing power of benefits, once received, for the rest of a beneficiary's life. Subsequent events also included adjustments to the tax rules so as to keep the Social Security and Medicare systems solvent. In 1977, for example, Congress raised the scheduled tax rate for 1979 from 12.1 percent of employers' payrolls to 12.26 percent of employers' payrolls—a seemingly small change that nonetheless involved millions of dollars.

SOCIAL SECURITY AND MEDICARE IN BRIEF

That fact brings us to the modern Social Security and Medicare programs. A few facts about who benefits and who pays for the programs highlight their pervasiveness. Social Security—that is, the Old-Age, Survivors, and Disability Insurance program—is by far the largest American social insurance program, with the greatest impact on individuals and families. In 1992, for example, 132 million American workers and their employers paid Social Security taxes and about 41 million Americans received Social Security benefits each month.

We think of Social Security beneficiaries as elderly individuals, and 33 million of them did fit this description in 1992. Because the program is so large and pays so many different types of benefits, that still leaves room for 3.2 million disabled workers and their spouses, 2.6 million children under 18, 620,000 people over 18 who have been disabled since childhood, about 300,000 young widows or widowers caring for young children, and another 120,000 persons aged 18 to 19 who fall into a special surviving elementary or secondary school student's category.

We know that Social Security costs a lot, and the numbers confirm this impression. In 1992, the program's revenues came to $341 billion and its expenditures reached $287 billion. Most of this money went for the payment of actual benefits, but about $2 billion was used to administer the program.

As for Medicare, it provided health insurance to 35 million beneficiaries in 1993. About 31.5 million of these people were elderly, and 3.5 million people were younger individuals with long-term disabilities or permanent kidney failure. The program, for reasons related to its political history, actually contains two separate types of coverage. Hospital insurance helps pay for hospital stays, and Supplementary Medical Insurance helps pay for inpatient and outpatient doctor and other medical services. Together, anticipated spending for these programs for 1993 is $146 billion.

ENDURING THEMES

These large, expensive, and complicated programs touch the lives of every American. No other programs provide more extensive protection, and no other federal domestic programs cost more. In the development of these programs, certain themes have endured as persistent policy issues and driven the political discussion. In particular, four general themes or issues illustrate the choices implicit in Social Security and Medicare.

The first issue concerns whether the benefits offered by the programs match contemporary perceptions of social need. Are the programs promising too much for the elderly, the disabled, and their dependents or too little? We use the shorthand label of "adequacy" for this theme.

The perception of Social Security's and Medicare's adequacy has varied over time. It has depended on the accepted limits to the government's behavior, on economic change, on other government benefits available, on the availability and generosity of private benefits, and on whether people regarded something like a stay in a hospital as desirable. To illustrate, the provision of retirement pensions by the federal government was highly controversial in the 1930s but much less so in the 1950s. As living standards improved, more Americans expected to retire, and retirement became widely perceived as a period of earned leisure. State welfare programs for the elderly provided real competition to the Social Security program in the 1930s and 1940s but declined as a threat to Social Security in the 1950s. Medical care became increasingly desirable as a good to consume in the 1940s and 1950s, and the supply of private health insurance increased exponentially in these decades.

Even as the range of benefits has broadened, the program still contains what some see as gaps and others regard as areas in which private and state programs need to be strengthened. Either way, most people agree that long-term care represents a contingency for which most are psychologically and financially unprepared. Some suggest that the list of Medicare benefits should be expanded to include payments for nursing homes and other long-term care services.

As the programs have matured, financing dilemmas have heightened. The second persistent theme or issue, therefore, concerns the financing of the programs. Do the programs have enough money to honor their promises? If Social Security has too much, should we spend the surplus or maintain it as an indirect mechanism for increasing national savings? If it does not have enough, how should we raise the money to finance the shortfall? We use the term "financing" as the shorthand label for this theme.

Financing dilemmas follow from the fact that social insurance programs are easier to begin than to sustain and are sensitive to economic downturns. At first, the money comes flowing in, and because none of the retired population is covered, little of the money goes flowing out. As a general rule of political behavior, early surpluses tend to get spent (in part because social needs are greatest as such programs begin), and taxes tend to remain low. The result is that mature social insurance programs have greater tendencies toward financial instability, in part because of anticipated outflows of revenues, but also because their short-term financing is increasingly dependent on the economy. Our programs escaped this problem for a long time because of unexpected growth in the number of people working and unexpected increases in wage rates, combined with relatively prudent expansions in the benefit levels and careful monitoring of the programs' financing.

In retrospect, this outcome is not surprising. We began Social Security in the middle of the Great Depression, when people were pessimistic about raising wage and birth rates. The economic emergency put a premium on short-range payments to people who were already old and unemployed. With the emphasis on short-range payments, little support emerged for social insurance, which depended on contributions from a labor force that was badly depleted by the depression. These social forces reduced the immediate pressures for benefit expansion in the social insurance programs. Then, the Second World War and the baby boom came along, expanded the labor force covered by Social Security, and reduced the percentage of the elderly in the population below the level that had been expected in the 1930s. In time, however, the sustained prosperity and period of fertility came to an end. Health care costs rose and the aging of the United States' population advanced. Thus, the programs have had to face threats to their solvency, and financing has gradually emerged as a major continuing theme of Social Security and Medicare policy.

This question has special relevance to the future. In the long-term we anticipate rising costs because of the aging of the population and because of growing expenditures on health care. The retirement of the baby boom generation presents particular problems. Some experts suggest that the system as structured cannot support the expense of paying retirement and health care benefits to the baby boomers. Others express confidence in the ability of Social Security and Medicare to solve future problems as they arise, based in large part on their history of meeting past crises. Indeed, the current controversies surrounding the financing of the programs involve a surplus in revenues, not a shortfall. At the same time, the problems in Medicare are more immediate and pressing. Most people agree that changes will be needed in this program within the next few years. For some, these changes invite the creation of national health insurance; for others, these changes are viewed as a political opportunity to cut back on the program.

Two financing proposals have enjoyed enduring appeal. One involves the introduction of general revenues. Instead of funding Social Security pensions from money raised by payroll taxes alone, this proposal would allow Congress to supplement the pensions with ordinary funds that come primarily from income taxes and government borrowing. Congress has, for the most part, resisted this suggestion, fearing that the use of general revenues would be hard to control and would lead to benefit increases that would be difficult to sustain. Even so, many indirect infusions of general revenues are made into the program, including the revenue produced from treating a portion of Social Security benefits as taxable income. The second proposal would put Social Security financing on a pay-as-you-go basis. In this approach, Congress collects, through payroll taxes or some other means, only the amount of money necessary to sustain the program on a current basis. This approach, however, has the benefit of keeping taxes low, avoiding the difficult problem of how to preserve the supposed surpluses in the program. This approach has the disadvantage of leaving the future to take care of itself, arguably bequeathing large burdens to future generations.

Supporters of these proposals often divide along the question of whether or not they wish to expand the program. Those, in the past, who generally favored expanding protections have traditionally favored general revenue financing, though given today's large federal deficits, few would currently advocate such a course. Conservatives such as representatives of the Chamber of Commerce in the 1950s and Daniel Patrick Moynihan in the 1990s, have tended to favor pay-as-you-go financing. In each case, the arguments have become very complex and often very cryptic, involving many hidden assumptions about the nature of our political system.

Questions about benefit levels and tax rates imply a third persistent issue or theme to which we attach the label "fairness." Even if we can agree on which benefits the program should provide and on how to finance them, that still does not mean that everyone pays his or her fair share and receives a fair amount. Instead, we need to fashion a relationship between an individual's contributions and an individual's anticipated benefits that will sustain the program financially and politically. What should be the terms of this relationship?

Some people believe that benefits should directly reflect contributions. They tend to favor quasi-private investment opportunities, such as Individual Retirement Accounts, over expansions of Social Security. Others consider it unfair that Social Security and Medicare benefits go to the rich. They view the relatively low living standards of many aged and disabled persons as manifestations of the program's lack of fairness. Yet others consider it unfair that lower-income beneficiaries receive proportionately larger benefits. Still others see problems with the fact that housewives receive no credit for the work they perform or the fact that some generations bear greater tax burdens than others.

A fourth persistent theme or issue involves the links between Social Security policy and other policy goals. Because the Social Security and Medicare programs are so large, they exercise powerful effects on many areas of policy. Examples include the labor force participation rates of disabled and elderly people, the price of medical care, and the effectiveness of fiscal policy (the use of tax rates) to protect the economy against inflation and unemployment. At times, policy measures that are in the best interest of the Social Security and Medicare programs conflict with other policy goals. How should we handle such conflicts? Our label for this question is "complexity."

Many feel that the program should work more effectively toward the participation of the elderly and the disabled in the labor force, rather than encouraging their withdrawal from work and from other social activities. Rehabilitation has therefore become a continuing public concern. Some people, including one of the present authors, have questioned public policies that, on the one hand, protect the civil rights of disabled people and guard against discrimination in the workplace, and, on the other, make withdrawal from the labor force an express condition of public aid. In this regard, the definition of disability as the "inability to engage in substantial gainful activity" has come into question.

Other people have raised questions about the double standards in public policy. Mothers of young children on welfare are encouraged, even required, to go to work; mothers of young children on Social Security are encouraged to remain out of the labor force. Without a doubt, Social Security, often working in concert with private pension incentives, has facilitated the trend toward early retirement among many who are able to work. Yet there are many other early retirees whose health and labor market circumstances greatly restrict the ability to find work. Whether the early retirement of able persons meshes well with changing demographic and labor force conditions constitutes an important policy issue. Some, concerned about possible shortages of entry-level workers in the next twenty years, believe Social Security and Medicare should do more to encourage later retirement. Noting substantial increases in life expectancies, they also suggest that the age of eligibility for Social Security benefits should be raised. Others disagree. They prefer that labor force and retirement age adjustments be made through the private, rather than the public sector. They warn of the potential that the legitimate needs of partially disabled or otherwise marginally employable older workers will be overlooked as retirement ages move upward. Thus, how to encourage later retirement of some without penalizing those who are not in a position to work remains an important policy dilemma.

Given such complexities, the programs are open to many misunderstandings about how they work. Many consider them the finest examples of effective government action; others view them as shell games and sources of inequities. Public opinion mirrors these contradictory views. The public strongly supports the programs but lacks confidence in their future.

This book marks an extended inquiry into these complex and sometimes contradictory programs. First, we describe the social insurance approach in both general and historical terms. We then describe the basic benefits of the modern Social Security and Medicare programs in some detail but with an eye toward explaining rather than using jargon to obscure. We then reconsider our general themes. First, we ask: does Social Security provide adequate protection for today's and tomorrow's old? Then we initiate a discussion in which we try to anticipate future financing problems of Social Security. Next we consider the fairness of Social Security in its treatment of particular groups, such as the members of racial minorities or of the baby boom generation, and we discuss the implications of the program's complexity and various notions of fairness. This is followed by discussions of two policy problems that transcend the boundaries of Social Security and Medicare—the nation's response to disability and to meeting and financing the health care needs of the elderly. We conclude by discussing the continuing relevance of the ideal of Social Security and with some general recommendations on how to reform Social Security and Medicare.

Any program that has the potential to overwhelm all other domestic priorities deserves this sort of inquiry.

The Social Insurance Approach

Before we can understand much about Social Security and Medicare, we need to consider the basic attributes of social insurance, the key device on which the nation relies to provide its citizens with social benefits. Social insurance, a near universal response of industrial societies to common hazards, has become the nation's preeminent social welfare technology. By discussing the various public and private means by which resources are transferred to protect citizens and by delineating some of social insurance's characteristic features, this chapter explains the reasons for social insurance's prominence.

Typically, transfers are discussed primarily as publicly funded income maintenance programs that shift resources from one group of citizens to another. Such government transfer programs provide cash payments, in-kind services such as health care, or commodities such as food stamps. The programs can be based either on the means-tested welfare approach or on the social insurance approach.

But welfare and social insurance do not exhaust the network of transfers that envelops our society. *Transfers*, in our opinion, include the numerous vehicles that individuals, families, employers, and government use to shift resources in ways that protect citizens against identifiable risks to their economic well-being or simply enhance that well-being. At any point in time, individuals are part of a vast constellation of transfers, sometimes as recipients and at other times as providers. Social insurance, welfare, and tax transfers supplement family and other private transfers, sometimes providing protection where none is available. We maintain that understanding social insurance programs involves comprehending this vast array of transfers.

PUBLIC TRANSFERS

There are three basic governmental mechanisms for transferring income from one group of citizens to another—social insurance, welfare, and tax transfers. Each tends toward somewhat different outcomes, with tax transfers benefiting higher income groups the most, welfare transfers being targeted to those with greatest financial need, and social insurance benefits having the largest poverty prevention and reduction effects. However, the decisions that need to be made are essentially the same. Benefits must be assigned to certain groups and revenues raised. How these benefits and taxes are structured— that is, deciding who benefits from and who pays for transfers—is the concern on which much policy debate centers.

One way of understanding social insurance involves thinking about its differences and similarities to private insurance. Part of social insurance's appeal lies in the reassuring ways it resembles private insurance. Robert Ball describes social insurance as a "form of group insurance operated by the government."[1] Just as a citizen who goes to work for, say, General Motors automatically receives life, health, and disability insurance, so nearly all American citizens participate in life, health, and disability plans run by the government. Primarily by pooling the resources of workers and their employers, *social insurance* programs—which include Social Security, Medicare, Unemployment Insurance, Workers Compensation, federal, state, and local employee pensions, and military pensions—provide protection against lost income and expenses arising from events such as retirement, unemployment, and illness. As we will see, however, social insurance and group insurance differ in important ways. If they did not, we would not need both. Instead, social insurance provides a different type of protection than does private insurance.

The economists' notion of a "transfer" enables us to get at some of the differences. At base, social insurance describes a means by which government transfers resources from one group to another. As we have already indicated, social insurance consists of a mechanism for raising revenues and another for distributing benefits. On one side of the ledger, social insurance programs are really just taxes that the government imposes on employers and employees. Like any government tax, the tax might be progressive, neutral, or regressive. On the other side of the ledger, social insurance programs are really just payments that the government makes to individuals or organizations. To use the economists' language, some of these benefits have no real cost to the economy since they simply transfer the command of resources from one person to another (I take from Peter to pay Paul). Other benefits involve real resource costs (the government causes medical services to be consumed).

If social insurance works in this manner, one might wonder if there is any difference between social insurance and welfare. Although both are governmentally mandated transfers of money, significant differences between the two types of programs exist. *Welfare*, by definition, involves the use of a "means test," and social insurance does not. A *means test*, as one might assume, tests a person's financial resources. One passes the test by not having too many resources. Thus, by design, welfare goes to those in financial need, primarily the poor. Aid to Families with Dependent Children (AFDC), Food

Stamps, General Assistance, Medicaid, and Supplemental Security Income (SSI) are welfare programs which are typically funded from the general revenues that state and federal governments collect. Social insurance goes to anyone who falls into a particular category, such as the injured, the unemployed, or the elderly, regardless of the person's resources. Congress and state legislators typically fund social insurance programs from earmarked taxes rather than from general revenues. Whereas welfare seeks to ameliorate the effects of poverty, social insurance works to prevent poverty and to lessen economic insecurity across all income classes. Interestingly, while many people think of welfare programs as receiving the lion's share of government expenditures, public assistance spending by local, state, and federal governments represents less than one-third of the spending on social insurance programs—about $120 billion in 1988 compared to $432 billion.[2]

Numerous public transfers are also structured less explicitly through the income tax system. Richard Titmuss referred to "*fiscal welfare*" as part of the large, submerged portion of the social welfare iceberg—the visible portions being welfare and social insurance programs.[3] Fiscal welfare includes tax policies that set deductions, tax credits, tax rates, and off-budget expenditures. Such policies usually distribute income in ways that are generally more beneficial to middle- and upper-income taxpayers.[4] For example, they have enabled some citizens to open Individual Retirement Accounts, thereby allowing the deferral of income tax payments on the interest from year to year until retirement age is reached.

One way to understand the importance of these transfers is to estimate how much tax revenue the federal government loses from tax expenditures.[5] One estimate puts the figure for lost revenues from tax expenditures in 1992 at $162 billion. This figure includes $63 billion for employer and individual pension contributions and earnings, $38 billion for employer-financed health insurance, and $37 billion for Social Security benefits that are not taxed. Other, less targeted transfers include the deductions that the federal government permits for mortgage payments.[6] This deduction cost the federal government $38.8 billion dollars in 1991, 80 percent of it going to the roughly 20 percent of taxpayers reporting at least $50,000.[7] Yet other aspects of fiscal policies, such as the decision to reduce federal income tax rates during the 1980s, have substantial influence on the economic well-being of citizens.

Very little differentiates a transfer through the tax system from a welfare or social insurance transfer, except that the former represents a less explicit transfer and the benefits of fiscal welfare are generally not defined as a type of social welfare payment. Also, tax expenditures (and off-budget expenditures such as the "S & L bailout") are generally more beneficial to higher income persons. There are, however, important exceptions such as the earned income tax credit, which seeks to offset the regressivity of the Social Security payroll tax for low-income workers supporting young children. Another exception is advocated in the final report of the National Commission on

Children, which calls for a yearly transfer of $1,000 through the tax system for each child in a family (which would then be treated as taxable income).

PRIVATE TRANSFERS

Although not typically discussed as transfers, private exchanges of resources within the family represent the nation's largest set of transfers.[8] Child-rearing, for example, costs money and shifts resources from parents to children. One economist estimates that it takes $82,400 (in 1981 prices) just to raise a child to age 16 in a middle-income family.[9] As any parent knows, the expenses rarely stop there. College, down payments on a home, and other payments lie ahead, up to the time when the parents die and leave an inheritance for their children.

Some of the transfers within a family, less visible than sending a check to the college of a child's choice, involve what the economists call "opportunity costs." A mother, who might be working, instead stays at home with her young child. This child receives services in the form of what one of us has called *"caregiving."*[10] University of Michigan economist James Morgan concludes that "the family is by far the most important welfare or redistributional mechanism," even taking into consideration welfare and social insurance programs. Assigning a value to housework and child care of $6 an hour, he estimates transfers within families to be the equivalent of 30 percent of the gross national product in 1979.[11]

Individuals do more than help one another in this informal manner. They also save money and invest it in instruments designed to meet future contingencies. A young couple with a newborn might buy a life insurance policy so that an unexpected death does not disrupt the household economy. A young woman, worried about losing her job, might put some of her paycheck in a savings account to provide a small cushion should she find herself out of work. Workers might participate in a long-term disability insurance program that their employer offers by having money withheld from their paychecks to pay the costs or "premiums."

The government does not permit this activity to occur in a vacuum. State governments regulate insurance companies. The federal government protects those who invest in banks or savings and loans (that is what people who open bank accounts are doing). These forms of regulation have led to significant unintended costs in recent years, as the federal bailout of the savings and loan industry and the state bailout of some insurance companies indicate.

As noted, the government also uses tax policy to subsidize private welfare benefits. Commonly referred to as fringe benefits, these private programs represent the major way that working Americans receive health insurance and an important way of providing protection against financial hardships due to disability. Along with fiscal welfare, these private *occupational welfare* benefits represent the hidden parts of social welfare.[12]

Clearly, occupational welfare provides one of the many examples of the interaction that regularly takes place between private and public transfers. Governmental subsidies encourage employers to provide fringe benefits by allowing employers to deduct some of their fringe benefit expenses from their income and in this manner to reduce their taxable income and lower their taxes. A dollar spent on health insurance, in reality, costs the company less than a full dollar, since that dollar will lower the taxes that the company might otherwise have paid. This policy represents a hidden transfer of money from all taxpayers to private companies and their employees.

THE CHARACTERISTICS OF SOCIAL INSURANCE

Despite the existence of other public and private transfers, we have also chosen to make a substantial investment in social insurance. Roughly half of everything that federal, state, and local governments spend on social welfare, including education, housing, welfare, veterans programs, health, social insurance, and other human services, goes toward social insurance expenditures that amount to 9 percent of the gross national product. The major social insurance programs cover nearly all workers and their families. Each month tens of millions of Americans benefit from these programs. Significantly, over 11 percent of all personal income going to American households comes from social insurance.

Here, in brief, is how such programs are generally structured. Utilizing social insurance principles, citizens pool their resources, thereby enabling them to share their risks, such as disability or the death of a wage earner, with others. Program costs are estimated for each social insurance program and are then divided by the number of people paying into the program. The amount each person (and/or employer) pays is called the *premium*. On a regular basis, employees and/or employers make premium payments (also called *payroll taxes* or *payroll tax contributions*). Then, when these risks which workers and their families are protected against occur, benefits are paid as an earned right. In other words, in exchange for a relatively modest premium payment, the insurer assumes the risk that would otherwise have to be borne by the individual and his or her family.

As the name implies, social insurance is a social mechanism that insures widely against identifiable risks to which large groups of citizens are subject. These programs share many of the characteristics we are about to discuss; however, program structures can vary considerably. For instance, although Social Security is primarily funded by payroll tax revenues, the federal Civil Service Retirement System and many state and local public employee pension systems are arguably funded primarily by general revenues (although some consider the governmental contributions to these programs to be the equivalent of employer contributions to Social Security). In social insurance programs, as in private insurance, some pooling of risks occurs, although some of the pools are broader than others. Social Security—Old-Age, Survivors, and Disability Insurance (OASDI)—draws revenues from nearly everyone in the country; workers' compensation, the social insurance program that covers industrial accidents, draws revenues only from employers in selected industries. OASDI operates through a broad trust fund; workers' compensation often functions by means of insurance policies purchased from private carriers. Differences abound. Still nearly all types of social insurance programs, like private insurance programs, involve payments of premiums and the possible receipt of benefits.

Much misunderstanding about what social insurance programs are supposed to do and how they work derives from a failure to recognize that they are not neatly structured to achieve only one end. Such programs seek to provide adequate benefits especially for low-income persons while also maintaining stable financing; they seek to reward work while also assisting those who cannot; they seek to expand access to health care while also containing hospital costs. The existence of many goals—not all of equal value—institutionalizes the need for compromise and balance and also necessitates complexity.[13] Programmatic outcomes must be evaluated, then, against a multidimensional standard, rather than a single goal.

Social insurance may resemble private insurance, but it is fundamentally different. The driving principle of social insurance programs is concern for *adequacy*—that benefits meet the basic needs of persons these programs are designed to protect. The emphasis on social adequacy is consistent with societal goals directed at providing for the general welfare, protecting the dignity of individuals, and maintaining the stability of families and society. Another difference: people choose to buy private insurance; they are often forced to pay taxes for social insurance. Because of this feature, social insurance programs are not hindered by what economists call "market failure" even though these programs are structured to accept all, that is, to include persons who for such reasons as illness or advanced age would not be considered suitable for many private insurance plans.

A hypothetical example illustrates the principle of market failure and, indirectly, the rationale for compulsory coverage under social insurance. Suppose that the ABC Insurance Company decides to sell disability insurance. It proceeds to set a price or premium for this insurance. In fact, the premiums vary depending upon the customer because, within certain legal boundaries, the ABC is allowed to discriminate. It can charge younger and healthier people less for this insurance than older and sick people. In this manner, it attempts to make as much profit as possible. But if someone becomes disabled, he can collect on the policy that ABC sold him. If too many people become disabled, the company loses money on its disability insurance. When the company raises its premiums to cover its costs, some people may decide that the price is too high. In this manner, a situation may arise where the product becomes unmarketable—too few people might want to purchase it at the market price to make it profitable for ABC to offer the insurance.

If the federal government decided to offer disability protection as part of social insurance, it would have two advantages over ABC. First, it could pool the risk broadly because of its coercive powers. Because everyone would contribute to the plan, the government is assured of a large revenue base to meet the costs as well as a good balance between "good" and "bad" risks. Second, it could raise the taxes indefinitely. If costs rose, so could taxes, enabling the disability plan to maintain is solvency.

This hypothetical example needs some tempering by reality. Government, like the ABC Insurance Company, is accountable to people. These people might object to higher taxes or might not want disability protection in the first place, feeling perhaps that disability constitutes a less pressing need than, say, health insurance. Nor would the public necessarily allow the federal government to price discriminate in the same manner as ABC, giving a completely different meaning to matching premium and risk in the public sector as compared to the private sector. In this manner, the design and maintenance of social insurance programs are every bit as demanding as marketing private insurance. The contrary nature of public opinion also makes social insurance difficult to run. We can pool risks broadly, but that requires us to cope with the diversity that is the United States of America. As some recent analysts of the system put it, "wherever we turn complexity intrudes. . . . It would be dumb to forget that we have more than one purpose and monomaniacal to structure public programs as if we did not." It can be no other way "for a polity that wants to affirm both self-reliance and mutual support, that believes both in the primacy of the market and in the necessity for collective action through government, that wants to rely on both national fiscal capacity and local political control."[14]

This sort of broad comparison between private and social insurance helps to illuminate the chief characteristics of social insurance. Private insurance depends on a search for profit. But, as noted, a concern for adequacy—that benefits meet people's basic needs—drives social insurance. The advantage of social insurance in this regard lies in the way that it helps to solve social problems; the disadvantage stems from a lack of limits that a market might otherwise set, though the political process, careful financing, and the linkage of benefit payments to payroll and other forms of taxation serve as a check.

Robert Myers, another central figure in the development of Social Security, explains why adequacy, for all of its inherent problems, defines the primary rationale for the existence of social insurance. Myers, who served as chief actuary of Social Security from 1947 to 1970 and directed President Reagan's National Commission on Social Security Reform, points out that the real reason for having social insurance programs is "that social benefits on a social adequacy basis can only in this way be provided to a large sector of the population."[15] Private insurance might meet the needs of some individuals;

only social insurance meets society's needs to provide widespread protection for the populace, provided these needs can be cogently defined.

Another way to think about this matter is to assume that society will simply not tolerate such things as poverty among the elderly. Given that fact, as actuary Reinhard Hohaus put it in a classic article, "social insurance endeavors to organize the budgeting . . . and the dispensing . . . through systematic government processes. Hence, just as considerations of equity of benefits form a natural and vital part of operating private insurance, so should considerations of adequacy control the pattern of social insurance benefits."[16]

At the same time, adequacy must somehow be blended with the principle of *individual equity* or social insurance will collapse. If someone contributes to social insurance solely for the relief of social distress, then the distinction between social insurance and welfare diminishes until the two concepts merge. The rationale for earmarked taxes becomes impossible to sustain. In social insurance, as in private insurance, individuals receive benefits that bear a reasonable relationship to their contributions. That is, the more they put into social insurance systems, the more they generally get out, either in monetary benefits or in the value of insurance coverage.

The concepts of adequacy and individual equity are not consistent with each other and lead to some of the complexity that is inherent in social insurance. The typical compromise can be found in the basic Social Security benefit formula. The higher your average wage, the higher your benefit, but the lower your average wage, the greater your return on your Social Security investment. To illustrate, someone earning $1,000 will receive a higher Social Security benefit than someone earning $500, but the higher benefit will not be twice as much as the lower benefit. In this manner, social insurance relates benefits to contributions yet, when properly managed, also recognizes some social problems as more pressing than others and some social groups as more needy than others.

The very concept of adequacy also raises a fundamental question of just how far social insurance should go. If it went all the way, its beneficiaries could rely upon it exclusively and not need to make other arrangements for their old age. If it went part of the way, its beneficiaries would have to supplement their Social Security benefits with private savings. Americans have chosen social insurance as a basis upon which individuals and their families can build toward their economic security. Except for the poorest individuals, our social insurance programs go only part of the way.

Programs like Social Security provide a floor, rather than a ceiling, of protection for two reasons. One has to do with the proper roles of the public and private sectors. The American proponents of Social Security have, with very few exceptions, never sought to crowd out private pensions and investments. If anything, the growth of the public programs has stimulated the growth of private programs. Survivors' benefits have not impeded the growth of the life insurance industry, nor have Medicare benefits halted the growth of private health insurance, even among the elderly, who now purchase "medigap" policies where once they bought nothing. The other reason has to do with fears that generous benefits will lead to socially unproductive behavior. Workers' compensation benefits never replace all of a worker's earnings for fear of creating an incentive for workers to injure themselves. Policymakers make efforts to keep workers' retirement incomes below the amount they could make from staying in the labor force.

If social insurance benefits are limited in amount, the conditions of eligibility and the *benefits* are nonetheless *defined by law*. That creates a strong sense of entitlement and greatly limits the discretion that agencies have in awarding benefits. To get social insurance, you do not have to know someone in city hall. You simply have to meet the objective conditions as specified in a shared body of law. Should disagreements arise, social insurance programs, almost without exception, provide for appeal procedures.

A sense of entitlement is further reinforced by the *earnings-related* nature of the benefits. Both the right to benefits and the amount of benefits are related to prior earnings in employment covered under a social insurance program. Thus, the economic security of a worker and his or her family comes from the individual's own work.[17] Thus, unlike in welfare programs, the right to benefits in social insurance programs does not require proving extreme financial need. Benefits are an *earned right*, not affected by savings or by total income from other sources. This adds to the *dignity* of social insurance beneficiaries and helps explain public support for social insurance programs. The lack of a means test also encourages workers to build savings and other forms of private protection as supplements to social insurance since their benefits will not be affected by their assets. As with other types of income, social insurance benefits are often countable for income tax purposes. But in fact, while there is no means test, many who benefit have little or no means.

The flip side of entitlement is *compulsory participation* and *universal coverage*. With few exceptions, social insurance coverage is compulsory and, ideally, includes nearly everyone in the category of people being protected. Some argue that this condition violates a citizen's fundamental freedom, but the Supreme Court has ruled otherwise. Voluntary participation would heighten the similarity between social insurance and private insurance, with the exception that social insurance would not be able to deny anyone coverage. The social insurance programs would end up carrying the greatest risks at increasingly high costs and would become financially untenable.

Of necessity, the characteristics of social insurance programs reflect taxpayers' and politicians' concerns for *stable financing*. Workers contribute directly to the financing of most social insurance programs, often through a very visible payroll tax contribution as in the case of Social Security and Medicare, and indirectly through the contribution made by employers on their behalf. This practice reinforces both the receipt of benefits as an earned right and the dignity of beneficiaries. Equally important, because contributions are linked to benefit payments, workers and their employers have a personal stake in the financial stability of these programs. That personal stake helps to ensure financial responsibility when benefit increases and other program changes are being considered.[18]

The contributions of workers and their employers to most social insurance programs go into *dedicated trust funds*, earmarked to pay for social insurance benefits and the cost of operating these programs. The highly visible nature of these trust funds helps ensure that these programs are adequately financed. The many safeguards that are incorporated include legislative oversight; the establishment of trust funds dedicated to social insurance programs; ongoing review of social insurance programs by actuaries, other financial experts, and independent panels; and legislation when changing economic and demographic conditions necessitate corrective action. Ultimately, however, it is the *authority and taxing power of government* that help guarantee the continuity and stability of social insurance programs.

The defining characteristics of social insurance now become clear. They include a concern for social adequacy, a concern for individual equity, a right to benefits that is clearly defined by law, universal coverage, and a concern for stable financing. Social insurance, like private insurance, protects against losses from identifiable risks. In the Social Security program, if not in all social insurance programs, both the right to benefits and the amount of benefits are related to prior earnings in employment.

Taken together, these characteristics produce programs that have a mildly progressive impact on the distribution of income in American society. Social Security benefits, for example, tend to be fairly progressive in that they involve substantial transfers from the rich to the poor and from the working to the non-working. The taxes themselves have a tendency to be regressive. The poor pay a higher percentage of their income for Social Security protection than do the rich. The payroll tax financing of Medicare's Hospital Insurance Program is, however, arguably progressive in that the payroll tax contribution of a person earning $135,000 in 1993 is more than five times as much for the same benefits as that of a person earning $26,000. But the distributive impact of deductibles and coinsurance—which can be considered a type of financing—is regressive because they are paid disproportionately by persons using the service.

Social insurance programs, unlike private insurance programs, involve a compact between citizens and their government. While specific provisions can be changed, the contributory aspects of these programs help increase the contractual nature of the relationship between government and the citizenry. Such aspects also reinforce the political necessity for the government to maintain the continuity of social insurance programs as well as the promised benefits. To a large extent this helps assure the program's existence for each birth cohort. Further, contributory financing provides an "institutional check against the political temptation to overpromise" by linking benefit liberalizations "directly to increases in a highly visible tax."[19]

Social insurance programs, particularly Social Security and Medicare, also involve a different sort of compact, one that links generations. Present generations of workers pay taxes to support current retirees. As each generation approaches retirement age, it begins to receive benefits, in a never-ending chain of contributors and beneficiaries. Thus, the taxing power of government and the notion of an intergenerational compact guarantee the continuity of Social Security and other social insurance programs. J. Douglas Brown, a labor economist who for many years defended the program from its critics by eloquently expressing the program's ideology, wrote of an implied covenant in Social Security, arising from a deeply embedded sense of mutual responsibility in civilization that underlies "the fundamental obligation of the government and the citizens of one time and the government and the citizens of another to maintain a contributory social insurance system."[20]

THE POLITICAL STRENGTH OF THE SOCIAL INSURANCE APPROACH

With some sense of what constitutes social insurance, we can begin to probe its political popularity and its potential weaknesses. Here we return to Social Security and Medicare, the chief social insurance programs in America and the main focus of this book.

Social Security and Medicare enjoy strong support. Periodic controversies and crises have arisen, such as a long debate over whether Medicare would lead to socialized medicine in America and financing crises in the late 1970s and early 1980s. The crises over Social Security funding have caused people to be wary of the program's future. Despite this fact and despite over a decade of highly effective conservative rhetoric about how social welfare programs undermine individual incentive and trap people in poverty, political support for Social Security and Medicare remains strong.

No single reason for this support suffices. Partial reasons include the fact that many people already benefit from the programs and see no reason to fear the loss of benefits in *their* future. Those who are less certain about the future of the program nonetheless indirectly benefit from such things as survivors' benefits, disability coverage, and old-age benefits for their relatives. The very size and range of the program implicate nearly all of us in it and make it difficult for dissidents to gain a wide audience. Universal programs have a wide pool of beneficiaries from which to gain political support. Universal programs also operate in every congressional district in the nation, unlike, say, farm-price supports which must depend upon fragile alliances between urban and rural constituencies.

Although this explanation helps to understand why Social Security remains popular, it does not explain how social insurance came to be so popular in the first place. Some argue that the Social Security program owes its success to the way its features mesh with widely held values. Robert Ball posits that, "on the whole, the social insurance approach to preventing economic insecurity has worked well because in a wage economy it is the right prescription for a large part of the problem."[21] But such an assertion is difficult to prove. Because Social Security became popular, that does not necessarily mean its popularity was foreordained.

Wilbur Cohen, another of the remarkable group of individuals who helped to create and nurture Social Security, regarded the success of Social Security as a matter of psychology and of popular perception. He said that people did not view Social Security as just another government program but rather they saw it as the very antithesis of a government program: a mechanism to give individuals greater freedom in their personal lives when they experience one of the "major vicissitudes of life."[22]

By preventing dependency and providing benefits as an earned right while simultaneously protecting individuals and families against economic insecurity, social insurance arguably helps underwrite human dignity, strengthen family life, and stabilize society. Especially during times of crisis or life course transitions, social insurance can serve to stabilize family life. While much care flows to and from family members of all ages throughout their lives, adults prefer not to be financially dependent on their children, their parents, or even like-aged family members during times of financial stress. Instead they prefer to rely on a combination of private savings and social insurance. Without social insurance, events such as unemployment, disability, death of a wage earner, and retirement would be far more likely to overwhelm most individuals and families. Such individuals and families might have no choice but to seek financial or housing assistance from other family members—an occurrence that often strains family relations. Or families might not be able to help. Moreover, by providing benefits to older family members, Social Security, Medicare, and other social insurance retirement programs free up young adult and middle-aged family members to concentrate more resources on their young children and on themselves.

By observing Wilbur Cohen in action, we can get closer to the basic assumptions of social insurance proponents.[23] Early in 1968, at a particularly bad moment for the Johnson administration with the country about to come apart over the Vietnam War and riots in the cities, Cohen, who served as undersecretary of Health, Education, and Welfare at the time, tried to interest the president in a new social insurance program. He saw such a program as an antidote to the considerable criticism the president had been receiving for his handling of the war and as a mean of reasserting the primacy of the Great Society over foreign affairs as the major focus of the administration. Cohen proposed extending coverage similar to that of Medicare to children in their first year of life.

Presenting his program, Cohen indicated his willingness to compromise on details, but he told the president that any plan should follow basic social insurance principles. These began with universality of protection. Cohen said that everyone should be covered with no exclusions. "This appeals to the egalitarian nature of the majority of the Americans and it thus includes all of the poorest people who otherwise are not effectively covered. To cover all the poor you cover the rich as well," Cohen argued. As he explained, "a plan limited to the poor may be desirable from the point of view of cost-effectiveness but it does not appeal to the 50% of the people who consider themselves middleclass, self-supporting, respectable, independent." Furthermore, the benefits should be contributory, with part of the cost borne out of a payroll tax or an *earmarked* income tax. According to Cohen, "This gives beneficiaries the psychological feeling that they have helped to pay for their protection. It is the reason why social security has been so popular and well-accepted. People do not want something that is called a hand-out or welfare."

When Cohen presented his child's health insurance plan in 1968, this sort of explanation carried great weight with policymakers who regarded it as a correct reading of the American character. Social insurance was how the government operated effectively in a culture that distrusted government. Social insurance stabilized existing families, rather than trying to create new family structures. Social insurance protected capitalism against some of its excesses and inherent weaknesses, rather than acting to socialize the economy. Social insurance reinforced the work ethic, rather than creating boondoggle make-work schemes. It exemplified the value of self-help, rather than providing a hand-out. It blended security and freedom in a soothing harmony.

Perhaps much of this is true, yet social insurance has served as the basis of other welfare states in countries with very different sorts of values. It is not social insurance in general that holds the key to the success of Social Security and Medicare but the American experience in particular. In this chapter we have tried to define some of the defining features of social insurance and to distinguish social insurance from private insurance. We now turn to the specific historical development of Social Security and Medicare in America.

The History of Social Security and Medicare

We did not always have a large and successful social insurance system in this country. The Social Security Act of 1935, like many landmark pieces of legislation, was a near thing. President Franklin D. Roosevelt slipped it through a window of political opportunity that opened in the middle of the depression and closed very soon afterwards.

This chapter contains a short historical overview of Social Security and Medicare.[1] We believe that history is the best way to explain the programs, in large part because history allows us to understand and appreciate the programs' complexity. Things that make little apparent sense in present time often have perfectly reasonable historical rationales. History, we realize, need not be science; we understand it as a subjective endeavor in which the historian's interpretive framework influences the outcome. We choose to portray Social Security and Medicare as distinctively American responses to industrialism.

TOWARD THE SOCIAL SECURITY ACT

Although the idea for the Social Security Act came from Europe, the sponsors of the Act used American ingredients in creating it. Americans inherited their designs for social insurance programs from existing European programs that responded to conditions created by the change from a locally oriented agricultural economy to a global, industrial one.[2] American social insurance proponents modified these designs to accommodate such traditions as federalism, judicial review, and a deep-seated distrust of central government.

To preserve the benefits of industrialism and to cushion workers against some of its shocks, European governments instituted social insurance programs in the late nineteenth and early twentieth centuries. Comprehensive social insurance programs arrived first in the countries that industrialized earliest, notably England and Germany. These western European governments used their authority to force workers to pool their resources and in this manner to create a fund to compensate workers for wage loss. Social insurance was born.

When the German government gave serious consideration to the passage of social insurance measures in 1878, social insurance entered its formative era. Germany took the lead because it experienced the greatest rates of industrial growth in the late nineteenth century and because it saw the rapid development of a labor movement with a socialist orientation. To cushion the impact of industrialism, to subvert the union movement, and to tie the interest of the laboring class to that of the nation-state, the emperor of the Reichstag, Otto Von Bismark, proposed state intervention on behalf of the wage earner through social insurance. By 1884, Germany had begun two social insurance programs. One covered industrial accidents; the other provided benefits in the event of illness.

Other countries soon followed Germany's example and produced social insurance laws that fit their economies and cultural conditions. Between 1919 and 1930, for example, eleven countries adopted compulsory unemployment insurance laws.[3]

The United States failed to participate in this first round of the passage of national social insurance laws. The reasons had less to do with the development of the American economy than with the political organization of the American state.[4]

Responding to a fear of societal disorder, a group of American reformers, who paid close attention to events in Germany and England, began to explore means of importing social insurance to America. The members of this group tended to be genteel reformers, rather than the workers directly affected by changes in the workplace or politicians who held elective office. Neither the workers, nor the politicians, nor the reformers themselves were accustomed to looking to the central government for the solution of society's problems. Unlike the European nations, America had a weak tradition of central government activity. Whereas Europe was divided into nations, America, a larger mass of land, was divided into states. Until well into the twentieth century, most governmental activity occurred at the state or local levels. For most of the nineteenth century, the federal government largely confined its social welfare activities to conferring grants of land upon distinct groups and localities.

For more than a century, the Constitution had carefully circumscribed the extent of federal power. This blueprint for the American government reserved "non-delegated" powers to the states and prohibited the states and the federal government from "depriving any person of life, liberty, or property without due process of law."[5] Because of these provisions, even a state law requiring a worker or his employer to contribute to a social insurance fund could be construed by a conservative Supreme Court as unconstitutional and hence invalid.

The courts did not hesitate to exercise their judicial powers to review legislative actions. In fact, many proposals passed state legislatures only to be held unconstitutional by the courts. Thus, in the absence of a strong Congress or of strong state legislatures, the courts played an important limiting role in public policy during the crucial period when social insurance programs began in Europe. The Supreme Court exercised what amounted to veto power over federal social legislation, not relenting until 1937 when it approved many of the programs of the second New Deal, including Social Security.

Although the constitutional constraints that prevented the passage of a national social insurance law were gradually overcome, the American political tradition of "federalism" guaranteed that states passed social insurance laws before the federal government. A national social insurance law came only in 1935, long after most European states had passed such laws. By 1935, however, nearly every state in the union already ran a social insurance program, called workers' compensation, that provided money and medical care to workers injured on the job.[6]

Despite the passage of many workers' compensation laws during the second decade of this century, the movement for a comprehensive social insurance program in America stalled during the 1920s. This decade marked a high point in the influence of private companies and trade associations over American economic life. Prosperity throughout the decade indicated to many the wisdom of allowing private companies to take the lead in providing social welfare services such as pensions.

Then, beginning in 1930, the depression slowly altered the institutional landscape. It was brutal, crushing the economy, in one historian's image, like a tin can in a vise. More than 15 million Americans lost their jobs. Between 1929 and 1933, the country's gross national product (the sum of all the goods and services produced) fell more than 30 percent; 5,000 banks and 90,000 businesses failed. Out of a feeling of desperation, people conceded to the government an expanded role in maintaining social welfare.[7]

But even the depression did not occasion a stampede toward federal social insurance laws. For one thing, the need for immediate relief outweighed the need for long-range social insurance programs. For another, the tradition of state preeminence in social welfare policy (with the exception of veterans' pensions) continued to hold sway.

Thus, when Franklin D. Roosevelt became president in March 1933, he did not call for the immediate passage of social insurance laws. Instead, he asked Harry Hopkins, a social worker with whom he had worked as governor of New York, to begin a program of emergency relief.

PREPARING THE SOCIAL SECURITY ACT

In early summer 1934, Roosevelt decided to have his administration prepare an economic security bill, covering both old age and unemployment. In

essence, Roosevelt's actions, coming as they did near the peak of his popularity, took control of social insurance proposals away from Congress, which
was debating old-age benefit and unemployment compensation bills, and
brought it to the executive branch.

As a first step, Roosevelt created the Committee on Economic Security
(CES), composed of cabinet members and cabinet-level advisers, to study the
problems and issue specific recommendations. Principal participants included Labor Secretary Frances Perkins, Relief Administrator Harry Hopkins, Treasury Secretary Henry Morgenthau, and Agriculture Secretary
Henry Wallace. These individuals debated broad points of policy. The hard
staff work that supported their efforts fell to a special group recruited from
outside of the government for the specific purpose of studying the field and
to a government committee of technical experts.

The predilections of the CES staff exercised a powerful influence over the
history of Social Security in America. Unlike those who would follow, this
staff worked with a clean slate, able to make a fresh and lasting imprint on
federal social policy. The intellectual orientation of these men and women
therefore mattered a great deal.

President Roosevelt chose Secretary of Labor Frances Perkins, a social
insurance expert, to head the effort and guaranteed that the CES would be
stacked with social insurance experts from top to bottom. Perkins appointed
Assistant Secretary of Labor Arthur Altmeyer to lead a group of government
employees assisting the committee. Altmeyer, like Perkins, specialized in
social insurance. When it came time to select a director for the CES staff,
Altmeyer chose Edwin Witte, a professor at the University of Wisconsin,
whom he described as an "outstanding expert in the field of labor legislation,
which . . . included social insurance."[8] Witte, in turn, relied on experts in the
fields of unemployment compensation and old-age security and on special
assistants that he selected from among his students in Wisconsin. As a result
of this pyramiding effect, the staff contained few people who were experts in
relief or welfare; nearly all of the administration's advisers aspired to be
experts in social insurance.

Social insurance, to which the staff was intellectually predisposed, also met
pragmatic political needs. It depended on the taxing power of the federal
government, which was explicitly sanctioned by the Constitution. It also
depended on a separate revenue stream, distinct from the government's general revenues, which provided at least a partial remedy for the federal government's notorious inability to raise money for social projects.

Neither the CES staff nor the president wanted to make a complete break
with the past. In fact, the Social Security Act of 1935 preserved many American social welfare traditions. In particular, the Act contained two features that
continued state and local control over social benefits. Unemployment compensation, a major concern of the CES and of the Congress, emerged from
the policy process as a state, rather than a federal, system. Public assistance

Figure 3.1
Milestones in the History of Social Insurance and Related Public Assistance Programs

1878   Germany debates first national social insurance program.

1911   England adopts an unemployment compensation program.
        Wisconsin starts first constitutional workers' compensation program.

1920   Vocational rehabilitation program begins.

1933   Franklin Roosevelt begins first term.

1934   Committee on Economic Security begins its work.

1935   Passage of the Social Security Act, establishing two social insurance programs—Social Security and Unemployment Insurance—and three public assistance programs—Aid to Dependent Children, Old Age Assistance (OAA), and Aid to the Blind (AB).

1939   Comprehensive Social Security Amendments, including survivors and dependents benefits, are enacted.

1950   Congress extends Social Security coverage to most groups of self-employed.
        Aid to the Permanently and Totally Disabled (APTD) program is enacted.

1954   Disability freeze is passed.

1956   Disability Insurance begins.

1960   Kerr-Mills program for the medically indigent begins.

1965   Congress passes Medicare and Medicaid.

1972   Social Security benefits are indexed to the rate of inflation.
        Disability Insurance beneficiaries receive right to Medicare.

1974   Supplemental Security Income program begins, replacing OAA, AB, and APTD.

1977   Congress passes Social Security financing legislation, raising Social Security taxes and adjusting benefit formula.

1981   Substantial cuts are enacted in major social welfare programs, including phasing out student benefits and minimum benefits in Social Security.

1983   Social Security compromise resolves financing problems for the foreseeable future.
        Use of diagnosis-related-groups (DRGs) incorporated into law to contain Medicare's hospital costs.

1984   Disability reform legislation responds to the controversy of people being removed from the disability rolls.

1985   Fiftieth anniversary of the Social Security Act.

1988   Medicare Catastrophic Health Care Act enacted.
        Most provisions of the Medicare Catastrophic Health Care Act repealed.

1993   President Clinton establishes task force on national health care reform.

grants allowed state and local governments to provide welfare to the indigent elderly, the blind, and dependent children. The Act provided, for the first time in American history, substantial federal financial assistance to the states to fund their "public assistance" programs.

In contrast to these public assistance programs, social insurance made the receipt of benefits a matter of entitlement and did away with the public welfare worker who scrutinized each applicant. Unlike some state and local relief efforts, the benefits came in the form of cash and allowed workers to spend them any way they wished. In addition, the benefits were portable and did not depend on either remaining in the employ of one company or living in one location. A worker carried Social Security protection with him from job to job.

Even with these advantages over poor relief, no groundswell developed for social insurance, in part because it was not a perfect substitute for the old poor law. In particular, the old poor laws, despite their often inhumane treatment of the poor, had as much flexibility as local communities cared to give them. In an emergency, the community could improvise relief measures such as vouchers good for groceries. The new social insurance programs followed rigid rules that did nothing for someone who had never worked. The states, for their part, often put conditions on the receipt of unemployment benefits that made them difficult to secure quickly. As for Old-Age Insurance, under the 1935 law the program was not scheduled to begin to pay regular monthly benefits until 1942.

Despite these problems, President Roosevelt and the CES persevered and created the old-age insurance program that came to be known as Social Security. It helped that the treatment of the elderly had become a hot political issue in an America that felt besieged by the depression. In the 1920s a number of states had passed limited pension laws for the elderly. These laws, nearly always administered by local authorities acting as the agents of state governments, provided very small pensions to a limited segment of the needy elderly population. In the 1930s these laws came nowhere near meeting the elderly's demand for relief. Old people, after all, were among the first groups to be fired during a recession. Many of the elderly had chosen to retire in places like California, and that exacerbated the problems of establishing a residence and thus becoming eligible for relief. In short, the elderly were a group with a high level of voter participation and many potential political grievances.

Just as the CES began its work, some elderly citizens formed an alliance that influenced depression-era politics and remained a political force until well into the 1950s. Led by Francis Townsend, a retired doctor living in California, the Townsend movement enrolled thousands of elderly members. They demanded that anyone over the age of 60 be paid a flat pension of $200 a month from the federal Treasury on condition that the recipient retire from the labor force and spend the entire amount of money within a month, a tremendous amount of money given that workers' monthly wages typically averaged $100 or less.[9]

Because the Townsend proposal linked the relief of the elderly with more general economic recovery, it gained a broad base of appeal. Spending their grants, elderly people would put more money into circulation, bid up the price of goods and services, and restore prosperity. "This plan is only incidentally a pension plan," Townsend said. "The old people are simply to be used as a means by which prosperity will be restored to all of us."[10] And they would also make room for the young in the labor force since the plan would, in Townsend's words, "create a scarcity of labor through this retirement system so that those people who are not old enough to retire will be in a position to demand and receive decent wages."[11]

CES staff members dismissed Townsend's plan as "fantastic and absurd" because they believed it to be impractical. They realized that it would take over half of the nation's income to provide pensions of $200 a month to everyone over 60. "It seems almost fantastic to estimate a solid, substantial insurance scheme in any such terms as that," said Perkins.[12]

Social Security was not the Townsend plan. It would not solve the problems of those already old and retired. Even though it would have its own source of funds, it would be difficult to finance. And if it continued the social insurance tradition of limiting coverage to industrial or commercial workers, it would leave many people uncovered. Even the committed advocates of social insurance who worked for the CES realized that Social Security alone would not be adequate. It would have to be accompanied by some form of welfare for those who were already old in 1934 and for those who had worked as the sole proprietors of small businesses or as farm laborers or in the thousands of other jobs that lay beyond the standard employer-employee framework (doctor, Rabbi, actor).[13]

The Social Security Act both improved upon existing state welfare programs for the elderly and started a new social insurance program known as Social Security. As matters stood, old-age pensions existed in twenty-eight states, and more than 180,000 people received them. But fourteen states had a 70-year-old age limit and required the recipient to have lived in the state for at least ten years. None of the states paid pensions to a person who had more than $3,000 worth of property, and the most any state paid was a dollar a day.[14]

Adequate state pensions paid to all who qualified without regard to political preference would be a costly endeavor for both the state and federal governments. If the number of elderly people grew and the economy did not improve, both reasonable future predictions in 1935, costs would continue to rise in the foreseeable future.

Here social insurance came to the rescue. To reduce the future costs of these "gratuitous" pensions, the federal government would eventually pay "earned" pensions.[15] These "earned," contributory pensions developed into the modern Social Security program.

Still, even earned pensions cost money, and just like welfare programs, the cost of a social insurance program for the elderly would rise over time. The reason was that, whether or not there was an extension of coverage, the percentage of the retired population eligible to receive Social Security would increase with the passage of time. Whatever else happened, old-age insurance would cost more in the future than when it started, and that did not begin to exhaust the problems of designing Social Security. Older workers who put only a little money into the system would be able to draw only a little out. For their pensions even to approach a reasonable level, they would have to receive subsidies from the other contributors, making future financing problems that much worse. Further, a system of earned pensions would mean that the old-age pension plan would have to build up a huge reserve in the early, cheaper years of the system to meet the costs that would arise in later years. The CES estimated that a "fully funded" pension plan could lead to the creation of a reserve fund as large as $70 billion in 1975, a huge amount of money from the vantage point of the 1930s.

To solve these implied problems, the committee staff recommended three things: an initial delay of five years between the first year of contributions into the system (from a payroll tax borne equally by employers and employees) and the first payment of regular monthly benefits, a system of gradually rising tax rates, which would handle the problem of long-range costs, and an eventual subsidy from general revenues, which would allow those already old to receive pensions that were partially "unearned" but not "free" as in welfare programs. It would also reduce the size of the required reserve.[16]

In looking toward the long run, the committee hoped to create a system of old-age insurance that was beyond the reach of the worst abuses of partisan politics. The CES asked Congress to put aside its present-day concerns and create a program that would be financially secure far into the future. It requested that Congress avoid legislating large benefits for elderly persons today so that the system would not go bankrupt tomorrow. Further, it wanted Congress to leave the administration of the program to trained professionals, who would resist taking actions solely for political gains.

Here then was a distinctively American response to the problems of old age, one that respected the traditions of federalism and recognized the perils of leaving pensions to the whims of popularly elected politicians. The Committee on Economic Security skillfully adopted a European institution and applied it to American conditions. Even so, the plan still needed to be approved in Congress, whose members were being pressed, by Townsend and others, to put money into the hands of the elderly and do it quickly.

THE SOCIAL SECURITY ACT IN CONGRESS

In January 1935 Roosevelt presented Congress with an omnibus social welfare measure that combined programs covering children, the unemployed, and the elderly in a single legislative package. It was, by far, the most comprehensive social welfare bill that any president had ever asked Congress to consider.

Because the legislation sought to establish a tax for unemployment compensation benefits and another tax for old-age insurance, Congress handled it as it did other forms of tax legislation. Tax bills began in the House of Representatives and then were debated in the Senate. Congress used special standing committees to analyze such legislation. Hence, the Committee on Ways and Means in the House and the Committee on Finance in the Senate held lengthy hearings on the legislation in the winter and spring of 1935.

A complication arose when President Roosevelt decided at the very last minute that he could not tolerate a deficit in the old-age insurance plan, even though yearly deficits were not scheduled to arise until the 1960s. Roosevelt dispatched Treasury Secretary Henry Morgenthau to appear before the House Ways and Means Committee with a new plan that would make the program "fully funded," without the need for general revenues.

Although businessmen and others raised many objections, the president had made up his mind and, in this instance, his opinion mattered most.[17] Indeed, the president's wishes went a great way toward explaining the eventual passage of the Social Security Act. He wanted the legislation, and Congress was in no position to argue with a popular president, who had won a resounding congressional victory in 1934. The president exercised crucial influence over the Act, beginning with his decision to turn its drafting over to Perkins and the social insurance advocates and almost guaranteeing that social insurance would finally have its moment on the national stage. Congress had no particular reason to oppose social insurance, just so long as the legislation also contained programs of more immediate benefit to the elderly and the unemployed.

The relevant standard of comparison continued to be the Townsend plan, which still attracted a great deal of attention. Its chief congressional proponent contrasted its generosity with the inadequacy of the administration's bill. Like many of his fellow legislators, the congressman ignored the Social Security bill's old-age insurance provisions completely since monthly benefits were not scheduled to begin until 1942. Instead, he concentrated on its relief features, which he said offered a "pauper's dole" to "God's beloved old people, who have read newspapers, who have studied the Bible, who have read books, who are intelligent, but who are pitifully helpless in their old-age. . . . I want to say these old people will resent it, and they will resent it bitterly," the congressman said.[18]

It was the old-age relief sections of the bill, however, that became its most popular feature. As another member of Congress announced, "Let me say frankly at the outset that the only part of the President's economic security bill that I am very greatly interested in for the moment, or that many Members are very greatly interested in, is section 1 of that bill [the relief section]."[19] Edwin Witte later suggested that if the other features had not been bundled together with it, the bill might never have passed.[20]

Sensing the popularity of old-age relief, Congressman Allen Treadway, the ranking Republican member of the House Ways and Means Committee, sponsored an amendment on the floor to make the non-contributory pensions more generous. By way of contrast, he called the old-age insurance program the "worst title in the bill, . . . a burdensome tax on industry."

Despite this and other efforts to defeat the old-age insurance sections of the bill, the House followed the lead of the Ways and Means Committee, passed the measure without further amendment, and sent the bill to the Senate.

Unlike the House, the Senate spent a great deal of time on the old-age insurance sections. Fifteen senators, including Walter George, who would subsequently become the chairman of the Finance Committee, voted to eliminate old-age insurance from the bill. It did not amount to a ringing endorsement.

Although the Senate eventually voted in favor of old-age insurance, it included an amendment that, if the House had concurred, would have seriously affected the program. It concerned the right of employers and employees who already had old-age pensions to opt out of the federal law. This proposal, drawn up by Sen. Bennett Champ Clark, known as the Clark amendment, remained in the bill until it was finally deleted by the conference committee charged with reconciling the House and Senate versions of the bill.[21]

The Senate devoted more attention to the Clark amendment than to any other single subject. Sen. Alben Barkley (later Truman's vice president) wondered if Clark's amendment would create a "competitive situation between the Government and private annuity or insurance companies, so that a lot of high-pressure salesmanship would be brought to bear on employers by private companies to adopt a private system in competition with the national system." Barkley speculated that the amendment would leave the federal system with the older employees, who, by the terms of the law, received subsidized pensions.[22] Such a situation might bankrupt the federal plan. Senator Thomas Connally agreed: "All the prosperous businesses will build up their own little plan, thinking they can save money by it, and there will be only the little wobbling, crippled corporations to participate in the Government plan," he said.[23]

Senator Clark disagreed. "If the high pressure salesmanship led to employers extending more generous treatment to their employees, I do not see that there would be any disadvantage to anybody," he said. He also called attention to the fact that some of the private pensions were more liberal than the proposed old-age insurance program since they had earlier retirement ages (particularly for women), disability protection, joint annuities for wives, and provisions for past service.[24]

Although businessmen and other conservatives supported the Clark amendment because they wanted to promote competition between the federal government and private insurance companies, the federal planners who had worked for the CES strenuously objected. Just like Senators Barkley and Connally, they argued that the Clark amendment would leave the federal plan with the worst risks to insure: relatively old workers who would not have many years in which to make Social Security contributions. The private sector could simply refuse to insure such workers and leave the load to the public sector, which would then face prohibitive costs. Social Security taxes would have to rise to cover the costs, driving more workers away from the system. Support for Social Security would be undermined by the fact that many workers would have chosen not to participate.[25]

In the end, Franklin Roosevelt insisted on the withdrawal of the Clark amendment for "further discussion." As he did on other aspects of the legislation, the president got his way. In doing so, Roosevelt allowed the social insurance system to spread the costs of retirement pensions broadly among industrial and commercial workers of all ages.[26] In retrospect, this action proved crucial to Social Security's success since, without it, Social Security might have degenerated into a welfare program and never achieved universal coverage or broad support. One could only imagine the pressures on Congress to eliminate Social Security, if the program were elective and covered only those on the edges of the labor force.

In August 1935, President Roosevelt signed the Social Security Act into law. Among many other things, the bill established a federal-state unemployment insurance program, and most importantly for our purposes, created an old-age insurance program that within a few years would be known as Social Security. In other words, the 1935 Social Security Act, although it lacked provisions for disability and health insurance, laid the basis for this country's modern social welfare system. It put the federal government in the pension business, giving industrial and commercial workers the right to a perfectly portable retirement annuity.

EARLY PROBLEMS IN SOCIAL SECURITY

For all that Social Security represented a policy breakthrough, few politicians rushed to endorse it in its early years. The fiscal discipline that a contributory old-age insurance program required clashed with the needs of the economy during the depression. Social Security, as it was planned by the president's advisers, took more money out of the economy in the form of payroll taxes than it returned in the form of retirement pensions. It reduced the amount of money in people's pockets at a time when most businesses were severely depressed. Old-age insurance would not begin to pay regular pensions until 1942, even though the payroll taxes would begin in 1937. That meant younger people would pay into the system for five years without any real assurance of ever getting anything back.

In theory, money just kept piling up in the old-age insurance reserve accounts when in reality many elderly people faced severe financial hardship. Not until 1967, when many of these elderly people would be dead, would the program begin to pay out more than it collected. By then, a reserve fund, estimated to have reached $38 billion, would make up the difference from interest on the fund's assets.[27]

This situation created a paradox. The creators of contributory social insurance regarded it as a means of keeping government expenditures within acceptable limits. Townsend promised his followers the moon; the president's Social Security program accepted the limits that restricted funds placed upon it. This responsible financing system, however, required the accumulation of large reserves in the early years of the program. The presence of these large reserves, in turn, presented politicians with a constant temptation to expand the program, creating large, unfunded burdens on the system that would arise in the future. In this manner, careful financing could lead to irresponsible spending and undermine all of the careful planning that had gone into the program.

The Republicans played upon this vulnerability in the program in the 1936 campaign. Alfred Landon put it this way: "We have some good spenders in Washington. With this Social Security money alone running into billions of dollars, all restraint on Congress will be off."[28] Many liberals and conservatives agreed with Landon.[29]

As early as 1937, a consensus had begun to emerge in favor of changing the old-age insurance program so that the huge reserves did not form. Ultimately, the financing issues were debated in a special Social Security Advisory Council established in 1937 by Senator Arthur Vandenberg, an influential Republican politician, Arthur Altmeyer, and others.[30] Social Security officials proposed and the advisory council accepted recommendations that, when adopted by Congress, substantially changed old-age insurance.

The events leading to the creation of the advisory council and the passage of the 1939 amendments illustrated the tensions between politics and program management. When the program was an idea, an abstraction, as it was in 1935, the politicians could dismiss many of its potential problems. The Social Security program before Congress in 1935 had no effect on any worker or employer until after the next election, and it was not the center of congressional debate. Although the Republicans could complain that the program was that generation's version of voodoo economics, the complaints failed to resonate with voters who had not yet paid a dime in Social Security taxes. Soon after the election, the abstraction of 1935 became the tax of 1937. Now Social Security had the potential to create problems for its sponsors, such as President Roosevelt, nor did the administration have as much political capital to spend in 1937 as it did in 1935. Roosevelt's political popularity was waning as the result of an ill-advised effort to pack the Supreme Court; his political influence was waning because he was perceived as a second-term, lame-duck president who could no longer blame his problems on his predecessor. All these things combined to produce a sense that something now needed to be done about Social Security, so that people could experience it as more than a painful tax.

The easy answer was to make the benefits more available and more plentiful. With surpluses forming, the easy answer also proved to be the expedient answer. In a felicitous and fortuitous manner, one could raise benefits, reduce future taxes, and lower the projected surplus. At the same time, one could not go too far or the result would be the Townsend Plan—a government giveaway to the elderly that would put a heavy burden on future generations. Social Security policymakers needed to decide just how far to go, and in making that decision, they would inevitably have to make important political and social judgments.

The resulting decisions, legislated in 1939, to pay benefits to dependent children, workers' wives, and workers' widows enhanced the adequacy of the program while compromising the individual equity goal of the system, the notion that benefit amounts should bear a direct relationship to prior contributions. A worker who died and left behind dependent children would get back more on his Social Security investment than would the worker who lived until old age, never married, and never had children. Here then was a shift toward a system that recognized certain social problems as more pressing than others and took steps to solve them.

Arthur Altmeyer believed that the changes embodied in the 1939 amendments would help to ensure the survival of social insurance at a time when its survival remained in doubt. Between 1935 and 1939, the Townsend plan had, if anything, gained in popularity, and congressional debate continued to be dominated by its supporters. In addition, the old-age relief programs (the state non-contributory welfare programs known as "Old Age Assistance," not the federal contributory old-age insurance program) had acquired a political following since they, unlike the old-age insurance program, were already paying benefits. Making old-age insurance more adequate also made it more politically attractive.

With the 1939 mixture of adequacy and equity, the American Social Security program had come of age. We owe our modern old-age insurance program as much to the 1939 amendments as to the original 1935 law.

THE 1950 AMENDMENTS

Although the 1939 amendments marked a significant step in the creation of America's social insurance programs, crucial elements were missing. One was broad coverage under old-age insurance since the program failed to cover farmers, the self-employed, and others outside the industrial or commercial labor force. Another was benefits that reflected America's postwar prosperity and the accompanying higher prices. A program created in the depression needed to be modified for a time of prosperity. After delaying the reform of old-age insurance through the war years and through the postwar conservative resurgence, Congress remedied these defects in 1950 and passed the most important amendments to the Social Security Act since 1939. As a result of the 1950 amendments, the old-age insurance program became America's most successful social welfare program.

After 1950, Social Security made up ground in a hurry. As late as 1940, veterans' programs and state programs, such as welfare and workers' compensation, continued to dwarf Social Security. Workers' compensation payments exceeded Social Security payments by a factor of six; veterans' programs cost fifteen times as much as Social Security. As late as 1950, more than twice as many people were on the state welfare rolls receiving old-age assistance than were receiving retirement benefits from the federal government under Social Security. The average monthly welfare payment was $42 in 1949, compared with an average Social Security benefit of $25.

Welfare predominated over Social Security because it was more widely available and offered its recipients a better deal.[31] As the statistics indicated, America had not yet come to accept social insurance as its primary means of providing aid for elderly persons, and a strong possibility existed that it might never come to do so.

Congress, for its part, appeared ready to accept welfare over social insurance. In the 1940s, although distracted by the war and the problems of postwar adjustment, Congress managed to raise federal aid to the elderly for welfare and to reduce the percentage of the labor force covered by Social Security. Tax rate levels for Social Security remained stagnant throughout the decade (as a result of legislative changes), even though the original law called for the tax rate to rise. Congress refused to raise taxes for something that appeared to have little popular support or that currently did not "need" the money. As if to underscore this lack of popularity, proposals to create an integrated social insurance system—uniting old-age insurance, unemployment compensation, and health insurance in one federal system—failed to go anywhere.

With Social Security in what might be called a crisis of inactivity, Congress proceeded in 1947 as it had in preparing for the 1939 amendments. It appointed an advisory council to study the situation and produce concrete recommendations. This council met in 1948 and issued a report that had a major impact on the future of social insurance. The council, it should be emphasized, met at a time when Congress was under Republican control and not predisposed to pass legislation requested by either the Social Security Board, which ran the program, or the Democratic president, Harry S Truman. The fact that the council ended up with a ringing endorsement of Social Security was nothing short of remarkable.

The 1948 council accepted the twin goals of preventing dependency and reducing the need for public assistance. Framing the problem in this manner, the council also telegraphed its preferred solution. The chosen method to reach these goals, not surprisingly, was the extension of social insurance. The council members looked forward to universal coverage under old-age and survivors' insurance, believing "the character of one's occupation should not force one to rely for basic protection on public assistance rather than insurance."[32]

The advisory council report served as a means of putting the agenda for Social Security expansion on the record in a congenial form. What previously took the form of recommendations from the Social Security Board and President Truman, both perceived to be remnants of the New Deal past, out of step with the realities of postwar America, now became the respectable conclusions of a bipartisan, independent body appointed by a Republican Congress. It marked a necessary but not sufficient step toward the expansion of the program. Report or no report, Congress continued to oppose Social Security expansion.

This situation changed in 1949. Truman won a surprising victory in the 1948 elections, and the Democrats regained control of both houses of Congress. The agenda, so carefully constructed by the advisory council, now fell into the hands of a group with the desire and power to enact it. They went along with the expansion of Social Security as a means of endorsing the continuation of a New Deal institution in postwar America, without having, at the same time, to make many hard choices. An expansion of Social Security did not imply a cutback in welfare. So long as the elderly continued to receive the same level of support from the government, it did not matter much whether this support came from welfare or Social Security. In addition, the political situation had changed somewhat with the creation of collective bargaining agreements in large industries, such as steel and automaking. These guaranteed pensions to workers that included Social Security payments, meaning that an increase in Social Security lessened the burden on large employers, reducing their resistance to an increase in Social Security taxes. Add to all these factors the careful way in which Social Security proposals were framed, and one had the makings of a watershed in Social Security history.

Creating its own mixture of adequacy and equity in 1950, Congress substantially modified the Social Security program, and in direct response the Social Security system revived. Eight million workers, most of whom were self-employed, were brought into the system; and average benefits were increased by about 80 percent (which compensated for the inflation that had taken place since the mid-1930s). In February 1951, for the first time, the number of its beneficiaries exceeded the number receiving old-age assistance.[33] It was a moment of epochal importance in the history of Social

Security, for it marked the point of no return. Social Security, not welfare, now defined America's approach to old-age security.

EISENHOWER

Social Security's triumph over welfare came just in time to withstand the challenge posed by the election of President Dwight D. Eisenhower. He was a Republican, the first member of his party to be president since the passage of the Social Security Act. Conservatives, who had been waiting for the right president, now expected a responsive audience for their ideas.

After the election of 1952, the Chamber of Commerce circulated a Social Security plan to its members, which they enthusiastically endorsed. This plan marked a conservative effort to remedy the perceived defects in Social Security.

The conservative critique began with the notion that Social Security was peculiarly vulnerable to expansion. Every time a new group entered the system, such as the self-employed in 1950, large surpluses developed. That was because, in the beginning, workers always paid more into the program than they received in benefits. Few of the self-employed qualified for Social Security pensions in 1951, yet nearly all of them paid Social Security taxes. Surpluses, according to the conservatives, were politically unstable. They tended to get spent by making present benefits more liberal. One could add disability benefits, raise the basic benefit level, add health insurance, create an early retirement program, or do any number of perfectly plausible things, all with the twin rationale that the country needed them and the program could afford them. When the future came, Congress could always make up any deficits by raising Social Security taxes or adding general revenues. Further, the conservatives believed that that was what the bureaucrats in charge of Social Security really wanted to happen. An adequate program for the elderly mattered far more to these bureaucrats than the preservation of a conservative, contributory financing scheme. Conservatives argued that the bureaucrats used conservative rhetoric to mask liberal objectives.

The Chamber of Commerce plan took as its objective to reveal, once and for all, the true costs of Social Security. It involved making Social Security coverage universal, abolishing federal subsidies to state old-age assistance programs and hence the state welfare programs for the elderly, and moving to a pay-as-you-go method of financing. The plan meant that a person would receive a pension, even if he had never made a contribution to Social Security and that this pension would be funded through payroll taxes. In this manner, workers would directly subsidize people who had never worked. As for the financing of the program, it would be sustained at first by the surplus in the trust funds. As the surplus diminished, payroll taxes would be set to bring in only enough money to pay for current pensions. Any rise in the benefit levels would require an immediate increase in the tax rate. In this manner, the plan's supporters hoped to discipline the program and keep its costs within reasonable limits.[34]

Although pushed by proponents of the Chamber of Commerce plan and by conservatives within his own party, such as Congressman Carl Curtis, to abandon Social Security, President Eisenhower endorsed the existing program instead. Responding to stockbroker E. F. Hutton's characterization of Social Security as tyranny, the president wrote that "it would appear logical to build upon the system that has been in effect for almost twenty years rather than embark upon the radical course of turning it completely upside down and running the very real danger that we would end up with no system at all."[35]

Social Security, begun by the Democrats with relative indifference and ridiculed by the Republicans, had acquired bipartisan approval by the 1950s. Both parties worked toward its extension and improvement.

DISABILITY AND MEDICARE

After 1950 old-age insurance was no longer controversial. At the same time, disability and health insurance remained highly partisan, highly contested, and highly controversial programs. The battles over enactment of these measures proved to be among the hardest in America's political history.

Disability insurance illustrated the incremental approach that policymakers took toward the expansion of Social Security in the 1950s.[36] At first Congress refused to support the payment of retirement pensions for the disabled, even though the advisory council had recommended such a measure in 1948. Then, in 1952, the House of Representatives voted to initiate a "disability freeze." The basic idea behind this notion was that a person unable to work because of a physical or mental impairment could be declared to be "disabled." Such a person could collect a pension at age 65, even though he had not worked for all of the years since the onset of his disability. In effect, the federal government "froze" his record at the moment of disability. The Senate failed to concur, and the measure died.[37] In 1954, however, the disability freeze was again debated, and this time it passed. The measure allowed states, acting through such agencies as the vocational rehabilitation program, to perform the administrative task of determining that a worker was "unable to engage in substantial gainful employment" (earn a minimum amount of money). Finally, in 1956, Congress initiated a disability insurance program under which workers were allowed to receive a disability pension at age 50. In time, this program became modified so as to permit disabled workers of all ages and their dependents to receive both a disability pension and subsidized medical care as well.

The fight over disability insurance served as a prelude to the even tougher political battle over health insurance. Efforts to pass health insurance as part of the Social Security program began in 1935 and continue to the present day.

In 1935, despite concern over the costs of medical care and a realization that these costs could be reduced through what reformers called "group budgeting," the framers of the Social Security Act failed to include health insurance. The reasons were many and varied. Most believed that unemployment and old age constituted more immediate risks than did the inability of workers and their families to pay for medical care. Some also believed that medical doctors might oppose a measure that would affect the way in which medical care was financed. At the time, as already noted, Social Security failed to cover many of the people in most need of national health insurance, and reformers consequently envisioned a program of federal grants to establish state-run health insurance programs.[38]

In the 1940s President Truman decided to make the passage of national health insurance a legislative priority. But although he pressed his case both in 1946 and after his victory in the 1948 elections, he failed to reach an agreement with the American Medical Association over how a health program would be run. Meanwhile, the private sector, acting through nonprofit community-based Blue Cross hospital benefit programs and through insurance plans subsidized by employers and labor unions, experienced a revolutionary expansion in health care coverage. By 1954, for example, unions were responsible for purchasing a quarter of the nation's supply of health care.[39]

Surveying the situation, Social Security officials began to concentrate their efforts on workers who had been left behind by the explosion in private health insurance. In 1951 planners in the Federal Security Agency, the forerunner of the Department of Health and Human Services, explored the idea of health insurance aimed at people who had already retired. Such people experienced particular difficulty in securing adequate coverage against the risk of ill health for two reasons. In the first place, elderly persons who had already retired seldom received health insurance through their former employers. Second, Blue Cross and the private health insurance industry hesitated to extend coverage to the elderly, because, in the jargon of insurance, they were "bad risks." Social Security, by way of contrast, could use its broad base and pool the risk of ill health across many individuals. In essence, this means that it enjoyed a comparative advantage over private insurance in financing health insurance.

The Medicare idea gained popularity slowly during the 1950s. At first, Congress and others interested in Social Security concentrated on the passage of Disability Insurance. With the accomplishment of this goal in 1956, attention shifted to health insurance. Even before Disability Insurance reached final passage, Wilbur Cohen, at the time a professor at the University of Michigan, called health insurance the most pressing need in the Social Security program. "No matter how high you raise the Social Security benefits," he noted, "you can't make them high enough to provide people with adequate health protection unless such health protection is put on a pre-payment basis. Consequently, it is my feeling that it is of prime importance to provide for an increase in Social Security benefits that will be earmarked specifically for payment of health costs. This can be done at a very modest cost."[40]

As with Disability Insurance, America took an incremental path toward national health insurance. In 1960, for example, Congress enacted a program that allowed states to fund medical programs for the elderly who were "medically indigent" and to expand the money available to pay medical costs for the elderly on welfare. These programs followed a "public assistance" format, which meant that they included a means test to determine whether the person applying for help was truly indigent. States were allowed considerable freedom in administering the programs; many failed even to establish such a program.

Social Security officials persisted in their argument that a social insurance approach would both protect the dignity of the nation's elderly people and avoid burdening the general taxpayer with the cost of their health care. Wilbur Cohen, by now a high-level official in the Kennedy and Johnson administrations, devoted a considerable amount of his time to formulating this argument and getting it heard in Congress. He noted that Medicare was not "new," but rather "a means of filling a gap in the floor of protection provided by monthly cash benefits under the Social Security program." Nor did Cohen believe that the proposal for Medicare amounted to socialized medicine. The administration proposal, as Cohen noted, "would not provide a single medical service . . . physicians' services would not be covered or affected and . . . the government would exercise no supervision or control over the administration or operation of participating institutions or agencies."[41]

The labor movement, concerned about obtaining health benefits for union retirees and eager to extend social insurance coverage, joined Cohen and his allies in efforts to pass health insurance. Nelson Cruikshank of the AFL-CIO lobbied particularly hard for the passage of Medicare, as he did on nearly every other important piece of social insurance legislation passed between 1945 and 1984.[42]

After many false starts, Medicare became law in 1965, the heyday of the Great Society. The actual terms of the law remained in flux until almost the moment of passage, but the idea of minimizing federal interference in the practice of medicine remained constant. As Congress prepared to meet in 1965, the legislation, drafted to reflect the ideas of Cohen, Cruikshank, and Social Security Commissioner Robert Ball among others, included such features as a guarantee of freedom of choice of physician and hospital. For the most part, the proposal excluded physician services and included the proviso that, "No supervision or control over the practice of medicine by any physician or over the manner in which services are provided by any hospital is permitted." Bills could be paid "in generally the same manner as is now customary in Blue Cross plans," and any group of hospitals "could designate a private organization of their choice, such as Blue Cross, to receive bills." In addition, due largely to the efforts of Senator Jacob Javits, the bill authorized "associations of private insurance carriers, exempt from anti-trust laws, to sell, on a nonprofit basis, approved policies covering health costs not covered under the Social Security hospital insurance program."[43]

The final bill differed in significant ways from the one sent to Congress. In particular, Congress deleted the Javits provision to allow private companies to sell plans and broadened the legislation to include doctors' services. As finally enacted, the Social Security Amendments of 1965 contained a broad health package that included three major components: Medicaid, subsidized medicine for most federally-assisted welfare recipients; hospital insurance, or Medicare Part A, intended for Social Security retirees; and the supplementary medical insurance program, known as "Part B of Medicare," which paid the doctors' bills and was also intended for retirees. This third program was optional, and beneficiaries had to pay extra for it. Unlike "Part A of Medicare," it involved the use of general revenues and did not depend on payroll tax contributions from workers and their employers.

The scope of the legislation came as something of a surprise to Social Security officials. Wilbur Cohen wrote the president that Congressman Wilbur Mills simply turned to him and asked him to consolidate all of the various proposals before the committee. "The effect of this ingenious plan is, as Mr. Mills told me, to make it almost certain that nobody will vote against the bill when it comes on the floor of the House."[44] Indeed, few people did.

Disability insurance and Medicare resembled each other in an important way. Unlike similar European programs, they illustrated the American dependence on private and state intermediaries in the administration of social insurance programs. Disability insurance, for example, relied on federally-funded state administrators to make the initial determination of eligibility. Medicare used "fiscal intermediaries" and local "carriers" to make payments to hospitals and doctors. Taken together, these programs revealed the complex state-federal, public-private partnerships that characterized American Social Security programs.

Social Security, even into the 1950s and the 1960s, operated in a distinctively American manner. If the notion that the government should limit its aid to the poor no longer controlled American social policy, the traditions of state and private involvement in the provision of social services remained. Few quarreled with this basic design, so long as the general model for American social policy involved a society in which men worked in stable industries. (Then, as now, the model largely ignored single-parent and two-wage-earner families, even though the numbers of both were on the rise during the 1950s.) These men provided for their families, with the aid of their unions and with the aid of a government that protected their retirement benefits, even as it took prudent steps to insure the vigorous growth of the economy. The American way of Social Security seemed to work. It appeared to minimize government interference in the private affairs of individuals and in the corporate affairs of the economy. It undergirded the operations of a dynamic industrial economy, with none of the paternalism that characterized the European version of the welfare state.

SOBERING REALITIES

By any measure, social insurance became the nation's largest and most successful social welfare technique in the period between 1950 and 1980. One might wonder, then, why anyone should be concerned about Social Security and Medicare. The answer, quite simply, is that things change. Indeed, economic and social conditions have changed more quickly than has Social Security, the nation's primary program for the economic and social condition of retirement. Some of the changes reflect the growth of the economy; others are the product of the last twenty years of erratic bust and boom.

Postwar prosperity both expanded and contracted the labor force. On the one hand, prosperity encouraged employers to hire people who were traditionally considered to be outside the industrial labor force. These people included African Americans who had worked as fieldhands in the agricultural south and women who had previously stayed home raising children. The mid-1960s, in particular, marked a period of considerable optimism concerning the nation's ability to integrate new groups into the mainstream. On the other hand, prosperity permitted those employees who felt tired or disabled to retire before the customary age of 65. Social Security, in effect, contained two early retirement programs. One concerned men and women who often elected to take early retirement, and the other involved men and women who retired either because of an impairment or inability to find work. Although distinctions between the two types of programs could be drawn, they often came to resemble each other, as in the case of a 63-year-old man with lower back pain who no longer wanted to assemble automobiles on a daily basis.

The changes in labor force participation that occurred in the 1960s proved disruptive to Social Security. The system was designed with a primary wage earner supporting a family in mind. But many families no longer resembled the traditional family for which Congress legislated family benefits in 1939. The rise of families with two wage earners, one or both of whom dropped out of the labor force from time to time to raise a family, resulted in new issues about the value and fairness of retirement, survivors', and spouse benefits for women.

Ironically, besides representing a potential difficulty for the program's short-term financing, the early retirement provisions of Social Security have also been perceived as a partial solution to unemployment. Though the 1956 amendments to the Social Security Act established the early retirement option for women, legislation extending this option to men was not passed until 1961, in the midst of a recession. A Kennedy administration's fact sheet accompanying the legislative proposal in 1961 explained that it "would help primarily that group of men who because of ill health, technological unemployment, or other reasons find it impossible to continue working until they reach 65."[45] The early retirement provision was also viewed by some as a means of reducing the high unemployment of the period by redefining some unemployment as "retirement." Thus Congressman Charles Vanik stated, "If 2 million male workers eventually retire under this program, 2 million job opportunities will be created, and unemployment will be reduced."[46] However, early retirement, like Medicare and disability benefits, also disrupted the long-range planning on which the system depended. A downturn in the economy might prompt more people to seek early retirement or disability benefits, increasing current costs in a manner that was difficult to anticipate.

As for Medicare, it was heavily dependent on the costs of medical care, yet, by the terms of the 1965 legislation, the federal government had absolutely no control over those costs. If customary rates or prevailing rates rose, the government had little alternative but to pay them. Changes in medical costs were not only difficult to anticipate, but they also increased the Social Security program's reliance on a constantly growing economy.

When the rate of economic growth slowed in the 1970s, Social Security began its passage through a crisis of confidence. In thinking about this crisis, we should note that it took a long time to arrive. As early as 1939, Social Security Administration bureaucrats had realized that a day would come when the system would spend more in benefits than it received from payroll taxes. At that time, the advisory council asked Congress to recognize the need for general revenues to supplement worker and employee contributions. In the 1940s, worried about a possible postwar depression, Congress even wrote this principle into the law, yet it soon thought better of the idea and repealed a provision that called for the federal government to make up deficits in the program through general revenues.[47]

In the affluent 1950s and 1960s, no one gave this matter a great deal of thought. Any crisis appeared to be a long way off and could be averted through careful planning and timely increases in payroll taxes. In the meantime, the program continued to enjoy the benefits of new groups entering the system and of larger than expected increases in wages, both of which increased total contributions into the Social Security accounts.

The crisis in Social Security financing began during the mid-1970s. In that decade, Congress decided to end the bidding to raise Social Security benefits before elections and to increase benefits in a scientific way. Led by conservative members who wanted to contain Social Security costs, Congress opted to "index" the program to the rate of inflation as measured by the consumer price index (CPI). If prices rose, benefits would rise. It seemed a safe bet for the program's solvency since conventional wisdom held that wages, which determined the money coming into the trust funds, always increased faster than prices, which would now determine money going out of the funds.

It seemed a safe bet, that is, until stagflation changed the conventional economic wisdom. During the early and mid-1970s and again in the late 1970s and early 1980s the CPI, which contained costly items like housing and gasoline, increased faster than average wages. Since Social Security benefits are tied to the CPI, their cost began to rise at a faster rate than expected. And since Social Security revenues are tied to a tax on wages, the program's income (relative to outgo) was less than anticipated. Adding to the problems, unemployment rose at the same time as prices did, a near impossibility in the standard economic analysis. That meant even less money came into the system than expected.

The result was a crisis. As one Social Security official explained, "our 1972 estimates turned out to be very wrong, very quickly. But if we had predicted what actually happened in the 1970s, we would have been practicing in an asylum."[48]

In response to the crisis, President Gerald Ford (and Jimmy Carter and Ronald Reagan after him) scrambled to keep the program solvent. A technical flaw in the indexing formula made the financial problems even more pressing by creating large and irrational benefit increases. And demographic changes, including increased life expectancies and declining fertility rates, also added to the financing problem. In 1977, after a painful political battle, President Carter convinced Congress to raise both the percentage of the Social Security tax and the amount of income subject to that tax. Benefits were also scheduled to be reduced slightly to bring them closer to what Congress had intended in 1972 (before the technical problem in the benefit formula arose).

Inflation and wage stagnation continued into the Reagan administration. When the president tried to correct the resultant problems with a tight money policy, a severe recession broke out. Inflation combined with widespread joblessness brought new problems to the Social Security system.

Questions arose just when alternative private sector investments, such as the much-touted Individual Retirement Accounts, appeared particularly attractive because of the high interest rates. Those with money in their pockets looked beyond Social Security for financial help. They compared private sector plans with a public sector plan they were accustomed to think about in private sector terms. Predictably, they found the latter wanting. It became fashionable to "zero it out"—that is, to assume it would not provide any benefits—in sessions between the young and their financial advisers.

Despite the growing criticism of Social Security, Congress and the administration joined forces to "save" the program. In December 1981, Reagan appointed a bipartisan commission, the National Commission on Social Security Reform, to propose solutions to the Social Security problem and report to the president at the end of 1982.[49] The commission's task was to find enough money to get through immediate financial problems and build a cushion for the future. Its proposal did just that. Other than that, the commission firmly believed that "the Congress in its deliberations on financing proposals, should not alter the fundamental structure of the Social Security program or undermine its fundamental principles."[50]

For their own reasons, representatives of both political parties on the commission wanted to save Social Security. Daniel Patrick Moynihan, the ebullient Democratic senator who served on the commission, argued that the key was getting the Republicans to agree that Social Security could be saved through "a combination of relatively modest steps." The alternative—a bankrupt Social Security system—was intolerable to officials who despaired over the fact that polls showed that half the nation did not think it would receive Social Security benefits. Moynihan asked readers of the *Washington Post* to think of what such a default implied: "That government is lying. That government is stealing. That government cannot be trusted. . . . We began to accept the idea that there are fundamental issues that our system cannot resolve. . . . We have got to stop that. There is a center in American politics. It can govern."[51]

Democrats Moynihan, former Social Security commissioner Robert Ball, former Congresswoman Martha Keys, AFL-CIO President Lane Kirkland, and Congressman Claude Pepper worked with Republicans Alan Greenspan (currently the chair of the Federal Reserve Board), Robert Beck (president of the Prudential Insurance Company), Senators Robert Dole and John Heinz, and Congressman Barber Conable and, together with administration figures such as White House chief of staff James Baker, budget director David Stockman, and others, fashioned a compromise. It should be emphasized again that the 1983 compromise left the program largely intact. Essentially, the experts agreed that the problem was in a temporary deficit that would take care of itself in time. In the 1990s, they argued, the system would enjoy a breathing spell. The retirement of the depression generation and the continued employment of the baby boom generation would generate an impressive surplus in the program. The retirement of the baby boom generation, everyone admitted, posed serious problems, but those problems could be handled by careful planning.

Each side sacrificed something. In the spirit of compromise the Democrats, led by Ball, accepted a permanent six-month delay in the annual cost-of-living adjustment—in effect, a roughly 2 percent reduction of benefits for all current and future beneficiaries. The Republicans acquiesced to small increases in Social Security taxes achieved by initiating already-legislated payroll tax increases earlier than scheduled. In addition, the commission recommended that the self-employed pay essentially the same amount as the combined rate for workers and employers. Both sides agreed to the treatment of up to one-half of Social Security income as taxable income for middle- and higher-income beneficiaries and to the extension of coverage to new federal employees.

In its deliberations, Congress used the work of the commission as the basis of the 1983 amendments. Additionally, Congress incorporated into those amendments a provision that will gradually increase the normal retirement age from 65 to 67, beginning in the next century, and used the 1983 legislation to initiate a prospective payment system for Medicare's Hospital Insurance program known as "diagnosis-related groups" (DRGs).

Shortly after passage of the 1983 amendments, other factors turned in Social Security's favor and increased its financial solvency. The smaller depression cohort began to retire and the larger baby boom cohort remained in the labor market. The disability rolls shrunk, in part because administrators made it harder for workers to qualify for disability benefits and to keep them, once received. And by the end of Reagan's first term, the economy entered a long and sustained boom, with low inflation, that lasted throughout his second term.

But Social Security was not free of all its problems. Now the problem seemed to be that for the next twenty-five to forty years there was too much, not too little. Large surpluses began to accrue in the Social Security coffers, spawning a new round of political debate, similar to the one in the late 1930s, over the government's ability to pre-fund the retirement of a large age cohort, in this case the members of the baby boom generation. New questions began to be raised about the desirability of the build-up. Could Congress avoid the temptation to use these funds for new products? Should a strategy be initiated to maintain large reserves as a means of strengthening the national economy in preparation for the retirement of the baby boom generation? Were Social Security's surpluses being used to help fund the federal deficit and hide large yearly deficits in federal general revenues? Should payroll tax rates be reduced and the system returned to pay-as-you-go funding?

Medicare, too, continued to pose complex dilemmas, as health care costs continued to rise, and as the entire health care financing system threatened to unravel. The baby boom's retirement also promised to challenge Social Security and perhaps change it. Indeed, plans for raising the retirement age were already on the books, and it seemed likely that some tax and benefit adjustment would be necessary thirty or forty years hence to maintain the system's financial stability.

As the century neared its end, however, it became clear that Social Security had wrought a permanent change on the nation's social welfare policy. In the 1980s, few people suggested a return to the traditional welfare system, with its means tests, case workers, and great variations from place to place. Instead, they worked hard to try to preserve the Social Security and Medicare programs so as to meet the challenges of the next century.

If history teaches anything, it is that the program is constantly under construction, constantly responding to new political and demographic forces.

We gradually came to accept a contributory, wage-related retirement system. Although it did not reflect popular preference during the depression, Roosevelt nonetheless slipped it through an open window of political opportunity. Social Security worked well in the postwar era, but that does not mean that it will work well in the next century. Only if we accept the program as man-made, rather than as a form of permanent truth or of irreducible evil, can we seriously sort out the policy options for the years that lie ahead. First, however, we need to understand more about how the current program operates, a task to which we now turn.

The Modern Social Security and Medicare Programs

The modern Social Security and Medicare programs, those cumulative results of nearly sixty years of legislation, affect all Americans, first as taxpayers and then as beneficiaries. Policy debates, which often take place on a global level and engage public attention from time to time, matter less to most people than do those intense moments when the program becomes a matter of personal decision and has a strong impact on their lives. These moments arrive for nearly all of us. They occur when, for example, an older worker makes plans to retire; when a young worker notices that he is paying more "FICA" than federal income taxes; when a recently widowed mother with young children applies for survivors' benefits; when a Social Security beneficiary wants to know how much he can earn without loss of benefits; when a hospitalized beneficiary is discharged before he feels ready to return home; when a medical secretary seeks reimbursement for services rendered by her office. Such mundane concerns put the public in touch with Social Security and Medicare.

We would be the first to admit that program details can be boring, and we urge the reader to use this chapter as a compendium of information, rather than to regard it as a well-formed essay on the nature of Social Security. Accordingly, the goal of this chapter is not to make the reader a benefits expert but rather to provide easy access to basic benefits information and to impart a sense of how the public experiences those benefits. Where possible, we have used special headings to mark the passages that describe the various types of benefits. We encourage the reader to skim over these descriptions, so as to gain a sense of the program's complexity and diversity. We try to be brief and to keep the use of jargon to a minimum. Starting with the point of entry to the programs, we describe each program and give a sense of the benefits available under that program and of how the program is financed.

APPLYING FOR SOCIAL SECURITY AND MEDICARE

When seeking information about Social Security and Medicare, most people use a special toll-free number (currently 1-800-772-1213). Most people want this information when they contemplate retirement, wish to receive a disability pension, or experience a death in the family. The Social Security operator can answer questions, initiate an application for benefits, schedule an appointment in a local office, or mail out relevant information. Since so many requests fall into routine categories, Social Security has tried to save money by resorting to an automated phone answering service. Without even speaking to another human being, simply by pushing a button on a touch tone phone, people can request applications, receive audiotaped information, and order pamphlets.

Some people want to meet someone in person rather than over the telephone. Although not encouraged to do so, people can still walk into any of the 1,300 Social Security Administration (SSA) offices. But the wait can be long. Walk-ins may be warned about the length of wait and advised that they might be better off using the telephone or making an appointment. Here is how SSA puts it in one of its most widely circulated public information pamphlets:

> Of course, you're always welcome to visit the office nearest you.
> But the easiest way to reach us is to call our toll-free number. . . . You can call from 7 a.m. to 7 p.m. every business day.
> If you'd prefer to talk to someone at your local office, the telephone service representative will be happy to give you the number.
> The Social Security Administration treats all calls confidentially. But we also want to ensure that you receive accurate and courteous service. That's why we have a second Social Security representative listening to some incoming and outgoing telephone calls.[1]

Here is how the system works in practice. Imagine you are 63 and considering retirement. You want to know how to apply for Social Security and Medicare, and you are a little vague about whether you qualify. You do not know the size of your potential benefit or whether your 61-year-old wife, who works and likes her job, also qualifies for a benefit. So you dial "411" and ask for the number of your local SSA office. The operator gives you the 800 number for SSA as well as the number of your local office.

You dial the local number. It is busy. You eat a sandwich and try again. The line is still busy. You watch a television program and try again. Still busy. Although you do not know it, Congress has forced SSA to list the local number in the book. For a number of years, this number had remained confidential, and casual inquiries were handled exclusively through the 800 number. But, as of the time of publication of this book, Congress and the Office of the Management of the Budget would not allow SSA to spend already-available funds for staffing the local offices, with the result that the phone lines are nearly always engaged.

Frustrated, you give up and dial the 800 number. This time your call gets answered, and you are greeted by a sufficiently pleasant voice. "Thank you for calling Social Security," says the voice, as you experience the inevitable disappointment that accompanies the realization that you have reached a recording. "A representative will answer your phone call in approximately two minutes." Indeed, you do get through to the operator. You want to know how much your benefit will be if you retire in the next few months and how to apply for that benefit. The 800 operator answers your questions clearly and without hesitation. These are, in fact, the types of questions the service is well designed to handle. For example, if you are over age 60, the SSA information operator can access your Social Security record and provide a close approximation of your benefits. Also, this operator can arrange an appointment, either by telephone or in person, with your local office, and if you wish, give you the telephone number of your local office.

For many beneficiary and public requests, the 800 number provides an effective, if bloodless, means of conducting business. Well-trained operators can handle most routine inquiries and often save a person a trip to a local SSA office. Updated computer systems provide quick access to earnings records and benefit projections, and clients are generally pleased with the service provided during visits to local offices, with 77 percent indicating in a 1986 study that SSA had done a "good" to "very good" job in handling their business.[2] Nonetheless, SSA's staff reductions, from 87,000 people in 1983 to 61,000 in 1990, have resulted in uneven services from place to place.[3] They have limited the agency's ability to provide special attention to persons with complex needs. As a result, telephone calls to local offices and visits to SSA can be enormously frustrating, with busy signals and long waits, occasionally followed by incomplete, erroneous, or only partially accurate information provided by a burdened staff. Complex situations, such as those requiring home visits to a house-bound applicant or the provision of translators by SSA, often are not handled well. Non-English-speaking people are expected to call the 800 number and visit SSA offices with someone who can translate for them. Although the SSA will arrange for translators as a last resort, translators are, as a practical matter, rarely available, especially for the more "unusual" languages.

With or without difficulties, nearly all who try eventually get through to SSA and receive the benefits to which they are entitled. We look now at the benefits themselves.

SOCIAL SECURITY: FINANCING WORKERS' BENEFITS

Workers earn retirement, survivors', and disability protections by paying Social Security taxes in employment covered by Social Security, which is to say, in over 95 percent of all the employment in the country. As most people now know, payroll tax payments do not go into a special savings account earmarked for particular workers and their families. Instead, these tax revenues mostly fund current benefits. Social Security financing is held together mainly by the taxing power of the government and the public's interest in sustaining the program along with the political pressures that follow. Current benefits come largely from the taxes paid by current workers, with the promise that the current workers will themselves receive benefits when they become eligible for them. In return for the taxes, SSA maintains a record of the earnings on which workers have paid payroll taxes. This record provides the basis for establishing eligibility to program benefits and determining the size of those benefits.

Workers contribute not to the general revenues of the federal government, but to three separate but interrelated trust funds. The first covers the Old-Age and Survivors Insurance program (OASI). The second finances the Disability Insurance program (DI), and the third pays for Medicare's Hospital Insurance program (HI). Payroll taxes account for most of the money that goes into these funds, but OASI and DI also receive general revenues from the income taxes that some middle-class and higher-income people pay on their Social Security benefits. The government also regularly adjusts the balance in all three trust funds to reflect the interest the federal government pays to the trust funds for money borrowed from the Social Security and Hospital Insurance trust funds.

It is difficult to know how to categorize this sort of transaction, for it raises the perplexing question of just what the money in the trust funds represents. In fact, the money in the trust funds goes partly to pay current benefits and 59administer the program and is also borrowed to help fund the other operations of the government (with interest returning to the trust funds). Perhaps the best way to think about the matter is to think of the money in the trust funds in the same way that one thinks about money in the bank: there if it is needed but actually not there in a physical sense because it is being spent by others. Just like a bank, the federal government must know how to manage its trust funds so as to make sure that the money is available when its customers, in this case Social Security beneficiaries, need it. But nothing guarantees the solvency of the trust funds, other than the faith and trust that people put in the United States government's continuity and ability to meet its obligations.

Something called the Federal Insurance Contributions Act governs the payroll tax contributions of wage and salary workers. Most pay stubs have a window called FICA (or, alternatively, show OASDI and HI payments separately). The figure(s) in the window(s) record the dollar amount withheld from earnings for Social Security and Medicare. Employees make payroll tax payments into the OASI, DI, and HI trust funds of 7.65 percent (6.20 percent for OASDI on earnings up to $57,600 in 1993 and 1.45 percent on earnings up to $135,000 for HI) (see Table 6.1). Employers must pay an equal tax. If it makes sense to talk about an average worker making average earnings, then we can say that the average employee's combined Social Security and Medicare tax is about $1,820 in 1993, with the maximum contribution being $5,529 for workers earning $135,000 or above.

Self-employed persons make contributions under the Self-Employment Contributions Act (SECA) at a rate that is the same as the combined rate paid by employers and their employees.[4] The large contribution of over $10,000 for those in the highest income brackets is mitigated by a tax rule that allows the self-employed to compute their taxes on a smaller base (net earnings from self-employment less 7.65 percent) and to deduct half of their payroll tax contributions from their income taxes.[5] In this manner, the Social Security trust funds get the full amount of the tax, and the self-employed person pays less tax, in a manner somewhat similar to the way in which employers fund OASDI, HI, and fringe benefits for their employees.

The exact amount of the earnings subject to the Social Security tax, called the taxable earnings base, may change each year according to a formula based on increases in the average level of wages. The idea is for Social Security to get a constant share of the economic pie, even as the pie grows. Without this automatic increase, a smaller and smaller proportion of earnings would be subject to taxation as inflation and economic growth resulted in increases in wages.

The system relies on elaborate rules that link contributions to benefits. Workers receive a "quarter of coverage" in 1993 for each 590 dollars they earn in a job covered by Social Security. In 1993 a worker can accrue up to four quarters of coverage by making 2,360 or more dollars that year. One does not have to work for more than a day or even an hour to get four quarters of coverage. All it takes is $2,360 in wages. The rules base eligibility for benefits on the number of quarters of coverage a worker has accrued.

To be eligible potentially for retirement and survivors' benefits, workers generally need one quarter of coverage for each year after 1950 or, if attaining age 21 after 1950, for each year after age 21 and before reaching age 62, or dying or becoming disabled before age 62. At least six quarters are needed but never more than forty. Disability coverage has its own rules. To be potentially eligible for disability benefits, workers also generally need credit for twenty out of the last forty quarters (five out of the last ten years), unless disabled before age 31, in which case fewer quarters are needed. For example, a person who is disabled in the quarter of attaining age 27 will only need twelve quarters.

SOCIAL SECURITY: THE BENEFITS

Most often, receipt of a Social Security pension is triggered by a worker reaching what is considered retirement age under Social Security. The death of a worker and long-term disability can also precipitate benefit flows. How much people actually receive each month depends on the type of benefit, prior earnings in jobs covered by Social Security, and sometimes the age at which a beneficiary first receives benefits (see Table 4.1).

The amount of the benefits generally depends on a concept known as the "primary insurance amount" (PIA). One can think of the PIA as the monthly benefit to which a worker is entitled if he accepts retirement benefits at the age he is first eligible to receive full retirement benefits (currently age 65). Social Security has a benefit formula that translates each worker's lifetime earnings in jobs covered by Social Security into a primary insurance amount. Benefit levels then get expressed as percentages of PIA. Surviving children of dead workers *may* receive 75 percent of the covered worker's PIA, and the monthly benefit for workers retiring at age 62 is *currently* 80 percent of the PIA.

Although these rules seem simple to understand, if rather arbitrary, they are riddled with exceptions that add to the system's complexity. Surviving children may get 75 percent of PIA, but this situation does not cover a family with several children. Each child does not receive 75 percent of PIA. Instead, the family receives a maximum amount. Nor does the program have just one benefit formula. Instead it has several, the most widely used of which is the "wage-indexed" benefit formula. By ensuring that Social Security reflect changes in the prevailing wages over a person's life, this formula helps main-

Table 4.1
The Value of Social Security in January 1993

Average monthly benefits*

All retired workers	$653
Aged couple	$1,106
Widowed mother/father and two children	$1,288
Aged widow alone	$608
All disabled workers	$627
Disabled worker, spouse, and child	$1,076

Maximum benefits for workers retiring at age 65 in 1993

Retired worker	$1,128
Total family maximum on retired worker's earning record	$1,692

*Benefits can be higher or lower.

Source: David Koitz, "Social Security: Brief Facts and Statistics," *CRS Report for Congress* (Washington, D.C., Congressional Research Service, January 4, 1993)

tain prior standards of living for retired workers as well as for disabled workers and surviving beneficiaries.

As a general rule, higher earnings result in larger benefits, but, as we have emphasized, the program attempts to balance adequacy and equity. Social Security assists individuals and their families to maintain adequate living standards. The system seeks to meet this objective through three distinct devices. First, it provides survivors' and family benefits. Second, it maintains a benefit formula that provides proportionately higher benefits to workers who have worked consistently at lower-paying jobs. Third, it contains an annual cost-of-living adjustment that adjusts benefits to the rate of inflation (see Table 4.2).

It helps in trying to make sense of this large and sprawling program to remember that it is primarily a retirement program, with a large portion of the money going to retired workers and their spouses. But even retirement, as defined by the program, brings with it a plethora of choices that center on when to retire and how much to earn in retirement. Workers may elect to start Social Security benefits at the earliest age—age 62—and by doing so accept a reduction (currently 20 percent) in all future Social Security checks to make

Table 4.2
Who Gets Social Security Benefits (as of February 1992)

Retired workers	25.3 million
Spouses of retired workers	3.1 million
Aged widows and widowers*	5.1 million
Children under 18 of deceased, disabled, and retired workers	2.6 million
Students aged 18–19**	0.1 million
Disabled adult children	0.6 million
Widowed mothers and fathers with dependent children	0.3 million
Disabled widows and widowers	0.1 million
Disabled workers	3.2 million
Spouses of disabled workers	0.3 million
TOTAL	40.6 million***

*Includes about 7,000 elderly dependent parents of deceased workers and special age 72 beneficiaries.
** Specifically, this category includes students aged 18 to 19 and two months who are children of deceased, disabled, and retired workers, and who are full-time elementary or secondary school students.
*** Due to rounding error, column does not add up to 40.6 million.

Source: Social Security Bulletin (Spring 1992), tables 1.B1, 1.BB3, 1.B4, 1.B5, and 1.B7.

up for the extra years of receiving benefits. Alternatively, workers may wait until age 65 to receive what SSA calls "full benefits" or plan to receive a monthly benefit that has been permanently increased beyond "full benefits" for delaying retirement past age 65. The choice of retirement age may also reflect the benefits of other family members, increasing or decreasing benefits available to spouses and other family members. Inevitably, then, calculations concerning health, employability, life expectancy, and one's preference for leisure over work all enter into the retirement decision. Further, the complexity of choices surrounding when to retire is further compounded by changes in the law that shift the age eligibility for full benefits and the value of early and later retirement benefits for future cohorts of retiring workers, especially today's young.

With these details as background, we can delineate the major benefits for retired workers.

Full retirement benefits. Workers born before 1938 are eligible for full retirement benefits, 100 percent of the PIA, at age 65. The full retirement age will increase gradually to 67 between 2003 and 2027, with accompanying reductions in benefits for early retirement. For all people born after 1959, the full retirement age will be 67. Some view this and related retirement age changes as benefit reductions, while others point out that these changes simply reflect lengthened life expectancies. Regardless, we should note that increases in the retirement age may be to the early decades of the next century what scheduled tax increases were to the 1930s and 1940s: parts of the law from which Congress retreats as the time for their implementation approaches.

Early retirement benefits. Most retirees begin receiving benefits before age 65. If a person claims benefits early, whether by choice or because of unemployment or ill health (but not disability), the benefits are permanently reduced for each month of retirement before the full retirement age. That works out to a benefit of 80 percent of the PIA if benefits are claimed before the year 2000 at age 62. The reduction in benefits will be larger for persons claiming early retirement benefits after 2000. Note, however, that the age of early retirement will not be raised in the future, even though the age for full retirement benefits will rise. That might cause much political attention to focus on early retirement and may lead to higher benefits for those workers who retire early.

Delayed retirement credits. Today benefits are increased for workers who choose to claim their retirement benefits after the full retirement age; for workers reaching age 65 in 1993, the increase amounts to about 4 percent a year up to age 70. The value of this credit is being increased gradually to 8 percent for each year of delayed retirement. Increases in this credit are being phased in gradually until 2009. Beginning with people who reach the full retirement age of 66 in 2009, the delayed retirement credit will be increased to 8 percent a year up to age 70. This change will go far toward eliminating the disincentives that keep employable people from waiting to age 70 to retire.

Special Minimum Benefits. This provision, an alternative way of computing the PIA, is designed to help workers who worked consistently at low-wage in jobs covered by Social Security. It results in the payment of a somewhat higher benefit than the person would have received if the regular benefit formula had been used.

Family members of retired and disabled workers may be eligible for an entirely different set of benefits, known as auxiliary benefits, although there is a ceiling, called the *family maximum*, on the amount of benefits that can be paid on a worker's earning record. By keeping a family's retirement income below the income it received before retirement, this family maximum provision eliminates a disincentive that may cause productive people to retire instead.

Auxiliary benefits take the following specific forms:

Benefits for older spouses. Spouses aged 62 and over are eligible to receive a benefit based on their own earnings or a benefit based on a percentage, ranging from 37.5 percent to 50 percent, of the retired worker's PIA. The choice of age 62 for this benefit reflected the judgment of policymakers who believed that it was normal for a 65-year-old man to have a younger wife. Accordingly, Congress first chose in 1956 to reduce the age of these benefits for wives as well as retirement benefits for women from 65, as it was in the 1939 law, to 62. Later, during a recession, Congress decided to extend these benefit options to men, in part, hoping that the retirement of older male workers would open up employment opportunities for younger workers. We should also note that the law also maintains an implicit analogy to early retirement in that spouse benefits are permanently reduced for each month of receipt before age 65 and that spouse benefits carry an entitlement to Medicare but only at age 65.

Spouse benefits for fathers and mothers. Regardless of age, the spouse of a retired (or disabled) worker who is caring for a child under 16 receives a full spouse benefit of 50 percent of the workers' PIA subject to the family maximum mentioned earlier. Other caretaking situations that also qualify a spouse for a full spouse benefit, regardless of age, include taking care of a mentally disabled or a physically disabled person (aged 16 or older), provided the disability began before age 22.

Retirement benefits for divorced spouses. Divorced spouses are generally eligible to receive the same spouse benefits based on the earnings histories of their former spouses as long as they had been married to the eligible retired worker at least ten years. Unlike married spouses, divorced spouses can receive benefits if the worker is 62 or older, even if the worker is not retired.

Children's and grandchildren's benefits. Unmarried dependent children under 18 (or up to age 19 if a full-time elementary or high school student) and even some dependent grandchildren under age 18 (or up to age 19 if a full-time elementary or high school student) of a retired or disabled worker may be eligible for a benefit equal to 50 percent of the worker's PIA. Again, this is subject to the family maximum.

Adult disabled children's benefits. The same benefits—50 percent of the PIA—may be payable in certain cases to the unmarried dependent disabled children of retired or disabled workers who are at least age 18, if the disability began before age 22. (They may also receive Medicare benefits after a twenty-four-month waiting period.) Adult disabled children's benefits generally do not terminate if the beneficiary marries another Social Security beneficiary.

We should emphasize again that these benefits are not simply entitlements based on age. Beneficiaries under age 65 can make $7,680 in 1993 without loss of benefits. If the person earns more, his Social Security benefit gets reduced by a dollar for every two dollars he earns. Should he earn a great deal, he will not be considered retired, and his Social Security benefit will shrink to nothing, though benefits will eventually be larger because of the provision that rewards delayed retirement. Note, however, how this provision favors the poor, who can earn a higher percentage of their former wages, over the rich. Someone between 65 and 69 can earn $10,560 in 1993 without penalty. Beyond that, the person's benefits are reduced one dollar for every three dollars he earns. The earnings test has been a subject of much controversy, with some arguing that it discourages work and others advocating its maintenance because they view Social Security as replacement for lost earnings and because mainly higher-income beneficiaries would benefit from its repeal. Increasingly this debate amounts to little more than a "tempest in a teapot." Ultimately, the phasing in of larger delayed retirement credits will essentially offset most benefit losses from the earnings tests.

Beyond these basic retirement benefits, the program maintains a full range of survivors' benefits that come complete with their own auxiliary benefits. Survivors' benefits refer to the set of benefits that the program pays to the family of workers who die before or after retirement age. Each month Social Security provides checks to over 7 million survivor beneficiaries: young children, surviving widowed mothers and fathers, aged widow(er)s, certain disabled widow(er)s, and in some rare instances, surviving parents. The major benefits for survivors are as follows:

Widow(er)'s benefits. Nearly all older widows and widowers are eligible to receive Social Security pensions. Spouses aged 60 and over and divorced spouses of workers covered under Social Security may be eligible for aged widow(er)'s benefits upon the death of the worker. Currently, the benefits generally range between 71.5 percent and 100 percent of the PIA plus delayed retirement credits where applicable. Taken at the earliest age today (60), widow(er)'s benefits are permanently reduced to 71.5 percent of the deceased worker's PIA (unless they inherit delayed retirement credits). This percentage increases to 100 percent if the benefits are first taken at age 65.

Surviving mother's and father's benefits. A widow or widower (of any age) may be eligible to receive surviving mother's or father's benefits of 75 percent of the deceased worker's PIA if caring for a child of the worker who is either under age 16 or disabled and entitled to survivor's benefits on the worker's record. Divorced surviving mothers or fathers must be caring for a natural or adopted child who is entitled to a child's benefits on the worker's record.

Disabled widow(er)'s benefits. Even without dependent children, widow(er)s and divorced widow(er)s aged 50 through 59 can receive monthly benefits equal to 71.5 percent of the PIA, but only if they themselves are disabled and their disability began within seven years of the worker's death. After a two-year waiting period, disabled widow(er)s are eligible to receive Medicare benefits as well—a benefit that is available to other widows at age 65.

Benefits for divorced and remarried spouses. The qualifications for benefits for divorced aged widow(er)s and disabled widow(er)s are essentially the same as for non-divorced survivors except that the marriage must have lasted for at least ten years.

Surviving children's benefits. Nearly two million children receive these benefits and 98 percent of all children are potentially eligible if a parent who works dies.[6] Many people (especially young people with children) have more life insurance protection under Social Security than through private mechanisms.

For example, consider a worker, who died in 1990 at age 35, who earned about $35,000 in 1989 and had an average earnings pattern before then. His survivors are his wife and two children, ages 8 and 10. By the time the youngest child reaches 18, this family could receive more than $177,000 in Social Security benefits, and this does not include any future cost-of-living increase.[7]

Surviving children under age 18, surviving children of any age who were disabled before age 22, and surviving children aged 18 and, in some cases, 19 who are full-time elementary or secondary school students are eligible for monthly benefits if a parent or, in some cases, grandparent was insured by the program at the time of death. Surviving children receive benefits equal to 75 percent of the deceased worker's PIA. Parents do not have to have been married for their children to be eligible.

Surviving parent's benefits. Under certain circumstances, the dependent parent aged 62 or over of a fully insured deceased worker is also eligible for survivors' benefits.

Workers below 62 may also receive disability benefits for long-term and severe disability, provided they can show to the satisfaction of the disability determination service in their particular state that they are unable to engage in substantial gainful activity. We explore disability policy in greater detail in Chapter 8. For now it is enough to state the basic concept behind the program. To be considered disabled, in January 1993 a person needs to be unable to make $500 a month because of a physical or mental impairment that is expected to last at least a year or result in death ($880 for blind people). A worker does not actually have to earn this amount to be ineligible for benefits; he just must be able to earn it. A worker must be unable to do any kind of work that exists in significant numbers in the national economy. The availability of jobs is not taken into consideration, although age, education, and previous work experience are.

Eligibility for DI benefits is reviewed periodically to see if the person's medical condition has improved and if the person is now able to work. Workers have the right to appeal within sixty days of receiving notice from Social Security if their application for DI benefits has been rejected (or if they are notified that their benefits will be terminated after a periodic review). Benefits stop if a worker recovers from the disabling condition and is therefore able to work. However, DI beneficiaries who are still disabled may have a nine-month trial work period, during which there may be no loss of benefits. Also, Medicare benefits may continue for three years after DI benefits cease because of a return to work.

Benefits for disabled workers. When workers covered under Social Security become disabled, they may be eligible, after a five-month waiting period, to receive monthly DI benefits for the duration of the disability. After twenty-four months of entitlement to such benefits, disabled workers (as well as disabled widows and widowers aged 50 through 64, and adult disabled children aged 18 or over who were disabled before age 22) are eligible for all Medicare benefits. Medicare does not, however, cover other family members (except for a spouse who is 65 or over).

Benefits for family members. Children under age 18, a child aged 18 or older who became disabled before age 22, a spouse who is caring for a child under 16 or for a disabled child, or a spouse (or divorced spouse) aged 62 or over may be eligible for monthly benefits. Benefits for family members of disabled workers are identical to those for family members of retired workers, except that the maximum amount a disabled worker's family can receive is generally lower.

SUPPLEMENTAL SECURITY INCOME (SSI)

Description of Social Security benefits would not be complete without reference to SSI, a program with numerous interactions with OASDI. SSI and Social Security are often confused, because SSA administers both, their names are similar, and some beneficiaries of Social Security also receive SSI as well. As a welfare program, the right to a SSI benefit is established by financial need.

In 1992, SSI provided cash benefits to an estimated 5.5 million low-income, aged, disabled, and blind persons. That amounted to a total federal and state expenditure of about $20.2 billion in fiscal year 1990. The government used this money to guarantee a minimum monthly income of $434 for a single person and $652 for a couple in 1993. Some states, such as California, supplemented this basic federal guarantee. Most SSI beneficiaries (3.3 million) are under age 65.

Local Social Security offices handle virtually all SSI applications. As noted, financial need, rather than prior employment in a job covered by Social Security, is a condition of eligibility. The person must have income and resources (assets) below a certain level. SSI beneficiaries are also almost always eligible for Medicaid benefits and for food stamps (except in California and Wisconsin, which add the value of food stamps to SSI to increase their state supplement).

For reasons that have to do with history and politics, blindness is always separated from other forms of disability, and blind people receive preferential treatment in SSI as they do in disability insurance. Unlike social security, SSI does not provide for early retirement; one must be 65 to qualify, unless, of course, one qualifies under the disability or blindness provisions. In fact, the great bulk of the caseload consists of disabled people, including 300,000 disabled children. A recent Supreme Court case has forced SSA, which administers the program, to reevaluate childhood disability applications denied since 1980. That should greatly expand the SSI rolls, perhaps by as much as 125,000 cases.[8]

MEDICARE

The Social Security Administration administers SSI but not Medicare. The Health Care Financing Administration handles this program, even though Social Security offices process enrollment applications and provide limited information about the program. The program and its paperwork are both very complex, often driving beneficiaries and medical offices to distraction. After assisting an elderly relative to negotiate the Medicare bureaucratic requirements, one person known to the authors commented in jest that Medicare paperwork is the federal government's secret weapon for killing off the elderly.

As we know from our review of the program's history, Medicare is actually two programs: Part A or Hospital Insurance and Part B or Supplementary Medical Insurance. The former deals with bills submitted by hospitals; the latter handles bills from doctors. Together they provide benefits to the aged (65 and over), the disabled, and persons with permanent kidney failure. The right to benefits is established primarily by payroll tax contributions and monthly premium payments by beneficiaries.

If Medicare is complex, it is also very expensive, a condition that has not escaped the attention of advocates of national health insurance who believe that health care financing could be made both more comprehensive and more simple. Estimated Medicare spending for 1993 is about $146 billion, with no sign that the costs will abate in the near future. Like everything else about the program, its financing provisions are very complicated. Part A works similarly to the rest of Social Security. Workers and employers pay taxes that go into a special trust fund. The government collects the HI tax as part of the FICA and SECA taxes. Part B relies upon a differing financing mechanism, premium payments by beneficiaries and federal revenues. The voluntary contributions of $36.60 a month in 1993 finance about a quarter of the cost of Part B. The government makes up the rest from general revenues (and a very small portion from interest from the trust fund's investments). The general revenue subsidy creates a strong incentive for people to participate in Part B.

Medicare has severe financing problems. Rising health care costs, a general lack of cost controls across the entire health care system, and the unwillingness of politicians to raise Social Security taxes above their present, already high, levels explain why Part A will go bankrupt around the turn of the century, without some sort of remedial legislation. One can predict that Congress will act on this matter, but its actions may well reflect the politics of the moment and are therefore difficult to predict. Social Security advocates view the remedial legislation as an important opportunity to gain a national health insurance program. Conservatives, however, regard the need for remedial legislation as a chance to increase the voluntary and means-tested features of Medicare. As for Part B, it is in no danger of going bankrupt in a formal sense, since its funds come from voluntary contributions and general revenues. The balance of the two may well shift in the future, with program beneficiaries asked to bear more of the load.

The great bulk of Medicare expenditures goes to pay for hospital costs for aged and disabled beneficiaries. To be eligible for reimbursement for hospital costs, a beneficiary must need hospital care, have it prescribed by a physician, and be treated in a hospital that participates in Medicare. (Nearly all do.)

Hospital Insurance benefits. Beneficiaries are responsible for paying only one deductible—$676 in 1993—per *benefit period* for hospitalization, a benefit period starting on the day someone enters a hospital and ending after they have been "out of the hospital (or other facility for 60 days in a row)."[9] After that, Medicare pays for the next 59 days of covered inpatient hospital care, including a semiprivate room, meals, special care units (e.g., intensive care), operating and recovery room costs, X rays, lab tests, radiation therapy, medical supplies, rehabilitation services, drugs provided by the hospital, and blood (except for the first three pints). Of course, beneficiaries still pay for telephone service, television, and the like (see Table 4.3). If further hospital care is needed, Medicare pays for the next 30 days of care, after the beneficiary makes a copayment—$169 a day in 1993. If further care is needed in a benefit period, a 60-day lifetime reserve which requires a daily copayment—$338 a day in 1993—can be used.

Copayment requirements and limitations on numbers of days of protection are two of the important reasons that many elders have purchased private medigap insurance policies to supplement Medicare. Without adequate me-

Table 4.3
Medicare (Part A): Hospital Insurance-Covered Services for 1992

Services	Benefit	Medicare Pays	You Pay
HOSPITALIZATION Semi-private room and board, general nursing and miscellaneous hospital services and supplies. (Medicare payments based on benefit periods.)	First 60 days	All but $652	$652
	61st to 90th day	All but $163 a day	$163 a day
	91st to 150th day[1]	All but $326 a day	$326 a day
	Beyond 150 days	Nothing	All costs
SKILLED NURSING FACILITY CARE You must have been in a hospital for at least 3 days and enter a Medicare-approved facility generally within 30 days after hospital discharge.[2] (Medicare payments based on benefit periods.)	First 20 days	100% of approved amount	Nothing
	Additional 80 days	All but $81.50 a day	$81.50 a day
	Beyond 100 days	Nothing	All costs
HOME HEALTH CARE Medically necessary skilled care.	Part-time or intermittent care for as long as you meet Medicare conditions.	100% of approved amount; 80% of approved amount for durable medical equipment.	Nothing for services; 20% of approved amount for durable medical equipment.
HOSPICE CARE Pain relief, symptom management, and support services for the terminally ill.	If you elect the hospice option and as long as doctor certifies need.	All but limited costs for outpatient drugs and inpatient respite care.	Limited cost sharing for outpatient drugs and inpatient respite care.
BLOOD	Unlimited if medically necessary	All but first 3 pints per calendar year	For first 3 pints.[3]

1992 Part A monthly premium:	None for most beneficiaries. $192 if you must buy Part A (premium may be higher if you enroll late).

1 This 60-reserve-days benefit may be used only once in a lifetime .
2. Neither Medicare nor private medigap insurance will pay for most nursing home care.
3. To the extent the blood deductible is met under one part of Medicare during the calendar year, it does not have to be met under the other part.

Source: Health Care Financing Administration, *The Medicare 1992 Handbook,* Baltimore, 1992.

digap protection, as many beneficiaries are, a long-term hospitalization can still be financially devastating. This risk to beneficiaries—especially those with low and moderate incomes—was one of the factors giving rise to passage of the Medicare Catastrophic Coverage Act of 1988. The act, which was later repealed largely because higher-income elders objected to shouldering much of its cost, eliminated all costs for covered hospital care (after the first day deductible) and added other protections, most of which are no longer available.

Under certain circumstances, HI also covers a substantial portion of certain types of home health care including skilled nursing, speech therapy, and physical therapy as well as hospice for dying persons. Also, following hospitalization, for beneficiaries requiring inpatient skilled nursing care or rehabilitation, Medicare may pay for the first 20 days of such care in a participating skilled nursing facility and most of the next 80 days—with the beneficiary responsible for a copayment for days 21 to 100 ($84.50 per day in 1993).[10]

Reimbursement for medical costs under HI is usually fairly simple because the institution that treats the beneficiary and the *intermediary*—the organization (usually an insurance company) with whom Medicare contracts to handle HI claims—take care of all the paperwork. However, beneficiaries often need to be involved with the paperwork as it relates to their medigap coverage or when unfavorable determinations are made regarding reimbursement (see Table 4.3).

Medical Insurance benefits. For those enrolled in the Medicare Part B Medical Insurance program, benefits (summarized in Table 4.4) provide for certain doctor's services, other medical and health services—including many surgical services, outpatient hospital services, diagnostic procedures—limited mental health care, certain self-administered drugs, radiation treatments, limited home health care and home dialysis costs.

MI will generally pay for 80 percent of approved charges for most covered services after the beneficiary has paid the MI deductible in a calendar year (the first $100 of approved charges in 1993). The deductible and coinsurance do not apply to certain services, such as home health visits. Beneficiaries may be responsible for additional costs since "approved costs" may be less than what is billed by the service provider.

MI beneficiaries also must pay the portion of a medical bill that exceeds what Medicare calls "approved charges," as well as services not covered by MI. Doctors and medical suppliers who accept assignment agree to accept approved charges as payment in full. Doctors file the benefit claim for MI beneficiaries. Even so, reimbursement under MI is often more complex than under HI.

While it increases the economic security and access to health care for millions of Americans, there is much Medicare does not do. Most notably, many people do not realize until it is too late that Medicare provides ex-

Table 4.4
Medicare (Part B): Medical Insurance-Covered Services for 1992

Services	Benefit	Medicare Pays	You Pay
MEDICAL EXPENSES Doctors' services, inpatient and out-patient medical and surgical services and supplies, physical and speech therapy, ambulance, diagnostic tests, and more.	Medicare pays for medical services in or out of the hospital.	80% of approved amount (after $100 deductible).	$100 deduct-ible,[1] plus 20% of approved amount and limited charges above approved amount.
CLINICAL LABORATORY SERVICES Blood tests, biopsies, urinalyses, and more.	Unlimited if med-ically necessary.	100% of approved amount.	Nothing for ser-vices.
HOME HEALTH CARE Medically necessary skilled care.	Part-time or inter-mittent skilled care for as long as you meet con-ditions for bene-fits.	100% of approved amount; 80% of approved amount for durable med-ical equipment.	Nothing for ser-vices; 20% of approved amount for durable med-ical equipment.
OUTPATIENT HOSPITAL TREAT-MENT Services for the diagnosis or treatment of illness or injury.	Unlimited if med-ically necessary.	80% of approved amount (after $100 deductible).	$100 deductible, plus 20% of billed charges.
BLOOD	Unlimited if med-ically necessary.	80% of approved amount (after $100 deductible and starting with 4th pint).	First 3 pints plus 20% of approved amount for additional pints (after $100 deductible).[2]

1992 Part B monthly premiums: $31.80 (premium may be higher if you enroll late).

[1] Once you have had $100 of expenses for covered services in 1992, the Part B deductible does not apply to any fur-ther covered services you receive for the rest of the year.

[2] To the extent the blood deductible is met under one part of Medicare during the calendar year, it does not have to be met under the other part.

Source: Health Care Financing Administration, *The Medicare 1992 Handbook,* Baltimore, 1992.

tremely limited protection against the cost of community- and institutionally-based long-term care resulting from chronic illness.

In providing this overview of the many, and often bewildering, provisions of Social Security and Medicare, we hope this chapter gives insight into not only the complexities but also the importance of these programs to individuals and families. We turn our attention now to examining policy issues and choices shaping the future of these programs and the citizenry they serve.

Does Social Security Protect Today's and Tomorrow's Old?

Having offered so much description, we can now turn to analysis. It is time to judge Social Security against some external criteria.

In this chapter, we examine the adequacy of Social Security protections, beginning with a review of the current economic status of the elderly population. As we examine the contribution of Social Security, we also discuss its shortcomings and whether it is likely to provide sufficient protection for elders of the future. We shall discuss the value of Social Security for future cohorts of elderly persons. And we shall see that simple stereotypes of the elderly as "all rich" or "all poor" do not provide a useful view of the elderly (or of any other demographic group).

It is important to recognize that the overall economic status of elderly persons is greatly improved since the early 1960s. Some interpret this improvement to mean that the elderly are "doing too well." Others consider the growing tendency to describe the elderly as "affluent" to be misleading, especially since many of today's elders—including large numbers of minority elders, the very old, and single women—still lack adequate financial resources and many other elders have only modest retirement incomes. Noting that there are many affluent elders, still others suggest that consideration be given to reducing benefits or raising taxes for this group. While some observers are convinced that elders of the future may receive little, if any, retirement protection from the program, analyses by others suggest that Social Security will be the mainstay of the economic well-being for today's young and middle-aged, when they are old.

THE ECONOMIC WELL-BEING OF THE ELDERLY POPULATION

The standard of living for today's elderly population far exceeds that which generally prevailed for elderly persons during the 1950s and 1960s because today's elderly have benefited greatly from the strong performance of the postwar economy as well as from expansions in Social Security and other public and private pensions. Economic growth allowed the nation to devote more resources to Social Security and to develop other pensions. By doing so, it helped institutionalize a relatively new and major period of "leisure"—the economists' term for activities other than paid work.[1] For workers during this period, the benefits of economic growth translated into increased ability to prepare for retirement through the accrual of rights to larger Social Security and other pension benefits, more equity in homes, and more savings. "From a statistical point of view," notes James Schulz, "the elderly in this country are beginning to look a lot like the rest of the population; some very rich, lots with adequate income, lots more with very modest incomes (often near poverty), and a significant minority still destitute."[2]

Whether measured as trends in median incomes, poverty rates, or wealth, the data confirm the improved economic status of the elderly population as a whole.[3] Median income of families, mainly elderly couples, headed by persons aged 65 or over as measured in inflation-adjusted 1989 dollars (what economists call real or constant dollars) increased from $13,620 in 1965 to $16,149 in 1970, $19,384 in 1980, and $22,806 in 1989.[4] Primarily reflecting economic growth and decisions made to improve the adequacy of Social Security, poverty for all persons aged 65 and over, as measured by the official U.S. poverty rate, declined from 35.2 percent in 1959 to 24.5 percent in 1970 and 12.6 percent in 1985—certainly a noteworthy success.[5] Since then the elderly poverty rate has fluctuated around 12 percent, 12.4 percent in 1991. (In 1991 persons 65 and over, living alone, were defined as poor if their cash incomes fell below $6,532. For those living with another person, the poverty threshold was set at $8,241.)[6] Moreover, this period saw significant improvements in the well-being of the elderly resulting from increased availability of in-kind benefits, most notably Medicare, Medicaid, and Food Stamps for low-income elders.

These and other trend data tell an important part of the story of the economic status of the elderly. To stop here might give the mistaken impression that problems of poverty prevention and other forms of income insufficiency are virtually solved for the elderly. But we need only pull apart some of these summary statistics to see the great diversity of economic circumstances of today's elderly. As warns Boston College economist Joseph Quinn:

. . . never begin a sentence with "The elderly are . . ." or "The elderly do . . ." No matter what you are discussing, some are, and some are not; some do, and some do not. The most important characteristic about the elderly is their diversity. The least interesting summary statistic is the mean because it ignores the tremendous dispersion around it.[7]

The data presented in Table 5.1 further highlight this diversity. Elderly individuals in the bottom 20 percent of the income distribution received an average of $4,221 in cash income in 1989, about 4.6 percent of all income going to all single elders. In contrast, those in the upper 20 percent received an average of $32,331, about 48.2 percent of aggregate income to single elders. The story is much the same for elderly couples, with the bottom fifth averaging $8,940 (5.7 percent of aggregate income) and the upper fifth averaging $75,091 (47.4 percent of aggregate income).

These and other data do not lend support to the growing stereotype that the elderly are a homogeneously affluent group, anymore than people of any age group belong to a homogeneous group. Some elders are very well-off.

Table 5.1
Average Cash Income (Post-Transfer and Pre-Tax) and Shares of Aggregate Income Going to Elderly Units in 1989 by Quintiles

Family Type and Income Quintile	Average Cash Income	Share of Aggregate Income
Elderly Childless Families[a]		
Lowest	$8,940	5.6%
Second	$15,967	10.1%
Middle	$23,381	14.8%
Fourth	$34,869	22.0%
Highest	$75,091	47.4%
Average	$31,657	
Elderly Unrelated Individuals[b]		
Lowest	$4,221	6.3%
Second	$6,806	10.1%
Middle	$9,414	14.0%
Fourth	$14,286	21.3%
Highest	$32,331	48.2%
Average	$13,414	

[a]Refers to households of two or more (mostly couples) with no children under age 18 headed by a person aged 65 or over.

[b]Refers to households consisting of a single person age 65 or over.

Source: Tables 32 and 33 in U.S. House of Representatives, Committee on Ways and Means, *Background Material and Data on Programs Within the Jurisdiction of the Committee on Ways and Means* (Washington, D.C.,: U.S. GPO, 1991), pp. 1197–1200. Derived from tabulations from the March 1990 Current Population Survey.

For example, among the 20.9 million households with people aged 65 and over in 1991, 10 percent reported receiving at least $50,000 in money incomes and 22 percent reported from $25,000 to $49,999. Others, such as the 23 percent who reported $15,000 to $24,999, may be comfortable, especially if they have accrued substantial equity in their homes and are in good health. But over 40 percent of elder households continue to have resources that seem likely to support more modest lifestyles, at best, even taking into consideration the value of homes and non-cash benefits such as Medicare. Among these households are the 28 percent reporting cash incomes of less than $10,000 and 30 percent reporting $10,000 to $19,999 in 1990.[8]

While only 12.2 percent of the elderly are defined as poor in 1990, a very different picture of the prevalence of poverty emerges when these data are

Table 5.2
Poverty Status of Elderly Persons
(percent below poverty in 1990)

All elderly persons	12.2
Men 65+	7.6
Married	5.3
Widowed	13.8
Divorced, separated, never married	16.1
Women 65+	15.4
Married	5.7
Widowed	21.4
Divorced, separated, never married	24.3
Black men	27.8
White men	5.6
Black women	37.9
White women	13.2
Black men living alone	44.0
White men living alone	13.1
Black women living alone	60.1
White women living alone	24.0
Persons 85 and over	20.2
Hispanic elderly persons 65 and over	22.5

Sources: U.S. House of Representatives Committee on Ways and Means, *Background Material and Data on Programs Within the Jurisdiction of the Committee on Ways and Means* (Washington, D.C.: U.S. GPO, 1992) and Bureau of the Census, "Money Income and Poverty in the United States: 1990," *Current Population Reports*, P-60, no. 175 (Washington D.C.: U.S. GPO, September 1991).

disaggregated in terms of racial and ethnic groups, gender, and age. On the one hand, married elderly persons have a relatively low incidence of poverty, with about 5.5 percent of married persons aged 65 and over defined as poor in 1990. On the other, elderly single women have very high rates of poverty; 24 percent of white and an astounding 60 percent of African American unmarried elderly women had below poverty incomes in 1990 (see Table 5.2). The data tell a similar story for Hispanic elders, 22.5 percent of whom were poor in 1990. Poverty rates are also substantially greater among the very old, with 12.6 percent of men and 24.1 percent of women aged 85 and over being poor compared to 6.4 percent of men and 12.3 percent of women aged 65 to 74.[9] In short, the very old, African Americans, Hispanics, and single persons, especially women, are at substantial risk of poverty.

The picture that emerges from these data is one of improvement in the economic well-being of the elderly, much of which can be attributed to Social Security. But this improvement falls short of preventing large numbers of elders from being in or at the edge of poverty and leaves many moderate- and middle-income elders vulnerable to potentially catastrophic financial situations such as death of a spouse or the cost of long-term chronic illness. Let us look further at the major income sources for the elderly.

THE CONTRIBUTIONS OF SOCIAL SECURITY TO THE ELDERLY

Although the most central source of income for the elderly, Social Security is but one of several (see Table 5.3). Social Security (along with relatively minor contributions from Railroad Retirement) accounts for 40 percent of all income going to elderly households in 1990. Assets income, pensions (public and private), and earnings are also major sources of cash income for elderly persons, respectively accounting for 27, 18, and 12 percent of all the income going to elderly households in 1990. Elderly households also receive public and private in-kind benefits (including Medicare, Medicaid, and employer-provided health insurance) and benefit from home ownership and a number of tax breaks directed at the elderly.[10]

Social Security, the most pervasive source of cash income, goes to roughly 95 percent of the households headed by elderly people. Its importance varies substantially by income group. Elderly households with less than $10,000 income received three-quarters of their cash income from Social Security in 1990, compared to about 30 percent for households with $30,000–$49,999. Earnings, assets income, and other pension income generally make more substantial contributions to middle- and upper-income elderly households than to low-income elderly households (see Table 5.3).[11]

As these figures suggest, Social Security plays a major role in reducing and preventing poverty. Imagine, for a moment, that the nation eliminated Social Security and all other cash and in-kind transfers. Now take a look at Table 5.4, which allows us to see what the effect would be. Without all these

Table 5.3
Importance of Various Sources of Income to Aged Units,
65 and over in 1990

		Total Family Income From				
All Aged Units	Units Under $10,000	$10,000– $19,999	$20,000– $29,999	$30,000– $49,999	$50,000– $74,999	$75,000 and over
Percent of Total Income From:						
Social Security and/or Railroad Retirement	39.9	74.5	59.9	42.3	29.5	19.8	10.1
Private or other public pension	17.7	4.5	15.2	22.0	25.3	23.1	12.1
Interest, dividends	27.3	6.4	16.3	25.0	30.3	37.1	51.1
Earnings	(11.7)	1.6	5.7	8.7	12.8	18.5	25.5
Public Cash Assistance	0.7	4.9	0.5	0	0	0	0

Source: U.S. House of Representatives, Committee on Ways and Means, *Background Material and Data on Programs Within the Jurisdiction of the Committee on Ways and Means* (Washington, D.C.: U.S. GPO, 1992), table 14, p. 1250.

programs, the poverty rate would have increased overnight in 1990 from 13.7 percent to 53.6 percent for elders and substantially, though less dramatically, for younger groups. In fact Social Security's specific contribution is to decrease elder poverty from 52.8 percent to 14.7. Without Social Security, $39.6 billion would have needed to be transferred to close the "poverty gap" in 1990; that is, to move every elderly person above the poverty line. Social Security (along with minor contributions from other cash social insurance programs) reduced that gap to $5.7 billion dollars. Though not means-tested, it would appear that Social Security does much to meet the needs of poor and other potentially low-income elders. As we have seen, Social Security substantially reduces the risk of economic insecurity, but whether it will continue to do so for today's young and middle-aged, now and in the future, requires further discussion.

Clearly, if one believes the program is destined for financial collapse, then it is only reasonable to conclude that today's young will receive little benefit, except those derived indirectly from protections extended to their parents. Given such a perspective, we would simply conclude that today's young, without doubt, are losers.

Our analysis, however, assumes the continued existence of Social Security. Of course, this does not mean that benefits and taxes will not be changed,

Table 5.4
Antipoverty Effectiveness in 1990 of Cash and Selected Non-Cash Transfers (Including Federal Income Taxes and Payroll Taxes)

	For All Individuals in Families or Living Alone	Individuals in Units with Unmarried Head and Children < 18	Married Couples with Children < 18	Individuals in Units with All Members 65 or Over
POVERTY RATE IN 1990 (percent in poverty)				
Cash Income Before Any Transfers	20.5	49.5	10.9	53.6
Plus Cash Social Insurance Benefits (other than Social Security)	19.7	48.6	10.3	52.8
Plus Social Security	14.4	46.6	9.6	14.7
Plus Means-Tested Cash Transfers	13.5	43.7	8.9	13.7
Plus Food and Housing Benefits	11.8	37.1	7.9	11.0
Less Federal Taxes	12.3	36.8	8.4	11.1
POVERTY GAP in 1990 (in billions of 1990 dollars)				
Before Transfers	124.4	33.4	15.0	39.6
After All Cash Social Insurance Transfers	70.5	30.0	11.7	5.7
Means-Tested Cash Transfers	52.5	20.4	9.0	4.2
After All Cash and In-Kind (food and housing benefits) and Taxes Transfers	40.6	12.2	6.9	3.4

Source: U.S. House of Representatives, Committee on Ways and Means, *Background Material and Data on Programs Within the Jurisdiction of the Committee on Ways and Means* (Washington, D.C.: U.S. GPO, 1992), tables 18–22, pp. 1304–13.

"downwards" or "upwards," or that new provisions will not be added or old ones revised in response to economic and demographic change. Nor does it mean that there are not major challenges likely to confront Social Security in the future.

To start, Social Security helps the young and the middle-aged in several ways. By providing the vehicle by which workers can, through modest payments over time, help protect themselves and their older relatives, Social Security frees up young and middle-aged workers to concentrate more of their resources on today's young children and helps stabilize family life. Older family members do not wish to depend on their adult children for financial support, preferring instead to rely on a combination of Social Security, other pension, and savings. Without Social Security, many elderly people would, of necessity, have to turn to their adult children for financial assistance and/or housing, a situation that could lead to emotional and financial strains within families and to a loss of dignity for many elderly persons.

Younger and middle-aged workers also gain immediate protection for their families through survivors' and disability insurance. Even if the risks being protected against do not occur, disability insurance and survivors' insurance have tangible worth. They generally provide the major source of disability and survivors' insurance for the young and middle-aged, providing protection that would be costly to duplicate privately. For example, it is estimated that for a worker aged 35 with average earnings in every year and a nonworking spouse aged 32 and two children under age 6, Social Security coverage provides the equivalent of a life insurance policy and a disability insurance policy, each with a face value of over $250,000 in 1993 dollars. And unfortunately, for some people the risks being protected against do occur. This is why there are 2.6 million children under age 18, 620,000 disabled adult children, 300,000 surviving spouses (mostly widows) caring for young children, 3.2 million disabled workers and their spouses receiving benefits each month, and another 120,000 persons aged 18 to 19 who fall into the special surviving student's category.

Importantly, Social Security also holds the potential to go a long way toward solving the retirement savings dilemma most workers must confront. Ideally, as James Schulz points out, workers should strive through Social Security, other pensions, and savings to maintain their pre-retirement standard of living throughout retirement.[12] To accomplish this objective, the worker must deal with a number of uncertainties since he does not know whether he will change jobs, whether he will become disabled, when he will retire, the rate of inflation, how long he will live, or whether he will die before his spouse. Social Security helps workers cope with those uncertainties.

As a mechanism for retirement savings, Social Security holds advantages for younger and middle-aged workers. Unlike private pensions, Social Security is highly portable. Workers can earn credit toward their Social Security retirement pension on nearly every job. Unlike nearly all private pensions, Social Security fully adjusts for changes in the standard of living prior to receipt of benefits *and* for inflation after receipt of benefits. The Social Security benefit formula works to replace relatively constant proportions of pre-retirement earnings for workers at different earnings levels: about 57 percent for workers retiring at the full retirement age who earned minimum wages throughout their lives, and 42 percent for those with average earnings. For workers, this means that even before they receive benefits, the value of their benefits is adjusted for rising wages and changing standards of living. Thus, because the anticipated growth of their wages during work lives will translate into larger benefits, the retirement benefits for today's middle-aged and young workers (and for those who follow) are likely to be larger on average and to have greater purchasing power. Analysis by Social Security's actuaries shows that while a worker earning average wages throughout his life and retiring at the full retirement age in 1990 would receive $9,104 in benefits in that year, a worker with a similar earnings history retiring in 2010 would receive $10,669 in 1991 dollars.[13] Annual benefits should be even larger for workers reaching the full retirement age in future years. For example, an average worker retiring at full retirement age in 2030 is estimated to receive about $13,127 in 1991 dollars. Of course, if these estimates were not adjusted for inflation, benefit amounts would appear gargantuan, fully $60,597 in 2030. Workers having earnings equal to the maximum wages that are taxable under Social Security throughout their work lives and retiring at full retirement age in 2030 can expect to receive about $21,000 (in 1991 dollars). We need to keep two things in mind, however. Because most workers are likely to continue to begin accepting benefits prior to the full retirement age, the actual value of benefits received by most retiring workers will generally be lower. Second, as larger portions of Social Security income become subject to the income tax, the after-tax value of benefits will decrease somewhat.

Now with these basic ideas, let us speculate about the standard of living for tomorrow's elderly and assess Social Security's future importance.

As with current retirees, the economic well-being of future retirees will be dependent on more than Social Security. Other pension income, savings, earnings, home ownership and health care coverage will also be important for the elderly as a whole and need to be taken into account. Since so much uncertainty about the future of the economy and the direction of public and private pension and health care policy exists, experts disagree about what the future will be. A few observers anticipate dire economic circumstances for those retiring 25 to 60 years into the future, unless social commitments to today's and tomorrow's elderly are radically reduced and efforts are directed at expanding private retirement savings.[14] Most analysts, while not complacent about the challenges that will face the U.S. retirement income system, reach less alarming conclusions.

While experts may differ substantially among themselves, they have reached some general agreement.[15] Two separate projections, one by the Congressional Budget Office (CBO) and the other by the Employee Benefits Research Institute (EBRI), a research institute sponsored by organizations that plan and administer employee benefits plans, suggest that Social Security will remain the main source of retirement income, especially for low-income retirees of the future. CBO projects that "for those in the bottom half of the retired population" in 2019, "some 60 percent to 70 percent of their income will come from Social Security" and for those in the upper half, about one-third.[16] These projections also suggest that private and other employer-provided pensions will act, as they are intended, to fill in the gap for higher-income retirees, providing 30 to 40 percent of the cash incomes for the upper half of the income distribution for baby boom retirees.

Using the EBRI model, Emily Andrews and Deborah Chollet compare the expected retirement incomes at age 67 of older baby boomers aged 25 to 34 in 1979 to workers aged 55 to 64 in 1979. They find that Social Security, while still the major source of retirement income, will become less important, with employer-provided pensions becoming more so. Robert Ball cautions, however, that targeting the analysis on the year the retiree turns age 67 overstates the importance of these other employer pensions. As retirees age, the value of employer pensions, as opposed to Social Security, generally diminishes as a result of inflation. As most workers with Social Security and an employer-provided pension age, Social Security provides a larger portion of their retirement income.[17]

Together, these analyses also suggest that the baby boom's standard of living in retirement is likely to at least equal that of current retirees.[18] Both projections suggest that the dollar amount (adjusted for inflation) of the baby boom's retirement incomes will be larger than that of today's retirees. How-ever, the Andrews and Chollet analysis suggests that replacement rates—that is, the proportion of pre-retirement income replaced by all pensions—will decline somewhat relative to today's retirees. They point out that:

> A gloomy prognosis for the baby boom in retirement seems unwarranted. Despite their greater numbers and relative handicaps in terms of earnings and career advance-ment compared to earlier generations, the baby boom's retirement years appear to be secure. . . . A greater number of baby boom retirees will receive pensions compared to workers now retiring, and their real retirement income will be higher, as will their Social Security benefits.[19]

These expected improvements in the cash income position of most future retirees should not be interpreted as suggesting that their future is entirely economically secure. Without significant public and private intervention, the potential cost of health and long-term care, will—as it does today—pose a major risk, especially as retirees reach advanced old age.[20] Income and wealth are likely to be distributed more unequally among baby boom retirees, than among current retirees.[21] John Palmer, the dean of Syracuse University's Maxwell School, describes this phenomenon as the "pulling apart of the 'haves' and the 'have nots' among the elderly in the future—with the economic status of those at lower income levels declining in the future relative to the status of nonelderly people, and the status of the well-to-do continuing to gain."[22]

Moreover, while poverty rates are likely to decline, poverty will likely be more concentrated on single people, particularly single women.[23] The CBO projection, for example, suggests continued high rates of poverty and of near-poverty for single people.[24] Two other analyses suggest the same thing. The EBRI analysis views single women, especially divorced women, to be at greatest economic risk. Although 97 percent of single women are expected to receive Social Security pensions, 43 percent will be poor or near-poor, according to the projection.[25] Michael Hurd's forecasts of the economic status of the elderly until 2003 identify single, widowed elders as the group at greatest risk. He predicts that most elderly couples will have an adequate standard of living.[26]

So, what are we to make of all this evidence with respect to the adequacy of Social Security for future retirees? If we believe most of the experts, Social Security will be the main source of income and provide the best hope for basic economic security for low- and moderate-income persons. Yet even so, many single women and others are likely to be at risk of poverty, just as they are today. The future, in other words, looks a lot like the recent past. As for middle- and upper-middle-income workers, it appears likely that Social Security will provide an adequate floor of protection. For these groups and for the highest-income workers, Social Security benefits will likely be supplemented by private and other employer-based pensions and by assets accumulated over a lifetime. Yet even many among the well-off need be concerned, as a House Ways and Means Committee report points out, that returns on savings and pension investments may not be as large as expected, that some private pensions may not survive, and that savings may not compensate for greater longevity.[27] And nearly all need be concerned with the risks posed by the cost of health and long-term care.

THE ISSUES

Summing up the discussion so far, we can see that Social Security does much to ensure adequate retirement incomes for current and future retirees, but it cannot do the entire job. It remains to assess how various policy proposals might move Social Security closer to or further from the goal of providing adequate protection, however that vague concept might be defined. Plainly, substantial numbers of retirees and current workers lack sufficient protection to ensure their well-being in retirement. Deciding whether and how to respond, and sorting out the extent to which Social Security should respond to shortages of retirement income, raise many important public policy questions. For example, is the economic risk of retirement to upper middle- and higher-income elders best addressed through changes in Social Security, private pensions, older worker policies, or some combination? Should the remaining risk of poverty and near-poverty in old age be addressed through changes in Social Security, welfare programs, or health policies?

Means-testing Social Security is one change that is often mentioned. This change holds many implications for the adequacy of the Social Security program. Of necessity, many Americans rely on benefits from welfare programs such as SSI or AFDC for financial support. The right to welfare, however, requires proving financial hardship through testing the amount of income an individual or family receives (income test) and/or testing the amount of assets (savings, stocks, value of equity in an automobile) an individual or family has. In other words, a person must prove that he or she is poor to get benefits, a process that citizens find distasteful and that tends to undermine the dignity of the individual. Although welfare programs target benefits to the most needy in society, they generally provide small benefits and are very vulnerable to budget cuts. If Social Security were means-tested, Social Security might develop some of the political problems that characterize welfare programs. Alternatively, means tests might lose their stigma.

In recent years, means-testing Social Security has been advocated primarily as a way of reducing government expenditures. This practice might also keep people who do not need benefits from receiving them, thereby targeting benefits to those most in need. We, however, side with the defenders of Social Security and oppose means tests. Means tests are difficult and costly to administer. They also create other problems. Let us assume we wanted to eliminate persons considered to be "better-off," say beneficiaries with $40,000 a year or more in income, from receiving Social Security benefits. To accomplish this task would require collecting income information from the over 41 million beneficiaries on a regular basis. How many people would we eliminate? Benefit rolls would be reduced by roughly 12 percent. At the same time, we believe that political support for the program would be reduced, because the program would no longer be seen as benefiting all income groups. Higher-income workers would no longer have an interest in sustaining the program. Although means-testing Social Security would undoubtedly save a substantial amount of money, these savings need to be assessed against the damage they might do to other program goals.

We believe that Elizabeth Wickenden, an active participant in Social Security policy discussions since the New Deal, puts the matter best:

Social Security owes its success and popularity to the fact that its benefits are certain, predictable and involve a minimum of inquiry into and control over the private and financial affairs of its beneficiaries. . . .

The best way to deal with widespread poverty is to prevent its occurrence. One cannot prevent poverty by a benefit based on its prior existence (however essential a network of such benefits may be to deal with unusual, individual situations).[28]

Cost-saving alternatives to means-testing do exist. Increasing the proportion of Social Security benefits that are subject to taxation is one such alternative, the implications of which will be discussed in the next chapter.

Another proposal that could affect the program's adequacy is to reduce the cost-of-living adjustment (COLA), an idea advanced in recent years primarily to limit federal expenditures. In 1983, as discussed in Chapter 3, the COLA was permanently delayed for six months, amounting to a roughly 2 percent cut in benefits for all current and future beneficiaries. More recently, the idea of delaying, skipping, or otherwise reducing the COLA has been advanced as part of various budget-deficit reduction proposals. With respect to the adequacy goal of Social Security, the difficulty here is that this step would undermine the economic security of beneficiaries, especially low- and moderate-income ones.

We believe the annual COLA is best understood as a mechanism to maintain the purchasing power of benefits once received, not as a benefit increase. Part of the rationale for the COLA is that it makes little sense to set up a social insurance system in which the purchasing power of benefits declines the longer people receive them. And giving the COLA only to lower-income beneficiaries would be administratively complex and would introduce a means test, which we oppose.

If the exigencies of the politics of the federal deficit require placing some of the burden of balancing the federal budget on Social Security beneficiaries, then further taxation of benefits will be better than eliminating or skipping the COLA, because it will place greater burden on higher- as opposed to lower-income beneficiaries.

One change already made, the scheduled increase in the full retirement age (discussed in Chapters 3 and 4), has important implications for the adequacy of Social Security. As noted in Chapter 4, the 1983 amendments to the Social Security Act legislated a gradual increase, from 65 to 67, in the age of eligibility for full retirement benefits over a twenty-four-year period beginning in 2003. A related reduction in the value of benefits for persons accepting early retirement benefits and for spouses of retired workers will be phased in beginning in 2000. Thus, for those first accepting early retirement benefits at the earliest possible age (62), the value of their benefits will ultimately drop from 80 to 70 percent of a full benefit. Spouses subject to the new retirement ages will experience similar benefit reductions. Widows and widowers first claiming benefits after age 60 will also have larger benefit reductions beginning in 2000, as their age for full benefits begins to rise to 67.[29]

Older workers in poor health and widows, widowers, and spouses with fewer options to retirement will bear the greatest cost of these changes. Economist Frank Sammartino, who has analyzed the implications of the retirement age provisions of the 1983 amendments, observes that older workers "in poor health, but whose health problems are not severe enough to keep them bedridden or completely unable to work, are likely to retire from 1 to 3 years earlier than workers in good health with similar economic and demographic characteristics."[30] If this pattern continues, there is reason to believe that the cost of the retirement age change will fall most heavily on lower-income early retirees as opposed to the large number of early retirees who are relatively healthy and more likely to leave work by choice and with higher retirement income expectations.

Advocates of this change argue that it is a fair and reasonable way of reducing expenditures. They point out that life expectancies, and hence the number of years beneficiaries receive retirement benefits, have increased and are expected to increase even further. Even after age 67 becomes the new normal retirement age, future beneficiaries will generally receive retirement benefits for more years than current beneficiaries. In the future the real value of Social Security benefits will be greater than it is today, even with the change in retirement age provisions. Moreover, this change, proponents point out, will encourage work effort on the part of the old.

Opponents of raising the retirement age argue that this change undermines the adequacy goal of Social Security, coming mostly at the expense of lower-income persons who are unable to work due to limited employment opportunities and poor health. There are better ways of encouraging work among the elderly, they argue.

Still others neither advocate nor oppose the rise in the retirement age. They point out, however, that, if the retirement age is raised, then perhaps disability benefits should be easier to obtain, particularly for older workers.

The adequacy issue touches not only the matter of disability but gender as well. In recent years the adequacy and fairness to women of Social Security, and indeed of the entire retirement income system, have emerged as particularly sensitive issues. Issues with a gender slant in terms of their politics include the high proportion of widows with incomes below poverty, the lack of disability protection for homemakers, and the inadequacy of benefits for divorced spouses. These issues also include the lack of credit under Social Security for time spent out of the labor force doing caregiving work at home, the fact that benefits paid to a retired couple in which both spouses worked are generally lower than benefits paid to a couple with a similar pattern of total earnings in which only one spouse worked, and the reality that a woman who works outside the home will often get what amounts to a higher benefit as a spouse than she will get as a wage earner in her own right.[31]

The current political interest in gender, along with the growing awareness of the needs of low-income elderly women, suggests that more attention may be given to these concerns, though a projected long-run deficit in Social Security may serve as a "drag" on such changes. Earnings sharing is one approach to solving problems related to gender. This approach would credit each partner with one-half of total household earnings in employment covered by Social Security for the years during which a marriage exists. Philosophically, it is very attractive because it treats marriage as an economic partnership, with each partner deserving an equal share of the fruits of their combined effort. While solving many problems, the proposal would leave other problems unsolved without major refinements, especially those affecting low-income divorced, widowed, and disabled women today. Also, to implement it without greatly increasing the cost of Social Security would require significantly reducing the benefits of future beneficiaries, including, in all likelihood, divorced men, married men, and married women who have a limited or no history of paid employment.

The adequacy issues for today's and tomorrow's low-income disabled, divorced, and widowed women are arguably more important than the equity issues concerning working women. Further, concentrating on making modest improvements in benefits for economically vulnerable and potentially vulnerable women may be more feasible, given scarce resources, than earnings sharing which would be very costly to implement. For example, recently, the more stringent test of disability for disabled widows' benefits was changed so that it is the same as the one currently applied for disabled workers' benefits. In a similar manner, benefits for disabled widows (and widowers, though there are relatively few) could be raised from 71.5 percent of a full benefit to 100 percent. Time spent out of the labor force to care for children under 18 or for disabled family members might be credited toward disability insurance and Medicare protection. Consideration could be given to limited earnings-sharing provisions for divorced spouses. And to assist low-income women who left the workforce to care for young children or other family members, credit for those caregiving years could be given toward the special minimum benefit, which provides an alternative way of computing Social Security benefits for workers who have worked for many years but at low wages.

Others argue that the issue should not be framed in terms of poor (and otherwise vulnerable) women versus working women, and that equity for all women requires gradually phasing in a modified earnings-sharing proposal. For example, such a proposal "could assure that a surviving spouse would inherit the combined wage credits accumulated by a couple during marriage so that a majority of widows and widowers could get the same or higher benefits than under today's system," and modifications could also be made in the case of disability.[32]

CONCLUSION

As we have discussed, Social Security has made an extraordinary contribution toward the well-being of the elderly. For this reason and because the program may have reached the outer bounds of what is financially acceptable, some counsel caution when reforms are proposed to improve the program's adequacy. They point out that across the board increases in the value of benefits would be extremely expensive and not called for, given the improved economic status of the elderly as a whole. More prudent actions are possible, however. Improvements in administration could open up access to Social Security (and SSI) for persons who are not fluent in English and others with special needs—who are more likely to be among the poor. Consideration could also be given to increasing the special minimum benefit and to changes such as the ones previously identified as addressing the special adequacy concerns of women.

Much of what remains to be done to prevent poverty and assist middle-income families is outside of Social Security's domain. As we will discuss in other chapters, there is more need to protect against health and long-term care costs, and there is need to make investments today in the future of the economy so that the promise of Social Security remains viable in the future. For those who are currently poor, much can be done to make SSI benefits more widely available. For the middle class, we must strengthen the private pension system. And for those on a trajectory toward economic insufficiency in old age, there is a need to intervene as early in their lives as possible through educational and employment opportunities, since economic need in old age is often just an echo of what has gone before.

Is Social Security
Financially Stable?

Asked about the future of Social Security, most young and even many middle-aged workers respond that they are not confident that it will be there for them. A 1991 public opinion survey indicates that 51 percent of persons aged 18 to 64 disagree that "Social Security will have the money to pay benefits" to them when they retire.[1] Yet, far more often than not, these same workers strongly support the program, in large measure because of protections provided to current elders. In this same survey, 78 percent report that they do not "mind paying Social Security taxes to support the program," a fairly high level of support given the antipathy of many Americans toward most taxes. While some financial planners simply discount Social Security as a potential source of retirement income for their clients, most academic and government analysts believe Social Security will meet its future commitments. Many would add, however, that benefit levels, age of retirement, and tax rates may need to be adjusted with changing economic and social conditions.

Some alarms were sounded in 1992 about program financing by Social Security's board of trustees (the secretaries of the Treasury, Labor, and Health and Human Services, and two public trustees appointed by the president). Each year, the trustees issue a report on the financial status of Social Security. Based on the most widely accepted assumptions about the economy and population trends, the 1992 report indicates that the combined financing of the large Old-Age and Survivors Insurance (OASI) and the smaller Disability Insurance (DI) trust funds is sufficient to assure the timely payment of benefits for roughly the next forty-five years. However, beginning in 2010, as the baby boom generation heads toward retirement, program costs grow quickly, primarily because "the number of beneficiaries is projected to increase more rapidly than the number of covered workers."[2] Thus, a significant and growing long-term deficit is projected for the seventy-five-year period over which cost estimates are made for the combined OASDI program, leading the trustees to recommend first study and then policy measures strengthening OASDI's long-term financing.[3]

Increases in the number of disability insurance awards since 1982 along with a decline in the proportion of disability beneficiaries whose benefits terminate (due to rehabilitation, recovery, death, or receipt of retirement benefits) produce a more immediate concern. To assure the timely payment of benefits past the mid-1990s, the short-term financing of DI requires prompt congressional action.[4] The DI shortfall is substantially offset by the extremely large annual surpluses ($55.5 billion in 1991 alone) that are projected for each of the roughly next twenty-five years in the combined OASDI trust fund. In other words, one quick and likely solution for the next quarter century would be simply to shift a relatively small portion of the anticipated yearly surpluses in the OASI account to the DI account. In fact, this is not very different from the strategy previously undertaken—though in reverse—in the early 1980s when a small portion of the DI payroll tax rate was allocated to OASI when the latter program was facing a shortfall.

No doubt Congress will have to revisit Social Security's long-term financing. As always, opinions vary about the magnitude of the problem and the preferred policy responses. Given at least thirty to forty years of adequate funding, some see no incipient crisis and suggest that decisions may be best postponed for twenty to thirty years in the future. Others, while seeing the problem as manageable, believe action is needed within a few years so as to avoid undermining confidence in the program. Still others interpret the emerging long-term financing problem as evidence of the need to alter the entire program.[5]

Experts like former Social Security Commissioner Robert Ball take the perspective that, as with all large systems, problems will arise from time to time, but there is every reason to think that the nation will continue to resolve such problems in a way that maintains the integrity and vitality of the program and its commitments. He writes:

Social Security is the most cautiously and conservatively financed of all government programs, deriving its revenues from dedicated taxes, making long-range cost projections based on objective actuarial analyses, and providing exhaustively detailed reports to Congress and the public. . . . There is no basis for claiming that future generations cannot count on Social Security being there when they retire. They have the power to see that the system remains stable and secure and that changes are made if needed. . . . The key point to bear in mind is Congress' clear legislative intent to provide for full funding of the program across a 75-year period.[6]

Other experts, also long-time Social Security supporters, such as Senator Daniel Patrick Moynihan and former Chief Actuary Robert Myers,[7] while not disputing the long-term viability of Social Security, find themselves vigorously opposed to Social Security accumulating huge trust funds to be followed by their depletion in the latter years of the retirement of the baby boom. Still other experts, such as Haeworth Robertson, another former chief actuary of Social Security, and Dorcas Hardy, another former commissioner, believe the program is headed for financial collapse unless radically altered.[8] Robertson writes:

During the past fifteen years (since 1975) Americans have devoted a great deal of time and energy to studying and worrying about Social Security. The concerns are real, not artificial, and indicate that there are serious problems underlying the design of Social Security. The public can no longer be tranquilized by public relations campaigns about how good social insurance is . . .

There is no reason for the country to continue with a social insurance system that is so controversial and unpopular and whose financial status must be constantly debated. . . . It is eminently more sensible for us to design a social insurance system that is understood and perceived as fair and reasonable by the majority of the citizens— one that will support rather than hinder the attainment of a healthy and productive economy.[9]

To understand why seemingly contradictory opinions abound about the stability of the program's financing and to develop a basis for making informed judgments about the adequacy of financing, students of the program need to understand (1) the way Social Security is financed; (2) the procedures underlying financial projections; (3) the most recent cost estimates; and (4) how the financing debate is shaped by differing views about the implications of population aging and the proper role of government in a market economy. Such knowledge will equip readers to draw their own conclusions about financing dilemmas and choices, including the significance of a growing surplus amidst a projected long-term deficit and the implications of population aging. One cautionary note: Social Security financing issues should not be reduced simply to technical questions. Analysis can yield important data about economic and programmatic trends, but politics and societal values provide the lenses through which these data are interpreted and acted upon.

FINANCING SOCIAL SECURITY

The ABCs of Social Security financing can be explained by drawing an analogy to your checking account. To manage your account, you need to balance income with expenditures. If too much goes out (your rent increases) or too little comes in (you lose your job), then you must either cut back spending or find another means of increasing your income.

The heart of Social Security financing, too, requires maintaining a favorable balance between anticipated income and expenditures. Income flowing into the Social Security "checking accounts," termed "trust funds," is generated primarily from taxing earnings (see Table 6.1) and, secondarily, from

Table 6.1
Scheduled Payroll Tax Contribution Rates
(Percent of income at or below taxable wage base* which is taxed for Social Security and Medicare)

Year	OASI	DI	OASDI	HI	TOTAL
For Employers and Employees Each					
1990–99	5.60	0.60	6.20	1.45	7.65
2000 and later	5.49	0.71	6.20	1.45	7.65
For Self-Employed Persons**					
1990–99	11.20	1.20	12.40	2.90	15.30
2000 and later	10.98	1.42	12.40	2.90	15.30

*In 1993 employees (and their employers) make payroll tax contributions on earnings up to $57,600 for Social Security (OASDI) and on earnings up to $135,500 for Medicare's Hospital Insurance program. Self-employed persons make contributions on "net earnings" up to these levels. Net earnings is calculated by deducting 7.65 percent, the equivalent of the employer's contribution, from gross earnings.
**One-half of the payroll tax for self-employed persons is deductible for income tax purposes.

Source: U.S. House of Representatives, Committee on Ways and Means, *Background Material and Data on Programs Within the Jurisdiction of the Committee on Ways and Means* (Washington, D.C.: U.S. GPO, 1991), pp. 78–79.

taxing a portion of Social Security benefits and from interest earned by investing the portion of the Social Security trust fund that is not needed to meet current expenditures in interest-bearing securities of the U.S. government.[10] (Expenditures, in turn, are a function of such factors as the number of people receiving retirement, disability, and survivors' benefits and the size of the benefits.) As with your own account, if less money flows in than expected because, for example, a recession has resulted in high unemployment and little wage growth, then eventually something will need to be done. Taxes may be increased or benefits reduced. Similarly, if program costs go up, perhaps because of inflation or a higher than expected number of disability beneficiaries, then off-setting revenue adjustments or benefit changes are likely to be needed. Of course, unlike you, the government has one major advantage. It can legislate increased taxes or benefit cuts (e.g., delay cost-of-living adjustments) in response to changing circumstances.

More concretely, it is important to understand that there are two Social Security and two Medicare trust funds, Old-Age and Survivors Insurance (OASI) and Disability Insurance (DI) trust funds and the Hospital Insurance (HI) and Supplementary Medical Insurance (SMI) trust funds. In 1991 taxes on earnings funded roughly 93 percent of the combined OASDI trust fund, the rest coming from income generated by loaning out the trust funds to the federal government and from revenues generated from treating up to one-half of Social Security benefits as taxable income for middle- and high-income beneficiaries.[11] Taxes on earnings funded about 89 percent of HI income, the rest coming mainly from trust fund investments.[12] In contrast, 73 percent of SMI's funding comes from an open-ended contribution from the general revenues of the federal government, with the remaining portion coming primarily from premiums paid by beneficiaries and secondarily from interest on the trust fund's investments.[13]

Once collected, most payroll taxes and other revenues for Social Security (and Medicare) are paid out in benefits. A relatively small amount, about one percent of Social Security revenues (and about 1.4 percent of Medicare's Hospital Insurance revenues), is used for administrative expenses.

Today most workers are no longer surprised to learn that their Social Security tax contributions do not go into a separate account to be saved for their own retirement. Instead, a record is maintained for each worker of the earnings subject to Social Security taxation, which later serves as the basis for determining eligibility and benefit amounts. Often this awareness leads to skepticism about the program's financing, since unlike private pensions, in which sound financial management requires large reserves to meet future obligations, Social Security's financing is not designed to build reserves sufficient to meet all future commitments. However, as Brandeis University economist James Schulz notes, pension experts generally agree that sound financial management of social insurance programs do not require building large reserves.[14] In fact, strong arguments can be made against fully funded reserves. Social Security shifted in 1939 from funding which would have resulted in the build-up of very large reserves toward a largely pay-as-you-go financing approach, in part, because of fears that large reserves would be vulnerable to inflation-based erosion, might be spent for other purposes, or might force the federal government to make large financial investments in private sector activities. As Schulz observes:

It is recognized that the taxing power of government guarantees the long-run financial integrity of such programs and that, unlike private insurance, it is appropriate to assume that the programs will operate indefinitely—with a consequent continuous flow of revenue. Moreover, the fact that public insurance is usually compulsory and covers most of the population, avoids the financing problems arising from a fluctuating number of participants. . . .

Thus we see that the main argument for nonfunding rests on the quality of the pension promise made by the government. To fulfill this promise requires that Congress ensure that over the long run the flow of funds remains in a "satisfactory actuarial status."[15]

PROJECTING SOCIAL SECURITY REVENUES AND EXPENDITURES

With this background, we are ready to discuss further how the government tracks Social Security's financing.

Because Social Security is sensitive to economic and demographic change, actuaries forecast the financial status of the program based on expected economic (price increases, rises in unemployment, wage increases) and demographic (birth rates and life expectancy) trends. Short-term (over the next ten years) and long-term (over a seventy-five-year period) estimates aid in making assessments about the likelihood that expected revenues will meet anticipated program obligations. To develop these forecasts the actuaries draw on past experience moderated by assumptions about future trends such as price increases, economic growth, wage increases, unemployment, birthrates, and life expectancy. Because no one really knows what the future will bring, the actuaries use three different sets of economic and demographic assumptions—ranging from optimistic to pessimistic. These assumptions, in turn, are adjusted as warranted by changing social and economic conditions.

Perhaps the major drawback of these projections is the tendency for their consumers—who include politicians, analysts, the press, and the public—to treat them as expected occurrences rather than as forecasts of possible futures, thereby attaching far more certainty to these projections than appropriate.[16] Because the contours of the future are uncertain, projections—especially long-term ones—are subject to error, and, not surprisingly, actual experience is almost always more or less favorable than forecasted. In fact, the history of the program tells us that continued policy and programmatic change, in response to shifting demographic, economic, and political forces, is almost the one thing that can be predicted with certainty. Nevertheless, projections provide useful indicators of probable experience, even forty, fifty or seventy-five years into the future. By doing so, they provide policymakers a useful tool for making the mid-course corrections that are necessary from time to time.

The actuaries have contributed many entries to the lexicon of Social Security, including cost rates, income rates, percents of payroll, and close actuarial balance. Rather mercifully, the 1992 trustees report includes explanations, in relatively simple English, of the most frequently used terms in cost estimates. (See Tables 6.2 and 6.3.)

In summarizing the major demographic and economic assumptions drawn through the forecasts in the 1992 trustees report, Tables 6.4 and 6.5 highlight the variation between the optimistic (alternative I), intermediate (alternative II), and pessimistic (alternative III) sets of assumptions. For example, beginning in 2015 the optimistic fertility assumption is that an average of 2.2 children will be born to each woman compared to an assumed 1.6 births under the pessimistic assumptions. Fewer children mean fewer workers (rela-

Table 6.2
Measures Used to Evaluate Social Security Financing

Taxable payroll is that portion of total wages and self-employment income that is covered and taxed under the OASDI and HI programs.

The annual *income rate* is the income to the trust fund from taxes, expressed as a percentage of taxable payroll.

The annual *cost rate* is the outgo from the trust fund, also expressed as a percentage of taxable payroll.

The *percentage of taxable payroll* is used to measure income rates and cost rates for the OASDI and HI programs. Measuring the funds' income and outgo over long periods of time by describing what portion of taxable earnings they represent is more meaningful than using dollar amounts, because the value of a dollar changes over time.

The annual *balance* is the difference between the income rate and the cost rate. If the balance is negative, the trust fund has a deficit for that year.

Annual balances are summarized for periods of up to 75 years and adjusted to include the beginning fund balance and the cost of ending the projection period with a trust fund ratio of 100 percent; the resulting figure is then called the *actuarial* balance: if the balance is negative, the fund has an *actuarial deficit.*

The *trust fund ratio* is the amount in the trust fund at the beginning of a year divided by the projected outgo for the year. It shows what percentage of the year's expenditures the trust fund has on hand. For example, a trust fund ratio of 50 percent would be six months' worth of expenditures.

The *year of exhaustion* is the first year a trust fund is projected to run out of funds and to be unable to pay benefits on time and in full.

Source: From Social Security and Medicare Board of Trustees, *Status of the Social Security and Medicare Programs: A Summary of the 1992 Annual Reports* (Washington, D.C.: U.S. GPO, April 1992), pp. 4–5.

tive to the number of future beneficiaries), and so this has a depressing effect on the system's financing. Of course, what is considered pessimistic from within the perspective of Social Security's financing, such as living longer, is not necessarily negative from an individual's or society's point of view.

These assumptions are reviewed and updated each year in response to analyses and judgments made about the implications of social and economic change. Changes in assumptions are usually introduced slowly over several

Table 6.3
Tests of Social Security's Financial Status

The *short-range test* is met if, throughout the next 10 years, the trust fund ratio is at least 100 percent. Or, if the trust fund ratio is initially less, but reaches 100 percent within the first five years and stays at or above 100 percent, and there is enough income to pay benefits on time every month during the 10 years, the short-range test is met.

The *long-range test* is met if a fund has an actuarial deficit of no more than five percent of the cost rate over the 75 years, and the actuarial deficit for any period of the first 10 years or longer is less than a graduated amount of five per-cent. If the long-range test is met, the trust fund is in *close actuarial balance.*

Source: From Social Security and Medicare Board of Trustees, *Status of the Social Security and Medicare Programs: A Summary of the 1992 Annual Reports* (Washington, D.C.: U.S. GPO, April 1992), pp. 5–6.

years to avoid abrupt transitions, but over time the significance of these changes can have a major effect on financial forecasts, sometimes increasing projected trust fund balances and sometimes decreasing balances. For instance, program costs are very sensitive to changes in what the actuaries call the "real-wage differential," essentially the difference between the yearly increase in average wages minus the increase in the cost of living.[17] A reduction in the assumed year-to-year increase in real wages results in projections of smaller trust fund balances, which is exactly what has happened as adjustments have been made in response to the growing caution about the future of the economy and wage growth. Thus, whereas the assumptions behind the most commonly accepted intermediate projections in 1982 assumed that real wages would grow (on average) by 1.5 percent per year beginning in 1989, the 1992 intermediate projections assume growth of only 1.1 percent per year beginning in 2005.

Each assumption can be questioned. Take, for example, a change in the intermediate assumptions for the ultimate fertility rate between the 1982 and 1992 trustees reports—2.10 beginning in 2005 in the 1982 report and 1.90 beginning in 2020 in the 1992 report. Interestingly, this change has been made during a period in which the fertility rate, roughly defined as the "number" of children the "average" woman is likely to have during her lifetime, has actually increased. In fact, 1991 is the first year since the early 1970s that the fertility rate has reached the replacement level (about 2.1), that is, the fertility rate necessary to maintain a roughly constant population size; yet the intermediate assumptions assume a steady decline to 1.90 in 2020. A

Table 6.4
Selected Demographic Assumptions Used in 1992
to Project Social Security Financing

Calendar year	Total fertility rate[1]	Age-sex-adjusted death rate[2] (per 100,000)	Life expectancy[3]			
			At birth		At age 65	
			Male	Female	Male	Female
Historical data:						
1940	2.23	1,532.8	61.4	65.7	11.9	13.4
1945	2.42	1,366.4	62.9	68.4	12.6	14.4
1950	3.03	1,225.3	65.6	71.1	12.8	15.1
1955	3.50	1,134.2	66.7	72.8	13.1	15.6
1960	3.61	1,128.6	66.7	73.2	12.9	15.9
1965	2.88	1,103.6	66.8	73.8	12.9	16.3
1970	2.43	1,041.8	67.1	74.9	13.1	17.1
1975	1.77	934.0	68.7	76.6	13.7	18.0
1976	1.74	923.2	69.1	76.8	13.7	18.1
1977	1.79	898.0	69.4	77.2	13.9	18.3
1978	1.76	892.4	69.6	77.2	13.9	18.3
1979	1.82	864.2	70.0	77.7	14.2	18.6
1980	1.85	878.0	69.9	77.5	14.0	18.4
1981	1.83	853.4	70.4	77.9	14.2	18.6
1982	1.83	827.8	70.8	78.2	14.5	18.8
1983	1.81	835.0	70.9	78.1	14.3	18.6
1984	1.80	828.2	71.1	78.2	14.4	18.7
1985	1.84	830.0	71.1	78.2	14.4	18.6
1986	1.84	822.8	71.2	78.3	14.5	18.7
1987	1.87	813.9	71.3	78.4	14.6	18.7
1988	1.93	821.9	71.4	78.4	14.6	18.7
1989[4]	2.00	801.2	71.6	78.6	14.8	18.9
1990[4]	2.08	802.5	71.6	78.6	14.8	18.8
Alternative I:						
1995	2.11	779.7	72.4	78.9	14.8	18.8
2000	2.14	769.8	72.8	79.0	14.8	18.7
2005	2.16	761.4	73.1	79.1	14.9	18.7
2010	2.18	751.5	73.3	79.3	14.9	18.7
2015	2.20	741.7	73.5	79.4	15.0	18.8
2020	2.20	732.3	73.7	79.6	15.1	18.9
2025	2.20	723.1	73.8	79.7	15.2	19.0
2030	2.20	714.3	74.0	79.9	15.3	19.1
2035	2.20	705.7	74.1	80.0	15.3	19.2
2040	2.20	697.3	74.3	80.2	15.4	19.3
2045	2.20	689.2	74.4	80.3	15.5	19.3
2050	2.20	681.3	74.6	80.4	15.6	19.4
2055	2.20	673.7	74.7	80.6	15.6	19.5
2060	2.20	666.3	74.9	80.7	15.7	19.6
2065	2.20	659.1	75.0	80.8	15.8	19.7
2070	2.20	652.0	75.1	80.9	15.9	19.8
Alternative II:						
1995	2.06	771.0	72.0	79.2	15.1	19.1
2000	2.02	740.5	72.6	79.7	15.3	19.3
2005	1.99	706.9	73.5	80.2	15.6	19.5
2010	1.95	682.0	74.1	80.5	15.8	19.8
2015	1.91	662.0	74.5	80.9	16.0	20.0
2020	1.90	643.6	74.8	81.2	16.2	20.2
2025	1.90	626.1	75.1	81.5	16.4	20.5
2030	1.90	609.4	75.4	81.8	16.7	20.7
2035	1.90	593.5	75.7	82.1	16.9	21.0

Table 6.4
(continued)

Calendar year	Total fertility rate[1]	Age-sex-adjusted death rate[2] (per 100,000)	Life expectancy[3]			
			At birth		At age 65	
			Male	Female	Male	Female
2040.......................	1.90	578.4	76.0	82.4	17.1	21.2
2045.......................	1.90	563.9	76.3	82.7	17.3	21.4
2050.......................	1.90	550.1	76.6	83.0	17.5	21.6
2055.......................	1.90	537.0	76.9	83.3	17.7	21.9
2060.......................	1.90	524.4	77.1	83.5	17.9	22.1
2065.......................	1.90	512.3	77.4	83.8	18.1	22.3
2070.......................	1.90	500.8	77.7	84.1	18.3	22.5
Alternative III:						
1995.......................	1.99	755.0	71.9	79.6	15.4	19.5
2000.......................	1.90	731.0	71.7	80.1	15.8	20.0
2005.......................	1.80	681.1	73.0	80.8	16.2	20.4
2010.......................	1.71	621.3	74.8	81.7	16.6	20.8
2015.......................	1.62	583.3	75.8	82.4	17.0	21.2
2020.......................	1.60	555.6	76.3	82.9	17.5	21.7
2025.......................	1.60	531.9	76.7	83.4	17.9	22.1
2030.......................	1.60	509.7	77.1	83.9	18.3	22.5
2035.......................	1.60	488.6	77.5	84.4	18.7	22.9
2040.......................	1.60	468.1	77.9	85.0	19.1	23.4
2045.......................	1.60	448.6	78.4	85.5	19.5	23.8
2050.......................	1.60	429.9	78.8	86.0	19.9	24.2
2055.......................	1.60	412.2	79.3	86.5	20.3	24.6
2060.......................	1.60	395.3	79.8	87.0	20.7	25.0
2065.......................	1.60	379.3	80.3	87.5	21.1	25.4
2070.......................	1.60	364.1	80.7	87.9	21.5	25.8

[1]The total fertility rate for any year is the average number of children who would be born to a woman in her lifetime if she were to experience the birth rates by age observed in, or assumed for, the selected year, and if she were to survive the entire child-bearing period. The ultimate total fertility rate is assumed to be reached in 2016.

[2]The age-sex-adjusted death rate is the crude rate that would occur in the enumerated total population as of April 1, 1980, if that population were to experience the death rates by age and sex observed in, or assumed for, the selected year.

[3]The life expectancy for any year is the average number of years of life remaining for a person if that person were to experience the death rates by age observed in, or assumed for, the selected year.

[4]Estimated.

Source: From Social Security and Medicare Board of Trustees, *Status of the Social Security and Medicare Programs: A Summary of the 1992 Annual Reports* (Washington, D.C.: U.S. GPO, April 1992), pp. 62–63.

good argument can be made that this assumption is too pessimistic and consequently increases the projected long-term deficit. But then arguments could be made that other intermediate assumptions are too optimistic. That is one reason that there are three sets of assumptions and why adjustments are made year to year as new experience provides more information on which to base what amounts to "best guesses" which have been arrived at through careful thought and analytical methods.

CURRENT FINANCING ESTIMATES

So what do the most recent forecasts tell us about the future of Social Security? The facts of the matter are relatively simple, though plainly inter-

Table 6.5
Selected Economic Assumptions Used in 1992 to Project Social Security Financing

| Calendar year | Average annual percentage change in— | | | Real-wage differential[3] (percent) | Average annual interest rate[4] (percent) | Average annual unemployment rate[5] (percent) | Average annual percentage increase in labor force[6] |
	Real GDP[1]	Average annual wage in covered employment	Consumer Price Index[2]				
Historical data:							
1960-64..........	3.9	3.4	1.3	2.1	3.7	5.7	1.3
1965-69..........	4.4	5.4	3.4	2.0	5.2	3.8	2.1
1970-74..........	2.4	6.3	6.1	.2	6.7	5.4	2.3
1975..............	-.8	6.7	9.1	-2.4	7.4	8.5	1.9
1976..............	4.9	8.7	5.7	3.0	7.1	7.7	2.4
1977..............	4.5	7.3	6.5	.8	7.1	7.1	2.9
1978..............	4.8	9.7	7.7	2.0	8.2	6.1	3.2
1979..............	2.5	9.8	11.4	-1.6	9.1	5.8	2.6
1980..............	-.5	9.1	13.4	-4.3	11.0	7.1	1.9
1981..............	1.8	9.6	10.3	-.7	13.3	7.6	1.6
1982..............	-2.2	6.6	6.0	.6	12.8	9.7	1.4
1983..............	3.9	5.1	3.0	2.1	11.0	9.6	1.2
1984..............	6.2	7.3	3.5	3.8	12.4	7.5	1.8
1985..............	3.2	4.2	3.5	.7	10.8	7.2	1.7
1986..............	2.9	5.1	1.6	3.5	8.0	7.0	2.0
1987..............	3.1	4.4	3.6	.8	8.4	6.2	1.7
1988..............	3.9	[7]4.8	4.0	.8	8.8	5.5	1.4
1989..............	2.5	[7]4.2	4.8	-.7	8.7	5.3	1.8
1990..............	1.0	[7]5.2	5.2	.0	8.6	5.5	.7
Alternative I:							
1991..............	-.7	3.6	4.0	-.4	8.0	6.8	.4
1992..............	2.3	4.4	2.6	1.9	6.8	7.0	.7
1993..............	3.9	4.8	2.8	2.0	6.0	6.5	1.2
1994..............	3.7	5.0	3.0	2.0	5.7	6.0	1.2
1995..............	3.5	5.2	3.0	2.2	5.8	5.7	1.2
1996..............	3.4	5.2	3.0	2.2	5.9	5.4	1.1
1997..............	3.2	5.1	3.0	2.1	6.0	5.1	1.1
1998..............	3.1	5.0	3.0	2.1	6.0	5.0	1.1
1999..............	2.9	5.1	3.0	2.1	6.0	4.9	1.1
2000..............	2.8	5.1	3.0	2.1	6.0	4.8	1.0
2001..............	2.8	5.0	3.0	2.0	6.1	4.8	1.0
2005..............	2.6	4.7	3.0	1.7	6.0	5.0	1.0
2010&later.....	[8]2.3	4.7	3.0	1.7	6.0	5.0	[8].7
Alternative II:							
1991..............	-.8	3.6	4.0	-.4	8.0	6.8	.4
1992..............	1.5	4.3	2.9	1.3	6.8	7.1	.6
1993..............	2.9	4.5	3.3	1.1	6.2	6.9	1.0
1994..............	2.7	4.8	3.6	1.2	6.0	6.6	1.0
1995..............	2.5	5.2	3.9	1.3	6.3	6.4	1.0
1996..............	2.4	5.4	4.0	1.4	6.4	6.3	.9
1997..............	2.3	5.3	4.0	1.3	6.5	6.2	.9
1998..............	2.3	5.3	4.0	1.3	6.5	6.1	.9

Table 6.5
(*continued*)

| Calendar year | Average annual percentage change in— | | | | Average annual interest rate[4] (percent) | Average annual unemployment rate[5] (percent) | Average annual percentage increase in labor force[6] |
	Real GDP[1]	Average annual wage in covered employment	Consumer Price Index[2]	Real-wage differential[3] (percent)			
1999..............	2.3	5.4	4.0	1.4	6.5	6.0	.9
2000..............	2.3	5.5	4.0	1.4	6.5	5.9	.9
2001..............	2.2	5.4	4.0	1.4	6.4	5.8	.9
2005..............	1.9	5.1	4.0	1.1	6.3	6.0	.7
2010&later.....	[8]1.8	5.1	4.0	1.1	6.3	6.0	[8].5
Alternative III:							
1991..............	-0.8	3.6	4.1	-0.5	8.0	6.8	0.4
1992..............	.5	4.0	3.6	.4	7.0	7.3	.5
1993..............	2.6	5.3	5.2	.1	6.8	7.0	.9
1994..............	2.4	6.8	6.4	.3	7.5	6.6	1.0
1995..............	.7	6.3	6.2	.2	8.3	6.4	.9
1996..............	-.7	4.2	4.8	-.6	8.0	7.4	.6
1997..............	3.2	6.8	5.0	1.8	7.4	6.9	.8
1998..............	1.7	5.8	5.0	.8	6.9	6.7	.9
1999..............	1.5	5.9	5.0	.9	6.9	6.7	.8
2000..............	1.6	6.1	5.0	1.0	6.8	6.7	.8
2001..............	1.6	6.0	5.0	1.0	6.6	6.7	.7
2005..............	1.4	5.6	5.0	.6	6.5	7.0	.5
2010&later.....	[8]1.3	5.6	5.0	.6	6.5	7.0	[8].4

[1]The real GDP (gross domestic product) is the value of total output of goods and services, expressed in 1987 dollars.

[2]The Consumer Price Index is the annual average value for the calendar year of the Consumer Price Index for Urban Wage Earners and Clerical Workers (CPI-W).

[3]The real-wage differential is the difference between the percentage increases, before rounding, in (1) the average annual wage in covered employment, and (2) the average annual Consumer Price Index.

[4]The average annual interest rate is the average of the nominal interest rates, which, in practice, are compounded semiannually, for special public-debt obligations issuable to the trust funds in each of the 12 months of the year.

[5]Through 2001, the rates shown are unadjusted civilian unemployment rates. After 2001, the rates are total rates (including military personnel), adjusted by age and sex based on the estimated total labor force on July 1, 1990.

[6]Labor force is the total for the U.S. (including military personnel) and reflects the average of the monthly numbers of persons in the labor force for each year.

[7]Preliminary.

[8]This value is for 2010. The annual percentage increase in labor force and real GDP is assumed to continue to change after 2010 for each alternative to reflect the dependence of labor force growth on the size and age-sex distribution of the population. The increases in real GDP for 2070 are 2.3, 1.3, and 0.3 percent for alternatives I, II, and III, respectively. The changes in total labor force for 2070 are 0.6, 0.0, and -0.5 percent for alternatives I, II, and III, respectively.

Source: From Social Security and Medicare Board of Trustees, *Status of the Social Security and Medicare Programs: A Summary of the 1992 Annual Reports* (Washington, D.C.: U.S. GPO, April 1992), pp. 57–58.

pretations of their implications differ. In the short run, the combined assets of Social Security's Old-Age and Survivors and Disability Insurance (OASDI) programs are expected to grow substantially. Even under the pessimistic set of assumptions, the Social Security "trust fund ratio" is expected to grow from about 100 percent in 1992 to 134 percent in 2001. (A trust fund ratio of

100 percent is sufficient to pay the next twelve months' outgo absent any additional funds.) It is generally considered desirable that the trust funds maintain a ratio of at least 100 percent to weather unanticipated downturns in the economy that may reduce revenues.[18]

The cloud on the short-term horizon concerns funding for DI. When the OASI and DI trust funds are considered separately, then the short-run financing of the larger OASI trust fund is more favorable and the DI trust fund is exhausted in 1997 under the alternative II intermediate assumptions; 1995 under the pessimistic alternative III assumptions. In the short-run and even for at least the next thirty years or so, a simple accounting procedure which reallocates a small portion of revenues from OASI to DI would be sufficient to handle any problem that might arise in the DI trust fund. In fact, there is considerable force of argument for simply treating the OASI and DI trust funds as one account. Of course, this suggestion does not negate the need to examine the causes of DI cost increases—higher than expected numbers of new awards and relatively fewer terminations.

The long-term picture is more complex and ultimately of greater concern. With the enactment of a combination of modest benefit reductions and revenue increases in the 1983 financing amendments, Congress eliminated virtually any possibility of a short-fall in OASDI for at least thirty-five years and also provided sufficient funding to eliminate the prior long-run deficit. By moving from pay-as-you-go to a temporary, partially advanced funding approach, the 1983 amendments allowed for yearly surpluses in the early years of the seventy-five-year estimating period to roughly offset the yearly deficits that followed. Consequently, for the six years following the 1983 amendments, the trustees have reported that—based on the most widely accepted assumptions about the economy and population trends—Social Security was financially sound over the next seventy-five years.[19] However, as Congressional Research analyst David Koitz points out:

the average condition of the funds did not represent the system's condition over the entire period. . . . Simply stated 40 years of surplus were to be followed by an indefinite period of deficits. With each passing year since 1983, the trustees' 75 year averaging period has picked up one deficit year at the back end and dropped a surplus year from the front end. This, by itself, would cause the average condition to worsen. However, in recent reports assumptions about birth rates, the growth rate of the economy, and wages have been lowered, causing further deterioration in outlook.[20]

Thus, under the intermediate set of assumptions, Social Security is no longer in close actuarial balance. The most recent report shows a modest long-term deficit in OASDI, of 1.46 percent of taxable payroll; that is roughly 10 percent of anticipated program costs over the seventy-five-year period. Without remedial action, the combined trust funds are exhausted in 2036 under the intermediate assumptions, 2019 under the pessimistic assumptions. Under the optimistic assumptions, however, the trust fund ratio continues to grow to an extraordinary level—enough to pay ten years of benefits in 2070 without any revenues—and is never depleted throughout the seventy-five-year period.

The reemergence of a long-term financing deficit as a future policy problem is best understood within the context of a Social Security agenda dominated by financing issues during most of the past twenty years. As previously discussed, since the mid-1970s Social Security has experienced two major financing problems leading to remedial legislation, most recently in 1983. Ironically, following the 1983 financing amendments, as annual surpluses began to accumulate along with favorable forecasts, a different type of financing question emerged. Is partial advance funding and the accumulation of large surpluses (to be spent down later) desirable? Does the Social Security surplus help hide the federal deficit? Now, perhaps more comfortably, we have opportunity again to ponder whether the Congress will need to act (and when) to strengthen OASDI funding.

FRAMING THE FINANCING DISCUSSION

Reasonable people can reach different conclusions about Social Security financing. (So can unreasonable ones.) In part, this is a function of the relative emphasis given to different pieces of information and of views regarding the likelihood of future stagnation versus future growth. But these differences often arise from fundamental disagreements about the proper role of government in a market economy. They, in turn, color interpretations of the ever-changing status of Social Security's financing and have much to do with the proposed interventions that follow. To some, the emerging long-term deficit is a crisis in the making, requiring radical changes to Social Security. To others, financing issues, like many other Social Security issues, can best be responded to through the existing monitoring processes which allow for ongoing adjustments such as those legislated in 1983.[21]

The most widely subscribed to view is that the Social Security financing, indeed the multiple challenges posed by an aging population, are surmountable through planned and careful policy adjustments. From this perspective, much of the challenge confronting Social Security lies outside the program. There will always be a need to monitor and adjust the program for changing social and economic circumstances. But economic (incentives for research and development) and social investment (high-quality schools) are more important to assure a standard of living capable of supporting all age groups in the future. With respect to financing, this perspective focuses attention on incremental change—more taxes or smaller benefits—and on doing what is necessary to strengthen the economy. Those adhering to this perspective are generally supportive of the social insurance approach to protecting against economic risk. They consider the emerging long-term financing problem as not requiring immediate action since OASDI taken as a whole is able to make full and timely payment of benefits for at least the next thirty years and probably longer. Under these circumstances, waiting twenty to twenty-five years before acting may make much sense, some would argue, as there is little reason to cut benefits today or raise taxes for a problem that is so far off. Others, concerned with the consequences of a long-run deficit on public opinion, might consider scheduling new payroll tax increases or benefit reductions (e.g., increase the age of eligibility for full benefits) forty or fifty years in the future.

Plainly, opinion is not uniform among those who do not see an immediate financing crisis. They may also differ, and often do, on desirable levels of protections and on the wisdom of specific policy proposals. Thus, some believe program benefits too generous for many beneficiaries; others believe women, minorities, and partially disabled retirees are not adequately protected. Some believe the COLA places the program in a financial straightjacket, while others argue that the COLA is absolutely necessary to the well-being of beneficiaries. And, as discussed, some within this perspective argue strongly for a return to pay-as-you-go financing, others for the maintenance of partial advance funding and the build-up of a large contingency fund ratio.

From the beginning of the program, there have always been articulate opponents who considered Social Security an inefficient intrusion into the private market. Rejecting social insurance approaches, they are more likely to favor means-tested public assistance approaches to protect against risks facing individuals and families when private efforts fail. Today they generally interpret demographic trends and the emerging long-term deficit as an impending disaster, requiring radical restructuring of Social Security. Marmor, Mashaw, and Harvey suggest they are largely "a contingent of conservative academics and popularizers of economic commentary, usually advocates of market discipline and strict limits on the scope of government, who accept society's obligation to maintain a safety net for the 'truly needy,' but who strenuously object to the government's providing income maintenance benefits to the middle class."[22] From within this view, not only is Social Security unsustainable in the long run, but it also contributes to current budget deficits because it represents such a large share of federal spending. Moreover, it is a source of intergenerational conflict, reduces national savings, and is an important cause of the slowdown in economic growth.

Thus, the emerging long-term financing problems of Social Security are, along with the shortfall in DI, seen as predictable and probably much worse than the government suggests because the cost projections are based on what is viewed as "a stunning series of shaky assumptions and misunderstandings."[23] The solutions, then, that sometimes follow are to phase out Social Security, substituting private approaches to retirement savings.[24] Others would radically reduce the scope of benefits, especially to middle- and higher-income beneficiaries by such provisions as eliminating the COLA, means-testing benefits, lowering the value of initial benefits, and substantially raising the age of eligibility for full benefits.[25]

More than anything else, it is these large differences in perspective that help explain why the circumstances surrounding Social Security financing are interpreted so differently and why the public is so often presented with such disparate images about the future of the program. Another element is the discomfort engendered by uncertainty. The future is not knowable. Making carefully reasoned estimates of probable futures—allowing for adjustments as circumstances change—is the best we can do. The alternative is to engender public mistrust by falsely interpreting actuarial projections as being able to say more about the future than intended. Or worse, we could dispense with making projections on the grounds that they yield less than perfect information about the future, an ostrich-like approach to social policy.

THE FINANCING ISSUES

Now let us explore several financing issues in greater depth, including the implications of and choices that follow from the aging of the population, the yearly surpluses anticipated through 2020, and the growing long-term deficit in OASDI.

Implications of Population Aging

No doubt demographic changes will place new pressures on Social Security and related public and private income protection and health care programs. Such pressures are probably best understood, however, as byproducts of public and private investments which have yielded a growing and longer-lived elderly population and declining birthrates, all part of a worldwide phenomenon referred to as "population aging." Investments during the twentieth century in sanitation, biomedical research, immunization, and social policies have resulted in fewer childhood deaths, more people reaching old age (and living longer thereafter), and a better quality of life for elderly persons and other age groups, too. The characteristic long-term declines in the fertility rate that accompany modernizing and mature economies have contributed to reducing the number of children relative to elderly persons. These changes, along with the aging of the baby boom generation, also mean projected increases in Social Security (and Medicare) costs—a challenge that will fall on the shoulders of today's young workers and children, who will be called upon to assist their parents' generation.

The demographics of population aging are often easier to agree upon than their implications. Under the Census Bureau's middle series population projections, the elderly population—persons aged 65 and over—is projected to increase from about 32 million persons in 1992 (12.6 percent of the population) to roughly 35 million (12.7 percent) by 2000, swelling to 70 million by 2030 (20.7 percent) and 79 million (20.6 percent) by 2050. More importantly, the very old—persons aged 85 and over and the age group with the greatest need for health and social services—are projected to increase at an even more rapid rate, from approximately 3.3 million in 1992 to 4.3 million in 2000, 8.4 million in 2030, and 18 million in 2050 when today's preschoolers reach retirement age. (See Table 6.6 and Figure 6.1.)[26]

Along with this increase in older people, the number of persons aged 18 through 64, the so-called working-age population, is projected to decline as a proportion of the entire population. The number covered under Social Security (3.3 in 1991) per beneficiary has been quite stable since 1975. However, under the Social Security Administration's intermediate projections, this

Table 6.6
Actual and Projected Growth of the Older Population: 1900–2080*
(numbers in thousands)

Year	Total Population of All Ages	65 and over		85 and over	
		Number	Percent	Number	Percent
1900	76,303	3,084	4.0	123	0.2
1910	91,972	3,950	4.3	167	0.2
1920	105,711	4,933	4.7	210	0.2
1930	122,775	6,634	5.4	272	0.2
1940	131,669	9,019	6.8	365	0.3
1950	150,967	12,270	8.1	577	0.4
1960	179,323	16,560	9.2	929	0.5
1970	203,302	19,980	9.8	1,409	0.7
1980	226,546	25,549	11.3	2,240	1.0
1990	249,415	31,224	12.5	3,050	1.2
2000	274,815	34,886	12.7	4,289	1.6
2010	298,109	39,705	13.3	5,702	1.9
2020	322,602	53,627	16.6	6,480	2.0
2030	344,951	69,839	20.2	8,381	2.4
2040	364,349	75,588	20.7	13,221	3.6
2050	382,674	78,876	20.6	17,652	4.6

*Projections based on middle series assumptions of the U.S. Bureau of the Census.

Sources: Senate Special Committee on Aging, in conjunction with the AARP, the Federal Council on Aging, and the U.S. Administration on Aging, *Aging America: Trends and Projections: 1991 Edition* (Washington, D.C.: U.S. GPO, 1991), p. 6, and Gregory Spencer, "Projection of the Population of the United States, by Age, Sex, Race, and Hispanic Origin: 1990 to 2050," *Current Population Reports*, P–25, no. 1018 (Washington, D.C.: U.S. GPO, November 1992), Tables G and H, pp. xiv, xv.

Figure 6.1
Number of Persons 65 Years (and 85 Years) and Over: 1900–2050

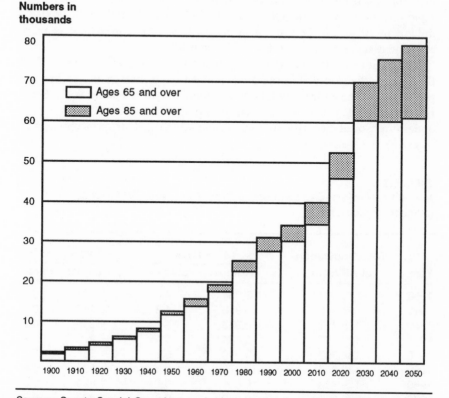

**Numbers in
thousands**

□ Ages 65 and over
▨ Ages 85 and over

Sources: Senate Special Committee on Aging, in conjunction with the AARP, the Federal Council on Aging, and the U.S. Administration on Aging, *Aging America: Trends and Projections: 1991 Edition* (Washington, D.C.: U.S. GPO, 1991), p. 6, and Gregory Spencer, "Projection of the Population of the United States, by Age, Sex, Race, and Hispanic Origin: 1992 to 2050," *Current Population Reports,* P-25, no. 1018 (Washington, D.C.: U.S. GPO, November 1992), Tables G and H, pp. XIV, XV.

number is projected to decline to 2.7 workers per beneficiary in 2015, 2.0 in 2030, and 1.9 in 2050.[27] Another way of expressing this changing relationship in the age structure of society is through the so-called "aged dependency" (also called the "elderly support") ratio, which is increasing. That is, the ratio of elderly persons (65 and over) to every 100 "working age" persons (18–64) has increased from about 15:100 persons in 1955 to roughly 21:100 today and is expected to increase to about 36:100 persons in 2030, the height of the retirement of baby boomers. Thus some ask, "Will future workers be able to afford Social Security and other income and health services needed by a growing aged population?"

Those who look only at the demographics of population aging often conclude that the burden will be too great. They interpret these trends as proof that the nation will not be able to sustain Social Security and related systems for baby boomers and those who follow. However, such predictions overlook many important facts. Most notably, that the aged dependency ratio only shows part of the "overall dependency burden."

Analysis using the "overall dependency" ratio (also called the "total support" ratio)—which defines children under 18 plus the elderly as the "dependent" population—leads to very different conclusions.[28] Because the proportion of the population under 18 is projected to decline, *never at any time during the next 65 years is the overall dependency ratio projected to exceed the levels it attained in 1964.*[29] Even from 2030 through 2050, the total dependency ratio is projected to be below (about 78:100) what it was during the 1960s (e.g., 83:100 in 1965) when most of the baby boomers were children. While the composition of governmental and private expenditures for younger and older Americans is quite different, careful analysis of all the facts surrounding dependency ratios do not support the gloomy view that changing demographics will overwhelm the nation's ability to meet the retirement needs of future generations.[30] (See Figure 6.2.)

As previously discussed, under the intermediate assumptions used to forecast the financial status of Social Security, the program is able to meet benefit payments through 2036, and there is plenty of lead time to deal with any problems that may occur. Additionally, experts generally expect that the economy will, over the long run, expand slowly, at perhaps an average of 1.5 percent to 2.0 percent per year after adjusting for inflation. This means that after adjusting for inflation, the income available per person—what economists call real per capita gross domestic product—would double in roughly every forty to fifty years, thereby enabling workers of the future to pay higher taxes, if necessary, while simultaneously enjoying considerably higher standards of living. Consequently, barring unforeseen disasters, the economy of the future seems likely to be able to support a mix of private and public efforts to meet the needs of all age groups.

Also, interpreting the changing demography of society in very pessimistic terms fails to recognize that some among today's elderly work and that policies can, if needed, be developed to encourage healthy older people to work longer and employers to retain them longer. Very significantly, they overlook the importance of basic biomedical research which has helped us to conquer diseases in the past. So, for instance, investments in biomedical research that have the potential to help us delay, if not eliminate, the onset of a disease such as Alzheimer's *may* result in substantial public and private savings, not to mention the *possibility* of a better quality of life.

One way to discuss this issue is to turn the question around by asking,

Figure 6.2
Young, Old, and Total Support Ratios: 1900–2050 (Number of people of specified age group per 100 people ages 18 through 64)

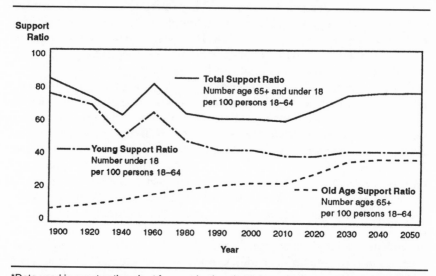

*Data used in constructing chart from projections based on middle series assumptions of the U.S. Bureau of the Census.

Sources: Senate Special Committee on Aging, in conjunction with the AARP, the Federal Council on Aging, and the U.S. Administration on Aging, *Aging America: Trends and Projections: 1991 Edition* (Washington, D.C.: U.S. GPO, 1991), p. 18, and Gregory Spencer, "Projection of the Population of the United States, by Age, Sex, Race, and Hispanic Origin: 1992 to 2050," *Current Population Reports,* P-25, no. 1092 (Washington, D.C.: U.S. GPO, November 1992), Table H, p. XV.

"What's the alternative to an aging society?" Plainly there is none and, one way or another, it will be necessary to provide needed income and health care support. Such support will be provided either through public programs or by having individuals and their families bear these expenses entirely by themselves. Of course, this does not mean that public institutions can or should remain unchanged. Clearly, if the economy performs substantially better or worse than anticipated, then Social Security and related systems will change, restricting or expanding protections as needed and as possible.

In short, while neither panic nor dire predictions are appropriate, demographic and economic trends must be monitored very carefully and preparations made for the retirement of the baby boomers through policies that maintain the integrity of Social Security and of private and public employee pensions. Policies that would encourage healthy older persons to work longer, investments that are directed at economic growth, and investments in basic biomedical research ought to be considered. Consideration also ought to be given to directing more resources at today's children, especially those who are poor, to ensure that they become self-sufficient and productive workers.

The "Surplus"

As discussed, Social Security is expected to take in more money than it spends for roughly the next thirty years. With the enactment of the 1983 amendments to the Social Security Act, the program shifted from the principle of pay-as-you-go to a temporary, partial advance funding approach. With this change came new controversy, this time over a surplus rather than a deficit. Looking first at the history and facts surrounding recent trust fund build-ups, we will then turn to the political controversy and choices regarding partial advance funding.

When the Greenspan Commission, Congress, and the president forged the plans and eventual compromises that resulted in the 1983 financing amendments to the Social Security Act, all parties agreed that the eventual legislative package should greatly reduce the possibility of an unexpected downturn in the economy which could create a new short-term financing crisis prior to 1990. (Even without the 1983 legislation, it was understood that as tax increases which were scheduled under the 1977 amendments went into effect in 1990, the program would experience yearly surpluses for many years and a large build-up of reserves.) As previously noted, another financing crisis on the heels of the 1983 amendments, it was thought, would undermine public confidence in Social Security and possibly in the nation's political institutions. To protect against this possibility, the 1983 legislation was crafted to keep the program solvent even if economic performance more nearly resembled the projections under the pessimistic short-term assumptions than under the most commonly accepted intermediate assumptions. Fortunately, the cautious short-term financing assumptions underlying the amendments combined with economic performance through 1990 that was generally favorable to the program's financing, to bring about a more rapid growth of trust fund ratios than had been anticipated in 1983. The ratio in the combined OASDI trust funds reached the desired 100 percent level in 1993, sufficient to cover one year's expenditures absent additional revenues. Under the intermediate assumptions, the actual dollar surpluses are projected to grow from about $56 billion in 1993 to $129 billion in 2001,[31] and even larger for many years to follow. While those involved in shaping the 1983 legislation were generally aware that the combined effects of the 1977 and 1983 legislation were to produce many years of surplus to be followed by many years of deficits, partial advance funding was not defined as either a particularly desirable or undesirable end in itself. It seemed largely to be an artifact of the successful 1983 legislative package that placed the combined OASDI trust funds on very solid financial footings for many years to come, and which also had the secondary benefit of reassuring the public about the future of the program.

Even in 1992, a yearly surplus of tax revenues over expenditures is projected for the next twenty-four years in the combined OASDI trust funds under the intermediate assumptions. When interest earned on trust fund investments is added to tax revenues, the yearly surplus is projected to continue through 2023, with trust fund ratios peaking at 335 in 2014; that is, in January 2014 the combined OASDI trust fund is projected to have more than three times as much in funds as will be needed to fund anticipated expenditures in that year. Following this roughly thirty-year build-up of large trust fund assets, yearly expenditures are projected to exceed revenues so that the trust funds are projected to be exhausted in 2036. "Under the more favorable conditions assumed in alternative I, the combined OASI and DI assets would continue to grow throughout the long-range projection period, reaching about 10 times annual expenditures. Under the more pessimistic assumptions in alternative III, the combined assets are estimated to be exhausted in 2019."[32]

What happens to the assets that are building up in the combined trust fund? All Social Security revenues go to the federal treasury, with the treasury issuing interest-bearing securities that are credited to the trust funds to be redeemed as Social Security pays for benefits and administrative costs.[33] Under the pay-as-you-go financing, the build-up of these claims against the federal treasury is relatively modest, ideally representing about one year's anticipated outgo. But under partial advance funding, the trust funds function, in part, as an accounting mechanism, allowing the yearly surpluses to be used for purchasing bonds that help finance federal debt. "Later, during the retirement of the baby boom, as the trust funds are drawn down, these bonds would be cashed in, thus requiring taxpayers at that time to pay increased taxes to redeem these debts to Social Security."[34] By roughly

2025, $1 out of every $6 of the program's outgo would be dependent upon their redemption. The government has never defaulted on the securities it posts to its trust funds, but the magnitude of the claims . . . has prompted many observers to ask where the Government will find the resources . . . given the large deficits it is running today. Basically, the Government will have three options: raise other taxes, curtail other spending, or borrow from the financial markets. There is nothing in law today that will dictate or determine what it will (or can) do then.[35]

The surplus issue is complex and enmeshed with questions of national savings, large federal deficits, and tax policy. There is much agreement that it does not make sense to build up and then deplete large reserves and that a policy of running yearly surpluses in Social Security while simultaneously running large yearly deficits in federal revenues is not desirable. Expert opinion, however, tends to be split on a number of questions—including whether the problem is primarily a Social Security or a federal tax policy issue; whether to return to pay-as-you-go financing or strengthen the partial advance funding approach; whether large reserves create too much temptation for congressional spending; whether action is needed now or ten to thirty years in the future.[36]

Senator Patrick Moynihan has proposed returning to pay-as-you-go financing by lowering the OASDI payroll tax through 2015, to be followed by payroll tax increases to maintain the long-run solvency of the program. Those favoring this approach argue that the current approach of running surpluses in Social Security and deficits in federal general revenues is dishonest budgetary policy. Even though Social Security's yearly surpluses are no longer counted when calculating the federal deficit, the money loaned from the reserves helps finance the federal debt and interest paid to the trust funds is not shown as interest payments on the national debt in the budget. In effect, the payroll tax, which generally places more burden on low- and moderate-income workers than the income tax, is being used indirectly to fund ongoing government operations. Lowering the payroll tax, it is argued, is less burdensome to lower-income workers, more honest tax policy, and removes the political temptation for Congress that the build-up of large reserves presents. Moreover, a proposal such as Moynihan's would place the program in close actuarial balance, thereby strengthening public confidence, and like most tax cuts be politically popular. As for the federal deficits, Congress would then need to address the deficit more directly, either through tax increases or benefit reductions.[37] Another concern is that the surpluses will eventually result in government involvement in private sector investment.[38]

There are two political arguments against returning to pay-as-you-go financing. One is that the baby boom generation may have a responsibility to help build a Social Security "nest-egg," thereby removing some financial pressures from the generations that will be supporting them during their retirement years. Resentment may undermine the willingness to support baby boomers if "boomers" are perceived as voting themselves a payroll tax decrease and those who follow increases. Second, it is argued that payroll tax decreases will place financial pressures on other parts of the federal budget because offsetting income tax increases will not be enacted. Third, tax decreases are easy to enact, but increases difficult. To reduce the payroll tax rate when future payroll tax increases may be needed in Medicare's Hospital Insurance trust fund in the near term may constrain our ability to deal with this impending problem.

There are also analytical arguments for other approaches. Some rest on the issue of timing, suggesting that action is premature since trust fund ratios have not yet reached the 150 percent level which advocates of this position consider desirable. As for the projected long-run financing problem, since Social Security is well financed for the next thirty years or so, it may be wise to postpone action for many years until future events provide a clearer picture of the program's financing. More importantly, viewed within the context of concerns over national savings and investment, the need for more savings provides a rationale for strengthening the partial advance funding approach by planning for modest increases in the payroll tax rate twenty-five to forty years in the future. Thus economists Henry Aaron, Barry Bosworth, and Gary Burtless view the build-up of Social Security trust funds as a needed opportunity to increase national savings and investment. They call for a policy of payroll tax increases in the future so that the trust fund reserves would not be diminished from their projected peak, coupled with a federal deficit reduction policy. As with Moynihan's proposal, depending on timing, this approach could resolve long-run financing problems and help strengthen public confidence. They write:

If fiscal policy is maintained so that additions to the national OASDHI trust funds add to the national savings, the resulting increase in national consumption will exceed the increased cost of social security benefits and come close to offsetting the increased cost of OASDHI benefits from a growing population of beneficiaries and rising hospital costs.[39]

There are some important lessons in the surplus issue. The first is that solutions to Social Security problems (the financing crisis of 1982) often create new problems (what to do about surpluses). The second is that Social Security issues are often complex and potentially connected to a host of non-Social Security concerns (the federal budget, national savings, faith in public institutions). The third is that politicians, analysts, and the general public are likely to favor different courses of action based on the relative value given to certain policy goals, for example, strengthening national savings or constraining congressional spending.

Long-Term Financing: The Choices

As noted, the 1992 trustees report calls for action "to strengthen the long-range financing of the OASDI program following the development of appropriate options."[40] This emerging financing problem provides an opportunity for us to explore various policy responses. The choices in one sense are fairly simple, involving some combination of tax increases, benefit reductions, and further taxation of benefits (with the proceeds dedicated to the Social Security trust funds). Other possibilities, such as means-testing Social Security, are possible but less likely because they involve radical departure from program principles. For the purpose of highlighting some of the choices and trade-offs surrounding choices, let us take a look at a few of the candidates for a legislative package.

On the tax side, payroll tax rates could be increased or the portion of earnings subject to taxation raised. Arguments against raising the payroll tax rate (and also in many cases against raising the taxable ceiling) are that it would burden business, hamper taxpayers in general and low-wage workers in particular, and hinder future generations of workers. Further, when the substantial deficit in the Medicare Hospital Insurance trust fund is considered, a solution that relies primarily on raising the payroll tax rate would require a very substantial hike, one that taxpayers, especially low-income ones, might find unacceptable. This view also overlooks the earned income tax credit which is specifically designed to offset this regressivity for low-income workers supporting young families and the progressive benefit structure which more than compensates for a regressive payroll tax structure. Others point out that the United States has not reached the upper limits of payroll taxation. In fact, payroll taxes and the overall level of taxation are substantially higher in many industrialized economies in the European Community and elsewhere. Moreover, given that changes in the OASDI payroll tax rate are not likely to be needed for many years, the real wages of future workers will generally be higher even if payroll tax rates are increased. One payroll taxation alternative avoids the problem of regressivity but adds to the costs of businesses. As with Medicare HI, a higher (or possibly the entire) proportion of earnings could be subject to the payroll tax for the employer but not the employee.

Another alternative on the tax side is to infuse the program with general revenues. In the past, there has been considerable support for some level of general revenue financing, beginning with the Committee on Economic Security and the 1937–38 and 1947 advisory committees on Social Security.[41] As federal deficits have mounted, however, it has become quite clear that general revenue financing, at least in the near future, is simply not feasible. Some would also add that it would set a dangerous precedent that would encourage unwise expansion of benefits, further politicize Social Security by drawing it too closely into budget debates, and erode the notion of Social Security as an earned right.[42] However, it is important to point out that many countries rely on this mechanism and that the income tax represents a more progressive taxing mechanism than payroll taxes. Also noteworthy is the fact that the Social Security program already has several significant indirect infusions of general revenues. The income generated from treating Social Security benefits as taxable income flows directly into the trust funds. Additionally, the trust funds are indirectly subsidized by the tax code which allows employers to deduct their share of employee's payroll tax as a business expense and by provisions allowing the self-employed some parallel tax deductions.

On the benefit side, raising the age of eligibility for full benefits beyond age 67 is one way of producing long-run savings. The 1983 amendments scheduled a gradual increase, from 65 to 67, in the age of eligibility for full retirement benefits over a twenty-four-year period beginning in 2003. A related reduction in the value of benefits for persons accepting early retirement benefits and spouses of retired workers and for nearly all widow(er)s will be phased in beginning in 2000. As discussed in the previous chapter, proposals to raise the age of eligibility for full benefits have numerous adequacy and equity implications. While saving money for the program and encouraging work, much of the savings will be produced by reducing the benefits of lower-income persons who are unable to work due to limited employment opportunities and/or health problems. Most proponents and opponents of this position tend to agree, however, that if further increases in retirement age are deemed desirable by Congress, then it should be done years in advance so as to give workers time to adjust their retirement expectations.

Revising indexing procedures could strengthen the program's financing, but this approach, too, has major implications for the income protection goals of the program. One of the important features of Social Security is the certainty of benefits. Prior to benefit receipt, the wage indexing feature of the program helps to maintain future living standards by adjusting promised benefits for changes in average wages in the economy, essentially guaranteeing a relatively constant proportion of pre-retirement earnings for workers at different earnings levels. Once benefits are received, the automatic COLA essentially guarantees their purchasing power, no matter how long the beneficiary lives. These same provisions, which are so important to maintaining the adequacy of Social Security, are also very expensive features of the program and important reasons why the program is vulnerable to economic change.

As previously discussed, the 1983 amendments permanently delayed the COLA for six months and, in recent years, the idea of delaying, skipping, or otherwise reducing the COLA has been advanced in the context of deficit reduction discussions. Also, as part of the 1977 amendments to the Social Security Act, changes were made in the benefit formula that effectively reduced benefit levels for future beneficiaries, making them closer to what Congress had intended in 1972 when the wage-indexing feature was first introduced.

Modifications in indexing procedures can do much to reduce anticipated long-run financing problems and to give Congress greater fiscal control over the program. Instead of being locked into yearly benefit adjustments or updates in future benefits, Congress could assess what it could afford prior to adjusting benefit levels. But, given that benefit payments seem assured for at least the next thirty-five years, does it make sense to reduce the benefits of today's beneficiaries (who are probably less well off than those who will follow) for a problem anticipated so far in the future? Moreover, instituting substantial reductions in the COLA, a COLA based on changes in the cost of living minus one percent for example, would substantially undermine the economic security of beneficiaries, especially low- and moderate-income ones for whom Social Security generally makes up a higher proportion of their total incomes. Such a change would structure Social Security in a manner that would result in less purchasing power of benefits the longer that people live. Another proposal, to give the COLA only to lower-income beneficiaries, would be administratively complex and would introduce a means test, which would arguably undermine the dignity of beneficiaries and the political support for the program. This is why some favor giving consideration to increasing the proportion of Social Security benefits that is counted as taxable income if the politics of the federal deficit or Social Security financing requires placing greater burden on beneficiaries.

Arguably, increasing the portion of Social Security benefits subject to income taxation is neither a benefit cut or tax increase. Currently, up to one-half of Social Security benefits are subject to taxation for persons whose incomes exceed certain base amounts—$25,000 for single taxpayers, $32,000 for married taxpayers filing jointly, $0 for married taxpayers living together at any point during the tax year but filing separately.[43] The proceeds from taxing benefits are credited to the trust funds, an estimated $6.2 billion in 1992, more in future years.[44] As inflation and real wage increases push more of the earnings of workers above these thresholds, more people will find their benefits subject to taxation and will be paying more. Even so, the benefits of low- and many moderate-income beneficiaries will not be taxed.

Taxation of benefits was one of the key provisions of the 1983 Social Security financing package. Given the choices between further cuts in benefits (skipping a COLA) or larger tax increases (more of a payroll tax increase), the National Commission on Social Security Reform and later the Congress accepted this provision which had previously been considered unacceptable by both the House of Representatives and the Senate. In the context of hard choices, this became an important part of the solution. Also, it had the advantage of ambiguity. Those preferring to resolve Social Security's financing problems through benefit reductions often viewed taxing benefits as a benefit cut and an indirect means test. Those preferring solutions relying on tax increases regarded the new provision as good tax policy, with higher-income beneficiaries appropriately being called upon to pay taxes on income (benefits) that had not previously been subject to taxation.

Very possibly, in the context of renewed discussion of long-term financing reform, further taxation of benefits will emerge as a prominent option. One suggestion would be to treat the entire benefit as taxable income (instead of up to one-half as is currently the case). Objections could be raised that some income would then be taxed twice. Another option would be to tax the non-taxed portion of the payroll tax contribution plus the equivalent of interest earned (through the wage-indexing features of the formula) on the employer and employee contributions, about 85 percent of benefits. One proposal calls for taxing up to 85 percent of Social Security benefits for single persons with incomes of $25,000 or more and couples with incomes of $32,000 or more.[45] If implemented in 1993, this change would increase revenues by roughly $38 billion over the next five years alone. This assumes that these tax revenues would be recycled back into the trust funds as is currently the case with receipts from taxing Social Security.

Depending upon one's point of view, further taxation of benefits can be regarded as a potentially important and equitable part of the solution to Social Security's emerging long-term financing problem. To some this would seem unfair because it further reduces the rate of return to beneficiaries, especially higher-income ones who already receive a smaller return relative to other beneficiaries. To others, this alternative has the virtue of maintaining the universal eligibility provisions of the program while also placing greater responsibility on middle- and higher-income beneficiaries. Still others, while advocating increased taxation of benefits, do not believe the receipts should be recycled into Social Security. Instead, they would use these new funds for deficit reduction.

Yet other proposals call for means-testing benefits. Means-testing could produce considerable savings and also target public spending to those in greatest need. But, as discussed, it would also radically alter the nature of the program, erode political support for it, undermine the dignity of benefici-aries, and break faith with beneficiaries—especially those eliminated—who had been promised benefits in return for payroll tax contributions. In other words, it is simply not possible to means-test Social Security without chang-ing it into a welfare program, a change that is damaging to the program and consistently opposed by the vast majority of the public.

In terms of the practical choices, we hope this discussion illustrates how important it is to assess various options in terms of trade-offs and differing policy goals. Thus, it becomes important to examine the potential savings against other policy goals such as adequacy, fairness, and maintaining public confidence. Would treating portions of social insurance benefits as taxable income be preferable to increasing the age of eligibility for full benefits or to a payroll tax increase? Can we afford further taxation? Should we lower the promised "floor of protection?" These are the kinds of questions that policy-makers and the public will be addressing once long-term financing problems work their way onto the public agenda.

"WILL SOCIAL SECURITY BE THERE WHEN I NEED IT?"

Let us conclude this discussion by taking a look at the bottom line, "Will Social Security be there for me and mine in the future?" We think the answer is assuredly, "Yes." While technical reasoning supports such a conclusion, the answer is perhaps most simply arrived at through political logic.

No matter what your view, a leap of faith is necessary. A negative answer assumes somewhere in the future that the political leadership of the United States will be willing to take the political risk of eliminating or dramatically scaling back Social Security protections, either because the economy of the future cannot sustain it or because the program lacks political support. An affirmative response assumes, whatever strains emerge, the continuity of an economy that can afford Social Security and the continuity of government and public support for the program.

Simply put, we believe that Social Security will continue, not only because the concept is fundamentally sound and the program's financing challenges are manageable, but also because it is too important an institution for Congress or any president to take the political risk of allowing it to go bankrupt. The well-being of American families is tied closely to the continuity of the program. In its absence, there would still be a need to provide for those who are old, disabled, or at risk because of the death of a worker. One way or another, the nation would need to transfer resources from the working to the non-working. Social Security provides a politically attractive mechanism that works well. Along with public support, the taxing power of the government guarantees its continuity and stability. No one disputes that new challenges and problems will arise from time to time, requiring mid-course adjustments. But to conclude from this that the political leadership will, with public support, allow the program to cease lacks credibility.

No doubt, if the economy of the future is more productive than currently anticipated, the likelihood (or scope) of future financing problems is diminished. If long-term economic growth is even lower. than projected, then plainly voters and public servants twenty or thirty years from now will need to decide to reduce the growth of benefits significantly or increase taxes or both. The point is that there is considerable lead time to respond to emerging long-term shortfalls should such problems occur.

Is Social Security Fair?

Questions are often raised about the fairness of Social Security, but usually with very different notions about what is fair and what the program is supposed to do. To some it is unfair that higher-income workers receive a smaller rate of return on their payroll tax investment than lower-income workers. To others it is unfair that retired workers with a history of higher earnings generally receive larger benefit checks. And others consider it unfair that Social Security benefits reflect much of the inequality and discrimination that is structured into our wage system and other social institutions.

As we will discuss in this chapter, these and other judgments are often made with little appreciation of the complexity of the program and with many unspoken assumptions. Such judgments are very sensitive to views about what constitutes justice in the distribution of social costs and benefits and about the extent to which Social Security as opposed to other institutions should (and can) correct for lifelong inequities.

Thus we begin this chapter by discussing several misunderstandings that sometimes mistakenly define intended (and generally beneficial) programmatic outcomes as inequities. We also make explicit various definitions of *fairness* as applied in the context of Social Security policy discussions. Next, we explore several contemporary discussions about the fairness of Social Security to young workers and future generations of retirees, to women and minorities, and to those who can and those who cannot work. By introducing these fairness issues, we hope to provide a basis to assist in making personal judgments about these matters.

MYTHS AND MISUNDERSTANDINGS

As we have suggested from the beginning of this book, critical analysis of Social Security requires an appreciation of its many goals and the values from which it derives. Critics, however, sometimes assess the fairness of the program from the vantage point of only one goal and with narrow notions of fairness which imply that the program seeks to realize only one value. Data highlighting the multiple effects of the program are often ignored or discounted. This failure to acknowledge the program's complexity often gives rise to specious criticism.

For example, Social Security is criticized with great conviction by some as "simply a middle-class entitlement," mainly serving the well off and doing little to eliminate economic hardship. Here Social Security is presented as wastefully directing hundreds of billions of dollars at persons who are not in need, while leaving many disabled and elderly persons in poverty or near-poverty. In a *Forbes* magazine article with the delicious title, "Consuming Our Children," the authors suggest "a remarkable number of social security recipients do not need the supplement."[1]

In fact, as intended, Social Security protects many middle- and upper-income citizens against risks of retirement, disability, and survivorship. But this does not mean that the program does little to prevent or otherwise reduce poverty. That most beneficiaries are middle-income should properly be interpreted as a sign of the program's success, not a weakness. Further, as previously discussed, studies and data indicate that social insurance programs, especially Social Security, do more to reduce poverty and inequality than other social programs and more than taxes.[2] Particularly for elderly persons, the program is a very effective antipoverty measure (see Table 5.4). Without Social Security, the proportion of persons aged 65 and over with incomes below the official poverty line would swell from about 12.6 percent in 1991 to roughly one-half, that is, over 16 million elderly persons.

Other data also dispel the criticism of Social Security as *just* a "middle-class entitlement," providing benefits mainly to financially comfortable people. About 62 percent of elderly persons aged 65 and over receive at least one-half of their total income from Social Security, and 85 percent of the very old (persons aged 85 and over) do.[3] As a source of income, Social Security is far more important for low- and moderate-income elderly persons. Among elderly households with less than $10,000 in yearly income, fully 60 percent reported in 1988 that they received four-fifths or more of their total income from Social Security as compared to 18 percent of households reporting $10,000 to $19,999.[4] Plainly, low- and moderate-income elderly persons depend more on and benefit greatly from this program, which is also why benefit cuts would greatly undermine their economic well-being. For example, a study commissioned by the American Association of Retired Persons indicates that if the 1988 COLA had been skipped, 331,000 beneficiaries—including elderly people, children, disabled, and widows—would have fallen below the poverty line. Of course, there are federal policies that are *disproportionately beneficial* to middle- , upper middle- , and higher-income people, such as the income tax deductions for homeowners and certain tax incentives for private pension savings, but Social Security is not among them.

Rather ironically, Social Security is also criticized with equal conviction (sometimes by the same persons!) as "little more than a welfare program." From this perspective, Social Security is disguised welfare, primarily benefiting low-income people who have not paid their fair share of payroll taxes. Believing that returns from Social Security should parallel market distributions, with those paying more taxes receiving proportionally more benefits, some condemn the program as unfair because it provides a smaller rate of return for higher-income workers relative to low- and moderate-income ones. Moreover, it unfairly forces middle- and upper-income workers to participate, foregoing alternative private investments that are viewed as yielding better outcomes.

Obviously, Social Security cannot be both welfare and a middle-class entitlement. That it is presented as both is testimony to the confusion resulting from overlooking how the program represents a compromise between the dual goals of adequacy and individual equity. As previously mentioned, the most important goal is *adequacy*, the principle that program benefits should be large enough to meet the basic needs of the citizens the program is designed to protect. This goal is reflected in (1) the benefit formula, which generally provides a proportionately larger benefit to persons (and their families) who have worked consistently in low-paying jobs, (2) the inclusion of benefits for survivors and other family members, and (3) an annual COLA that maintains the purchasing power of benefits once received.

Another important goal in Social Security is *individual equity*—a dominant goal in private insurance but not so in social insurance. This is the principle that persons ought to receive a return that is directly proportionate to their contribution. While adequacy is emphasized, the benefit formula in Social Security provides for a blending between these two goals. The result is that while Social Security generally replaces a larger proportion of previous earnings for low-income workers, higher-income workers usually receive larger benefits—in effect an acknowledgment of greater payroll tax contributions.

If we, as a nation, were unconcerned with providing widespread and adequate protection against loss of income due to retirement, disability, and death of a breadwinner, there would be no need for Social Security: we could rely entirely on private savings, private insurance, and other private solutions (e.g., the family). By doing so, however, we would guarantee that a substantial proportion—possibly a majority—of citizens would not have adequate protection. Thus it is the desire to provide a basic floor of protection under the entire citizenry that provides the strongest rationale for Social Security and for the emphasis on the adequacy principle. Moreover, the retirement and disability savings of middle- and upper-income people are often subsidized through other public vehicles, including tax write-offs that facilitate private pensions, Individual Retirement Accounts, and accrual of equity in homes. Thus, while Social Security is designed to provide special retirement, disability, and survivorship protection to those at greater economic risk, the parallel needs of better-off citizens are also met through Social Security in concert with other public mechanisms which are disproportionately beneficial to them.

Two other features of Social Security—the lack of means-testing and compulsory participation—are sometimes viewed as unfair, criticisms that again arise primarily from a lack of understanding about the complexity and multiple goals of the program. In the case of means-testing, it has previously been pointed out that political support for means-tested programs is limited and the benefits low. Means-testing would most likely undermine the rationale for payroll financing and the widespread support for the program. Moreover, it would erode the dignity of beneficiaries. Thus what may appear as a way of assisting those at greatest risk would most likely move them further from the social and economic mainstream.

Similar difficulties would result from making participation in Social Security voluntary. Some have argued that it is out of keeping with American values to require workers to participate in these programs and that participation should be voluntary, allowing workers to opt for other forms of protection (e.g., private savings, life insurance, Individual Retirement Accounts). At first glance, voluntary participation in Social Security and other social insurance programs seems very appealing.

But voluntary participation would not work. Unlike the way private insurance operates, almost everyone in the work force must participate in certain social insurance programs—namely, Social Security, Medicare's HI program, unemployment insurance, and workers' compensation—and coverage cannot be denied to any worker, even if very ill. Since private insurance companies generally accept only the healthiest citizens into their health, life insurance, and disability plans, voluntary participation would leave the least healthy for government-run programs. Because no one is turned away from participating in a social insurance program, making Social Security or Medicare's HI program voluntary would leave them with the most expensive risks, thereby undermining the programs' financing and ultimately its political support. Therefore, participation must be compulsory to ensure a balance of "good" and "bad" risks.

Moreover, if participation in a program like Social Security were voluntary, some people might use their contributions to make poor investments or might find the press of current needs so great that they could not save at all. When the risks they would have been protected against eventually occur, would they then be left to reap the consequences of their poor choices? Probably not. More likely, small welfare benefits would be provided at cost to taxpayers. Thus compulsory participation protects the public from paying for those who might choose not to participate now but later become dependent on public assistance.

As this introductory discussion illustrates, judgments about the fairness of Social Security are informed by different and sometimes contradictory notions of justice. Viewing Social Security as a "middle-class entitlement" assumes that expenditures directed at middle-income beneficiaries are wasteful and that poverty reduction should be the driving purpose of the policy, that a just policy is one that is singularly responsive to the greatest human need. Accepting this as the sole standard of fairness for Social Security, however, ignores the goals of preventing poverty and supporting the living standards of non-poor beneficiaries as well. It also ignores an important political lesson: that the poor are often best protected when they participate in programs protecting all income classes. In contrast, some consider Social Security an unjust intervention because it is mildly redistributive, because it is not based solely on the individual equity principle. Those criticizing the program as resembling a welfare program implicitly assume that market outcomes are just and that government should not seek any redistribution through Social Security, but simply provide benefits proportional to prior contributions. Those finding compulsory participation unfair may object to a perceived procedural injustice, to what is considered an unnecessary constraint on individual action. But, as explained, without universal participation, the social benefits of Social Security cannot be realized. In short, the lesson to be learned here is that discussions about the fairness of Social Security are often more complex than they first appear.

THE FAIRNESS ISSUES

From this introduction, we hope one gains an appreciation of the importance of making explicit the various ways of assessing the fairness of Social Security and of how one-dimensional views of the program can lead to faulty conclusions. No matter how well intended, such assessments often overlook many highly valued goals the program seeks to achieve. A balanced examination of Social Security requires recognizing that the program represents compromise and blending of many goals. Or, as Marmor, Mashaw, and Harvey put it: "All programs are compromises. Hence, all programs contain contradictions. Moreover these contradictions are not accidental. They respond to sets of political preferences."[5]

With this as background, let us take a look at some of the major issues that are often framed in terms of fairness.

Women and Social Security

We begin, then, by returning to the equity and adequacy issues of special concern to women, initially discussed in Chapter 5. In doing so, we hope to illustrate why different conclusions can be reached about what changes should be made in Social Security to address these concerns, and why, as Schulz points out, there "is widespread agreement that social security provisions related to women need to be reformed but no consensus on how to do it."[6]

Let us review a few points. There is no question that Social Security is the single most important and effective source of retirement income for women during their old age. There is also no question that women, especially single women, the very old, and minority women, are at greatest risk today and in the future of inadequate resources in old age. It is this adequacy issue—this threat to economic well-being—that many consider the most important fairness issue affecting women. Among women living alone, nearly one-quarter of white women and three-fifths of African American women report below-poverty incomes in 1990.[7] Analyses based on the Pension and Retirement Income Simulation Model (PRISM) suggest that while the elderly, as a group, will be better off in the future and poverty further reduced, an even larger majority of the poor and near-poor elderly will be single women, especially divorced women.[8] Related adequacy concerns include the high proportion of widows with incomes below poverty, the lack of disability protection for homemakers, and the inadequacy of benefits for many divorced and widowed women. That time spent out of the labor force doing caregiving work at home generally reduces women's Social Security benefits often compounds these problems. Moreover, many see this as devaluing the contributions of all who provide care and unfairly penalizing women who perform the bulk of such work.

There are also other issues that are often cast as unfair because they violate the principle of individual equity. Benefits paid to a retired couple with two earners are generally lower than benefits paid to a one-earner couple with a similar pattern of total earnings, although as Regina O'Grady-LeShane of Boston College points out, this issue is declining in importance because increasingly fewer women are and will receive a benefit based only on their marital status.[9] A second individual equity concern is that the earnings of women who work outside the home often do not contribute to the value of a woman's retirement benefit (though it does provide important disability and survivorship protections). Spouses of retired workers are eligible to receive a benefit equivalent to one-half of their spouse's benefit or what they have earned based on their own employment, whichever is larger. Similarly, widows receive benefits equivalent to the higher of what was earned on their husband's or their own earnings history. Consequently the payroll tax contributions of women often do not increase the value of their retirement and survivor benefits since they are better off accepting a benefit based on their husband's earnings. Yet a third concern could be considered an individual equity issue for women as well as an important adequacy issue. Given that roughly one-half of all new marriages end in divorce, and that divorce often greatly reduces the protections afforded women through Social Security, some argue that the joint interests of women in the accrued value of a household's Social Security are not well protected.[10]

As AARP analyst Laurel Beedon observes, the issues of greatest concern to women exemplify the "sometimes uneasy tension" between the twin principles of adequacy and individual equity.[11] Initially, benefits for the wives of retired workers and for aged widows of covered workers were established as part of the 1939 amendments to the Social Security Act. Ironically, the seeds of many of today's equity concerns can be found in this legislation which substantially improved the adequacy of the program for covered workers and their families.[12] For it is the provision of spouse benefits that creates the disparities between one- and two-earner couples that are a source of concern to many. This provision also gives rise to the anomalous situation that finds women making payroll tax contributions but often receiving relatively little in return since they are already eligible for benefits based on their spouse earnings. This legislation assumed that most women were married for life and would not participate as workers in the labor force. These assumptions are clearly outmoded today when divorce is common and most married women spend a significant portion of their married life in the labor force, though usually at lower earnings levels than men. (In fact, such assumptions were questionable as a basis for policy even in 1939, given the great diversity of life circumstances for women and their families.)

Problems such as poor protection for divorced spouses and inadequate incomes for many widows are a function of the interaction of changing social circumstances with the design of the program and the labor market experience of women. Although participating in the paid workforce at very high levels, women are more likely to reduce or leave employment to care for others. They also receive relatively low wages due to such factors as direct discrimination through wage differentials, rigidities in the workplace that do not facilitate caregiving or part-time employment, and opportunities lost from taking on caregiving responsibilities. Census data indicate that the earnings of women in full-time jobs in 1989 were roughly 70 percent of their male counterparts. Even where women hold the same position as men, they generally earn less.[13] And, as O'Grady-LeShane's research highlights, the caregiving activities of women and lower earnings are eventually reflected in smaller Social Security benefits.[14] Moreover, when roughly one-half of all new marriages are expected to end in divorce,[15] protecting the joint interests of men and women in a household's Social Security pensions is becoming increasingly important.

The problem definition and the policy prescriptions that follow are highly dependent on whether Social Security is viewed as the most appropriate vehicle for correcting "gender-based inequities in the labor market" and on "whether the definition of 'work' should . . . include unpaid work in the home and community."[16] As Beedon points out, these questions have implications for other aspects of the program. Answering them in the affirmative could lead to changes which "would diminish the connection that maintains popular support for the program—that benefits are 'earned' and have no connotation of 'welfare.'" Changing Social Security to offset fully labor market inequities would be very costly and might radically alter the program. An alternative strategy could be based on the assumption that the main causes of the income problems confronting women in old age have more to do with lifelong inequities in labor market and family institutions, thus requiring that effort be directed at reforming those systems while simultaneously seeking changes in Social Security and related programs that improve the well-being of women. While this approach does not let Social Security "off the hook," it allows for what some consider more realistic and incremental changes in the program such as modified earnings sharing at divorce, modest improvements in benefits for disabled widows, and adjustments that incorporate some recognition of the cost of caregiving to women. But it, too, is not without cost and, given projected long-run deficits, it is likely to be viewed by some as infeasible, while others would consider it too narrow an approach to a problem requiring large-scale reform.

Racial and Linguistic Minorities

Questions about fairness of the treatment of racial and linguistic minority groups by Social Security have been raised, both concerning the overall effect of the program and specific administrative practices. One set of issues concerns whether minorities are systematically discriminated against by the program because of generally shorter life expectancies and lower earnings. The other set of issues concerns whether members of linguistic and/or racial minorities are sometimes poorly served by such factors as staffing limitations and the limited translation services. Whether Social Security is viewed as discriminating against minorities depends substantially on whether the program is considered the proper mechanism to correct for systematic and lifelong inequities confronting members of many minority groups.

Several factors have led some to conclude that Social Security is unfair to minorities. Generally smaller wages and lifetime earnings for members of minority groups result in the absolute value of benefits being smaller, on average, than that for non-minorities. Minority youth are more likely than white youth to enter the labor force earlier and therefore can expect to work more years before receiving retirement benefits. The generally shorter life expectancies of minorities imply that minorities are less likely to collect retirement benefits for as many months as non-minorities. As groups, certain minorities—primarily African Americans, Hispanics, and Native Americans—have shorter life expectancies *at birth* and *at age 65* than white Americans, an indication of the lifelong effects of racial, ethnic, and economic discrimination on health and well-being. For example, white females in

1987 had life expectancies at birth of 78.9 years, compared with 73.6 for black females, 72.2 for white males, and 65.2 for black males. For persons reaching age 65, the life expectancy gap narrows. At age 65, life expectancy in 1987 was 18.8 years for white females, 17.1 years for black females, 14.9 years for white males, and 13.5 years for black males.[17]

Concerns such as these were highlighted in a report by the National Center for Policy Analysis, a conservative think tank studying private alternatives to Social Security. It concluded that because blacks have higher mortality rates than whites, "the vast majority of adult blacks would be better off if the [Social Security] system were abolished." Similar concerns have led some to consider separate retirement ages for different racial groups, a proposal that most consider highly impractical. (Interestingly, essentially the same argument can be made about men and women. But it would be patently absurd to argue that because men have higher mortality rates than women, Social Security unfairly discriminates against men and ought to be abolished, or alternatively to argue for lower retirement ages for men.)

Plainly, once again, the reality is more complex. For example, taking strong exception to the National Center for Policy Analysis report and the notion, as reported in the *Washington Times*, that Social Security "transfers wealth from black to white, young to old and poor to rich," Robert Myers writes:

Just as in any private pension plan, those who retire in the early years of operation receive "good buys" in order to make the program effective. However, transfers do not occur, on the average, from poor to rich and from black to white.

The National Center for Policy Analysis, which is given as the source for such views, has made faulty analyses when it entered into the field of actuarial computations. Any elements favoring higher-paid persons are more than offset by the weighted-benefit formula and their generally later retirement.

The flaws . . . are especially evident in the blacks versus whites comparison. Using life expectancy values at birth, instead of at age 20, is faulty.[18]

Similarly, a special study panel, the 1979 Advisory Council on Social Security, studied this issue and concluded that "social security does not treat minorities less favorably than it treats the majority population. However, the treatment of minorities is complex because various aspects of social security affect minorities in diverse ways."[19]

Because of shorter life expectancies, members of minority groups are, in fact, less likely to receive retirement benefits. But this is offset by three factors. First, minorities are more likely to receive disability and survivors' benefits. Second and more important, the adequacy feature of the Social Security benefit formula provides proportionately larger benefits to lower-income workers than to middle- and higher-income persons. Consequently, minority persons, who, on average, are more likely than non-minority persons to be in low-paying employment, generally receive proportionately larger benefits than non-minority persons.[20] And finally, because Social Security represents a larger portion of the retirement incomes of low- and moderate-income workers, it is an even more critical source of income protection for most minority persons who receive benefits than for most non-minority persons.

The entire nation should be concerned about the continued effects of limited opportunities and discrimination in education, employment, and housing in all regions of the country, and national, state, and local policies ought to address this ongoing problem. Nor should we take great satisfaction in knowing that, because minority persons are more likely to be low-income persons, Social Security offsets some of the negative impacts of racial and ethnic discrimination. But we should be cautious about suggesting that it is Social Security as opposed to other societal circumstances that is primarily responsible for the income and wealth disparities between minority and non-minority populations. On the contrary, Social Security is one of the few institutions that ameliorate these disparities.

To suggest that the benefit structure of Social Security does not systematically discriminate against minorities at risk does not mean that there are not aspects of the Social Security program in need of improvement. For example, there is some recent evidence of probable discrimination in the administration of the Disability Insurance program. A recent report of the General Accounting Office (GAO), the investigative arm of Congress, found that the chances of winning a successful Social Security (or SSI) disability appeal was 8 percent lower for African Americans than for white Americans. Similar differences in disability appeals were found for each of the past thirty years.[21] The GAO study suggested that at "the administrative law judge level, the largely unexplained racial differences in allowance rates calls into question the equity of treatment between black and white appellants under the Disability Insurance and Supplemental Security Income programs."[22] Importantly, the Social Security Administration has responded quickly by initiating an administrative review of the appeals process and by indicating intention of taking actions that are necessary to ensure impartial and equitable treatment of each applicant.

While some notable improvements in service have occurred with the modernization of SSA's computer system,[23] recent cuts in the Social Security workforce may have been particularly deleterious to non-English-speaking and other minorities as well as groups requiring special attention for their claims (e.g., persons with AIDS). Service to the public is less personal, and persons with complex cases sometimes "fall through the cracks." Local SSA staff are often overworked and demoralized. Consequently, more errors are occurring in the administration of claims and benefits, and outreach efforts have been reduced. Some eligible people, it has been suggested, are being provided with incorrect information or being discouraged from pursuing their cases by staff who are overworked and unable to provide proper assistance; as a result, they may not be receiving benefits to which they are entitled.[24] Many of the people served by Disability Insurance and other programs have limitations that make even the simplest transactions difficult without assistance. Specifically, functional illiteracy as well as physical and mental impairments of both younger and older individuals create many obstacles to access.[25] Staff cuts, it is argued, have exacerbated access problems, with fewer workers available for outreach and efforts directed at serving populations with special needs such as those who do not speak English. Moreover, since staff reductions were implemented primarily through attrition, and since there is more attrition in offices serving low-income minority populations, there have generally been more staff reductions in district offices serving minority populations. Though unintended, the effects are discriminatory. Having recently acknowledged many of these problems, SSA has launched its new Metropolitan Office Enhancement Project intended to improve conditions and services in 140 inner-city offices.[26]

Finally, there are a number of policy reforms that would be particularly beneficial to low-income and otherwise vulnerable groups—groups disproportionately composed of minority persons. Because minority persons are more likely than whites to become disabled or partially disabled in middle age, improving the administration of the program and liberalizing the definition of disability for older workers in the Social Security and SSI disability programs would be particularly beneficial. Increasing Social Security's special minimum benefit, which is designed to improve the adequacy of benefits for workers who have worked full-time for low wages throughout most of their work lives, would also aid many minority persons. And increasing the income guarantee under the SSI program and reforming the SSI assets test so that it does not prevent many poor people from receiving SSI benefits would provide significant assistance.[27]

Notch Babies

The "Notch Baby"[28] issue provides a good example of how the resolution of one problem often leads to another, albeit in this case a far less important one. And it provides an equally good example of how perceptions about what is fair can differ.

The saga of the notch babies begins with the enactment of the 1972 amendments to the Social Security Act. These amendments introduced a benefit formula allowing for automatic cost-of-living adjustments, which serves the important purpose of maintaining the purchasing power of benefits once received. Unfortunately, this benefit computation method (which applied to persons first eligible for retirement benefits in 1972 or later) contained a "flaw" that interacted with unexpected changes in the economy—higher than anticipated inflation and relatively lower wage increases—to "over-index" benefits (what has also been referred to incorrectly as "double-indexing"). The result was that benefits were being given to many new re-tirees that were greater than they should have been. Social Security began to replace unreasonably high proportions of pre-retirement earnings for all beneficiaries. Even larger benefits were projected in the future, so large that Social Security was projected to pay benefits higher than the wages of some persons retiring in the twenty-first century.[29] Obviously, this would place an unsustainable financial burden on the program, and it would not be sensible public policy. In fact, as early as the mid-1970s, it was the cause of roughly three-fifths of an unprecedented, large, projected long-run financing problem.

In 1977 Congress resolved most of the long-run problem by substituting a new benefit formula that reduced replacement rates (and benefits) to the more realistic levels that Congress had originally intended in 1972. Future benefits were lowered ("notched-down"), for workers born from 1917 through 1921—the "notch babies"—and maintained at these "lower" levels for all workers born after 1921. Before Congress corrected this problem in the benefit computation method, many people born from 1910 to 1916 received unintended windfalls from Social Security. In fact, because of special transition provisions in the 1977 law, many "notch babies" also received more modest windfalls.

There are two ways of looking at what happened and two conflicting views about what is fair. Those considering the notch to be a great inequity concentrate on the fact that benefits for many workers born from 1917 through 1921—the "notch babies"—are lower than they would have been in the absence of the 1977 legislation. Indeed, the 1977 amendments created an anomaly whereby substantial differences in benefits might result for workers with roughly identical work histories, but born in different notch transition years. Arguing that this unfortunate byproduct of the corrective legislation is a major inequity, the National Committee to Preserve Social Security and Medicare and some elders advocate reforms that would be beneficial to the "notch babies." The committee has suggested that the notch issue is "an inequity so obvious that it undercuts public confidence in the fairness of the entire Social Security system."[30]

Nearly all analysts and most elder advocacy organizations hold the other view about the fairness of the notch. Schulz points out the "real inequity was that those born before 1917 (who worked well beyond age 62) received benefits larger than Congress had intended (i.e., windfalls), not that those born after 1916 received too little."[31] In fact, it is not just the "notch babies" whose benefits have been reduced. Persons born after 1921 actually "lose" more than the transition "notch babies." Extending the logic of the "notch baby" advocates, one could argue that baby boomers "lose" more than the "notch babies" and that their children "lose" even more than that. But, if Congress had not acted in 1977 to fix the flaw in the benefit formula, the program's financing would have rendered Social Security unsustainable. That would not be fair to anyone! Another approach to correcting this flaw might have been to reduce benefits to everyone born from 1911 through 1916 back to a level closer to what was intended in 1972. But this would hardly be fair given the short lead time and the fact that many had already begun receiving their Social Security benefits before the 1977 legislation was passed, nor would it have been politically or administratively feasible.

Yet another approach, as proposed in some bills that have come before Congress, is to lengthen the transition period.[32] But this would only perpetuate the problem and it, too, would be unfair. For example, one proposal would cost $23 billion plus lost interest to the trust funds in the first five years and $300 billion (in nominal dollars) over the lifetime of those affected. One has to ask whether it would be fair to use Social Security trust funds for benefit increases primarily to higher-income beneficiaries, given the impending retirement of the baby boom generation and projections suggesting the need to respond one day to a manageable, but nevertheless emerging long-run financing problem in the combined Old-Age, Survivors, and Disability Insurance trust fund.

Others have suggested that "correcting" the so-called notch problem would not be a fair and useful public expenditure for other reasons. A General Accounting Office report shows Social Security beneficiaries who are most "affected by the notch tend to have higher incomes, greater asset holdings and fewer health problems."[33] Second, if Congress wants to spend Social Security trust funds on expanding protections, it could be argued that there are more pressing needs, such as those of many very old widows, prescription drug costs, and long-term care for the elderly and other groups. Third, studies by the National Academy of Social Insurance and the General Accounting Office suggest that the notch issue is a policy problem for which doing nothing is the fairest and most prudent response.[34]

In short, the notch issue illustrates that, in a complex program, we may have to live with a few inequities. Such inequities are, as in the case of the notch, the lesser of two evils, given the alternatives, or so we would hope.

Will Successive Generations Receive Fair Returns?

One view of Social Security is that it is unfair because the program is redistributing income from young to old and placing a very heavy burden on tomorrow's workers while failing to provide what critics consider a fair return to today's young. A *Forbes* magazine article suggests that Social Security is a major cause of the "great transfer of wealth from young to old" since 1973.[35] Calling for a new "generational accounting," Boston University economist Lawrence Kotlikoff argues that it is time "for our leaders to put an immediate halt to the ongoing redistribution to current Americans from future" Americans, a redistribution that has been greatly hastened by Social Security.[36] Similarly, others consider it unfair that the implicit rate of return on Social

Security investments is higher for current generations than for those who follow. They suggest that today's young—especially higher-income workers—will not get their money's worth out of Social Security and would do better by making private investments. Such judgments are often backed by analyses showing differences in rates of return in benefits for particular groups of workers relative to their employee and employer payroll tax contributions. Thus Anthony Pellechio and Gordon Goodfellow conducted analyses of the value of Social Security benefits, before and after the enactment of the 1983 amendments, to persons aged 40 and 55 in different family and work situations. They found the effects of the amendments diminished the net gains for all age groups, but especially younger ones, and that within generations some groups (e.g., higher-income couples with both partners employed) pay more in the combined employee and employer payroll taxes than they receive in benefits.[37]

Assessments of the value of Social Security to successive generations and groups within those generations are very sensitive to the methodological assumptions and the standard of fairness that are applied in an analysis. As a recent report by Congressional Research Service analyst Geoffrey Kollman makes clear, there is no definitive answer to the question of whether various groups of workers get their money's worth out of Social Security, nor is it necessarily sensible to ask such a question given the goals of the program.

Social Security today has social as well as insurance goals and is not comparable to a private annuity or insurance system. If social security were a strict annuity system, each worker's potential return on contributions would be the same, and the program could be evaluated against other methods of savings for retirement. However as a "social insurance" system, social security was deliberately designed to give a better return on taxes to some workers than to others. . . . Hence, some analysts of the program would argue that it is incorrect to evaluate the program's worth by simply measuring the speed or rate of return of the "typical" worker's contribution, because such computations do not illustrate the program's social features, such as its anti-poverty value.

Other analysts would argue that it is appropriate to evaluate the system this way because it illustrates the program's inequities. They contend that the relatively wide variance in payback times . . . illustrate how these social features unfairly lower many workers' potential return from the system.[38]

Returns are declining for new generations of beneficiaries primarily because in the "early years of Social Security, decisions were made to enable workers nearing retirement age to receive benefits even though they had made relatively small contributions." This was also done each time benefits were increased, so that those nearing retirement age became eligible for the new benefits. But "because the basic structure and major benefit liberalizations in Social Security have generally been in place for a number of year, future retirees will not reap such large returns." However, it is a mistake to conclude from this that Social Security is a bad investment and is unfair to younger workers. Had Social Security failed to blanket in workers approaching retirement, the system's adequacy goal would have been compromised. And to have done so would not have been fair in another sense since the economic welfare of workers retiring earlier in the history of the program was generally far worse than that of future retirees.[39]

In the future it will take longer for Social Security to pay back the employee and employer payroll tax contributions and the equivalent of interest that could be earned on parallel "investments" to various groups of beneficiaries. In other words, they will receive smaller rates of return on the taxes they and their employers paid on their behalf than those who entered earlier in the history of the program (even though the benefit amounts that future beneficiaries receive will generally be larger).

But this does not mean that Social Security is a bad buy. As economist Henry Aaron points out, most money's worth analyses place little or no value on the social ends served by Social Security and the value of special benefits such as inflation protection.[40] Second, money's worth analyses generally overlook the fact that the program is designed to provide different rates of returns to different types of workers (married versus unmarried, high versus low income). Third, while future rates of return are declining and while private investment toward retirement should be encouraged, Social Security can be counted on, still, to give a reasonable rate of return, and, as noted, to provide protection against inflation generally not available through other mechanisms. As Ball notes, "Social Security actuaries have calculated that, on average, workers who are in their early 20s today can expect to get somewhat more than the full amount of their own and their employers' contributions compounded at an interest rate that exceeds prices by two percent—a reasonable rate of return for a safe investment.[41]

For a few workers—for example, those who never marry and have the highest earnings throughout their lives—alternative investments might have a greater rate of return. But very few people really know early in their lives that they will, "for sure," never marry and be high-income workers throughout their lives. As Merton and Joan Bernstein observe, assessments of money's worth "*after* the race is run" seem inappropriate because, for individuals, anticipated outcomes could change in an instant with disability, marriage, or childbirth.[42] Moreover, as the October 1987 stock market crash and other events highlight, alternative investments involve considerably more risk, and without Social Security many—even some previously high-income workers—would be worse off in later life.

Additionally, it can be argued that by underwriting the dignity of individuals and helping to stabilize families and society, the program has value to each generation beyond the dollar amount of benefits provided. In a speech made in February 1987 before a colloquium on Social Security sponsored by the city of Philadelphia, Nelson Cruikshank noted:

It's not just old people who benefit in their retirement years from Social Security; young people benefit now. They know they have a secure future to look forward to, but they also know that the burden of caring for mother and father or for grandmother and grandfather is partly relieved for them. No American family should be confronted with the dilemma of whether we should take care of grandmother's health problems or grandmother's security and her decent living or send daughter Mary to college. That decision should not be forced upon any American family. So taking care of the parents and the grandparents also relieves some of the burden that would otherwise fall on younger people, who have their own problems educating their children, paying for their homes, and meeting the problems of income security.[43]

Fairness to Children

There are many indications that the state of the nation's children is not good. Investments in public education have been lagging, as have support for services that assist children at particular health, social, and economic risk. In tests administered in 1988 to 13-year-olds from Ireland, Korea, Spain, the United Kingdom, and the United States, U.S. students scored lowest in math and second lowest in science. The mean scores on verbal Scholastic Aptitude Tests have declined from 466 in 1967 to 422 in 1991.[44] U.S. infant mortality rates from 1986 to 1988 ranked twentieth among industrialized countries, behind nearly all of western Europe, Hong Kong, Japan, and Singapore.[45] Reflecting increased separation, divorce, and birth to unmarried parents, "the number and proportion of children living with one-parent families increased dramatically," from 5.8 million (9 percent of all children) in 1960 to 15.9 million (25 percent) in 1990.[46] And epidemics of drugs and AIDS are leading Senator Moynihan and others to warn of the growth in the number of "no-parent" families.

Income is distributed more unequally today, than twenty years ago, and it is children who are often among those on the wrong end of the curve. As measured by the official U.S. poverty rate, poverty declined among children from 27 percent in 1960 to a low of 14.0 percent in 1969, then leveled off for a few years, increasing to about 20.0 in 1981. During the recovery years of the 1980s, the childhood poverty rates remained close to this level, and 21.8 percent of the nation's children were poor in 1991. That is 14.3 million children. While most poor children are white (8.8 million), an astounding proportion of the nation's minority children are poor—46 percent of African American children (4.8 million) in 1991. Among Hispanic children who are classified among all races, 40 percent (3.1 million) were below the poverty level in 1990.[47]

The failure to invest adequately in the children, especially those who are poor, does not bode well for the future of the nation and is obviously unfair. To some, the problems of today's children find their origins in too many resources being directed at today's old. In 1990 the federal government spent, on average, roughly ten times as much per elderly person as was spent on each child.[48] Federal spending on Social Security, Medicare, and other elder services has increased and poverty among the elderly has declined while poverty among children has increased. Children's initiatives are constrained by large federal deficits and fixed commitments to Social Security, Medicare, and defense spending, and little willingness to raise taxes. Thus, reducing spending on Social Security and other elder-serving programs is one way to provide more services to children.

Framed in this manner, Social Security is inequitable to children. But there are other ways of looking at the problem. Others warn against assuming that there is a causal relationship between the increases in poverty of children and declines in poverty of elderly persons. They point out that the very old (85 and over) and the very young (under 5) continue to have the highest rates of poverty of all age groups. Moreover, rather than causing childhood poverty, Social Security actually protects many children from poverty through survivor, disability, and other auxiliary benefits and, by protecting elderly persons, allows families to devote more resources to the young. In fact, while a substantially higher proportion of federal transfers are directed at the elderly, a substantially higher proportion of state and local government spending is directed at the young, primarily through public education. Within the family, while care is often provided to disabled elderly persons, the great expenditures of time, caring, and internal transfers of money are directed at young children.

Another view is that the causes of the problems of children lie outside Social Security, and have more to do with the economy, short-sighted attitudes, and *intragenerational* inequities related to class and race. The relatively slow growth of the economy and loss of manufacturing jobs since the mid-1970s reduces employment and earnings possibilities for young families, the first line of defense against childhood poverty. Skepticism about government and taxpayer reticence to raise needed revenues at the federal, state, and local levels reduce needed investment in children. Callousness and an unwillingness to view caring for children—especially those at risk—as a combined responsibility of the family and the community are undermining the well-being of children. While there may be some inequities between generations, generally it is the *intragenerational inequities*, such as the growing inequality of income in society, that should be of greatest concern; that is, the inequities within particular generations and within the entire society. Viewed this way, defining Social Security as a cause of the problems of children is interpreted as a vehicle for scapegoating the elderly, not a means of strengthening the nation's investment in children or responding to those under greatest stress.

Fairness, the Earnings Test, and Retirement Age

That Social Security exerts a variety of effects on work effort should not be surprising. After all, it is designed primarily to replace earnings lost due to retirement, disability, or death. Thus, it should not come as a shock that the program is chiefly responsible for making "retirement" a period of institutionalized leisure in American life, and that the availability of benefits often figures into the work and retirement plans of covered workers and their family members.

Issues surrounding the behavioral effects (e.g., work incentives) of Social Security often move onto the public agenda under one of two conditions. Either the behavioral effect is defined as maladaptive in some way (removing needed workers from the labor force, discouraging savings) or as unfair. Elsewhere we discuss the behavioral effects of Social Security on work effort (see Chapters 5, 8, and 10). Here we briefly review one issue, whether the earnings test (also called the "retirement test") unfairly penalizes work efforts of beneficiaries. We refer readers interested in reviewing the equity issues surrounding the raising of the age of full eligibility for Social Security to Chapter 5, which addresses both the adequacy and equity implications of this change.

The earnings test has been substantially liberalized over the years. Benefits are currently reduced by one dollar for every three dollars of earnings that beneficiaries make beyond a certain earnings ceiling—$10,560 in 1993 for persons aged 65 through 69, and $7,680 in 1993 for persons under age 65. (Beneficiaries aged 70 or older are not subject to this earnings test.) The earnings ceiling is adjusted each year to reflect increases in average wages. In the long run, the effect of the earnings test will be greatly diminished because the value of the credit provided for delaying retirement past normal retirement age is scheduled to gradually increase—a change that, when fully phased in, will compensate for benefits lost due to the earnings test.

Even so, the earnings test is unpopular because it is perceived as penalizing and discouraging work effort and taking needed income away from beneficiaries. In fact, it provides some work disincentive, especially for those earning between $10,000 and $30,000 a year.[49] Periodically, there are proposals to eliminate or phase out the earnings test for people aged 65 to 69. Few wish to oppose the idea of "encouraging and rewarding the work effort" of older persons.

There are other considerations. In the short run, it is fairly costly to eliminate the test, and the bulk of the benefit of removing the earnings test would accrue to higher-income beneficiaries—a rather poor use of scarce resources when there are other changes in Social Security that could help lower-income beneficiaries much more. To do so only for people aged 65 to 69 would cost about $27.4 billion from 1993 to 1997, with half the benefits—about $14 billion—going to households with family incomes of at least $63,500 in 1992. The Congressional Budget Office (CBO) estimates that only "5 percent of the additional benefits would go to those with family incomes below $28,000."[50] As for whether eliminating the earnings test would result in more work effort, CBO's analysis concludes that existing data, research, and past experience provide very little evidence that a change in the earnings test will lead to a substantial increase in the employment and work efforts of older people.[51]

This issue concerns whether entitlement to retirement benefits under Social Security ought to be simply based on age or on both age and loss of income from paid employment. It also revolves, as we have often found to be the case, around competing notions of what is fair. The fact that Social Security is supposed to protect against loss of earnings due to retirement, disability, and death provides the rationale for the earnings test. When earnings are not lost, many would argue that benefits should not be paid. Others would argue that it is inequitable to make payment of Social Security benefits dependent on reduced work effort. Still others would respond that it is inequitable to make primarily low- and moderate-income workers pay for a change that primarily benefits high-income beneficiaries. An alternative also under consideration is to keep the earnings test but significantly increase its limits. This approach would enable most low- and moderate-income beneficiaries who must work "to make ends meet" to do so without losing any benefits due to the test.

Other equity considerations follow from the scheduled increase in the age of eligibility for full benefits. As discussed elsewhere, advocates of this change argue that it is a fair and reasonable way of reducing expenditures. They point out that life expectancies—and hence the number of years beneficiaries receive retirement benefits—have increased and are expected to increase even further, and that even after age 67 is phased in as the new normal retirement age, beneficiaries of the future will generally receive retirement benefits for more years than current beneficiaries. Moreover, the real value of Social Security benefits in the future will be greater than it is today, and this change will encourage work effort on the part of the old.

Opponents argue that this change is particularly unfair because much of the savings will be produced by reducing the benefits of lower-income persons who are unable to work due to limited employment opportunities and/or health problems. The provision will affect a disproportionately large number of minority workers and workers in employment requiring arduous labor. Better ways, they argue, can be found to encourage work among those elderly who are willing and able. They contend that, at a minimum, eligibility criteria for disability benefits should be liberalized for older workers if a later retirement age is to be phased in.

CONCLUSION

As discussed, Social Security equity issues can and often are framed in a variety of ways. As we hope this chapter illustrates, discussion of the fairness of the program is most productive when students, policymakers, and concerned citizens approach the topic with an understanding of the complexity of the program and the various ways that fairness is defined.

Disability as a Policy Problem

Disability confounds the conventional wisdom about Social Security. As an area of social policy, it presents problems as complex as any that can be found in the entire field. Although we do not have the definitive solution to these problems, we believe it important to explain the nation's approach to disability and to see how disability fits into the Social Security system.[1]

PROBLEMS IN DISABILITY POLICY

We begin with a paradoxical fact about disability policy. Disability is the least important part of Social Security, but Social Security is the most important part of disability policy. Statistics help to illustrate the paradox.

In 1991 the nation spent $264 billion on benefit payments for Old-Age, Survivors, and Disability Insurance. Approximately $237 billion went for Old-Age and Survivors Insurance benefits and approximately $27 billion for Disability Insurance benefit payments.[2] In other words, the nation spent more than eight dollars on Old-Age and Survivors Insurance for each dollar it devoted to Disability Insurance. These benefits went to 4.5 million Disability Insurance beneficiaries, compared to 36 million beneficiaries of Old-Age and Survivors Insurance. Old-Age and Survivors Insurance beneficiaries topped Disability Insurance recipients by a factor of eight.

If one looks at how the nation spends its disability dollars, a very different picture emerges. Even if disability constitutes a small percentage of Social Security spending, the nation still devotes a significant amount of money to disability. The best available estimates, prepared by the Rutgers Bureau of Economic Research, put the level of 1986 disability expenditures for the working-age population at $169.4 billion. This figure includes $75 billion in federal expenditures for such programs as Social Security Disability Insurance, Supplemental Security Income, Medicare, Medicaid, Food Stamps, and

Veterans Compensation. Of these various programs, Social Security Disability Insurance is the most widely available and the most expensive. Indeed, it accounts for about 30 percent of all the nation's expenditures for public and private income transfers related to disability and even more if one considers that the receipt of Disability Insurance also entitles a beneficiary to Medicare coverage after a wait of twenty-four months.

The $169.4 billion disability budget equalled 4 percent of the nation's gross national product, and it amounted to $1,136 for each person between 18 and 64 years of age. These numbers reflected a substantial increase in disability expenditures that had taken place since 1970, when the nation spent $19.3 billion on disability. In real dollars, we spent three times as much on disability in 1986 as we did in 1970 when "only" 1.9 percent of our gross national product went for disability.

We consumed our increased disability expenditures as retirement pensions rather than investing in rehabilitation services for people with disabilities. In 1970 the nation devoted a nickel of each of its disability dollars to direct services, such as rehabilitation, that were designed to encourage people to reach their maximum potential. (The figures do not tell us anything about the amount of money spent on disability prevention, such as immunizations). In 1986 this nation put only two cents of each of its disability dollars into direct services. By way of contrast, we spent about 51 percent of our 1986 disability dollars on monetary payments from the rest of society to people with disabilities and forty-seven cents of each disability dollar for medical care.

The harm in this social arrangement stems from the disservice done to people with disabilities by equating government aid and a retirement pension. Persons with disabilities should not have to retire from the labor force in order to receive government aid, but the Social Security program forces many to do just that.

There has been a great public outcry against this practice. People with disabilities have staged protests against the unfairness of our public policies. Almost always, these protests have centered on the passage of civil rights laws to grant equality in the workplace and access to public accommodations. Seldom do these protests stray into the technical details of the Social Security Disability Insurance Program.

Nor have Social Security administrators done much to change the Social Security Disability Insurance program to reflect the needs of persons with disabilities. The fact remains that, since disability represents such a small portion of the entire Social Security program, Disability Insurance is a low priority item on the Social Security policy agenda.

Disability Insurance flares up occasionally as an issue, becomes controversial, then quickly gets forgotten. In the late 1970s, some policymakers, including Joseph Califano, President Carter's secretary of Health, Education, and Welfare, regarded Disability Insurance as an example of a program that had gotten out of control. Too much money was being spent too fast. Too many people who had recovered from disabilities remained on the rolls. The program provided too few incentives for people to work. In the early 1980s, other policymakers reacted with concern to the Reagan administration's efforts to prune people from the disability rolls. Too many people were being removed from the rolls without concern for their health and welfare. Both of these controversies led to remedial legislation. Soon after passage of legislation, however, Disability Insurance became a forgotten part of Social Security policymaking.

When policymakers do focus on Disability Insurance, they often concentrate on the effects that program changes will have on old-age and survivors insurance. Some in Congress watch expenditures in Disability Insurance anxiously, fearful that unexpected rises in program costs will make funding the entire program more difficult. Concern with financing is both useful and inevitable, yet it ignores the problems of persons with disabilities and fails to recognize the injustice of forcing people with disabilities to retire.

Throughout this book, we have argued that our Social Security program represents a creative and effective blend of adequacy and equity. In the area of disability, however, one might question our argument. As a nation, we need to decide just what constitutes an adequate response to disability. At present, we give those who can demonstrate that they are unable to engage in substantial gainful employment a retirement pension. This practice makes sense for those who are truly unable to work. In many cases, however, a more adequate response might be to give many people a job, a partial pension, help with attendant care—anything but a permanent ticket out of the labor force.

As matters stand, Disability Insurance is an all-or-nothing proposition. One either receives a full pension, based on average earnings, family composition, and the other factors common to Social Security, or no pension at all. The program is structured in such a way that someone is either totally disabled or not disabled at all. A person cannot get partial payments. Hence, a person who qualifies with lower back pain receives just as much as someone who loses all of his senses and all of his limbs.

It might be more equitable to pay some people more than others, based solely on the severity of their impairment. In the workers' compensation program, for example, states routinely provide benefits for what they call "permanent partial disability." In that program, which comes to the aid of workers who have been involved in industrial accidents, the object is to restore workers to the level of earnings they received before their injury. In many states, one may continue to work and still get workers' compensation benefits and, in general, the more severe a person's impairment, the more he receives from the program.

Social Security simply does not operate that way. A person who gets a Social Security pension receives permission from the federal government to retire. The program takes such factors as his average wage or the number of people in his family into consideration, yet it does not consider that people who are more impaired may need more money in retirement. To some extent, the program compensates for this problem by granting people with lower incomes and shorter times in the labor force a higher return on their Social Security investments but that might not be enough. To put this matter another way, disability adds dimensions to the problems of adequacy that the program is not designed to accommodate.

Nor does the harm of the link between Social Security and disability policy end there, for Social Security benefits become the entry point for other benefits. Social Security bundles Medicare with retirement benefits, making it difficult for someone to receive Medicare alone.[3] That can prove devastating to a person who needs only medical coverage to remain employed. As the system stands, the person has no other recourse but to retire on disability benefits and remain retired for a substantial period of time, as much as two years, before he qualifies for Medicare. With rare exceptions, such as the cases of people with kidney failure or those between 65 and 70 making too much to qualify for Old-Age Insurance, no public mechanism exists to permit someone to receive Medicare alone. Since it is difficult to frame such coverage as anything but an expansion of the program, such coverage may not arrive for a long time.

Whether a person will want to return to work after two years of enforced inactivity on the disability rolls, even with Medicare coverage guaranteed for up to three years, is a question that the overwhelming number of people answer in the negative. Almost no one leaves the disability rolls and goes back to work. For some people, disability pensions are themselves disabling. That is why it would be useful to help people in need but to stop short of disability pensions. We might begin to think about affirmative aid that assists a person to find, keep, and enjoy a job rather than negative aid that pensions a person off to an uncertain world of leisure.

We need to be careful about these things, of course. We would not want to destroy our relatively well-developed system of disability pensions and put a punitive and badly financed system of social services in its place. We emphasize that people on the disability rolls do not choose to be there, and many would gladly give up their secure pension for a secure job. The trouble is that secure jobs, particularly for older workers with health problems, are not easy to find in contemporary America.

Although these problems are easy to delineate, the solutions are not self-evident. We can illustrate this point by demonstrating how difficult it is to define disability, to gain an accurate count of disabled people, or to rehabilitate persons with disabilities. Recently passed civil rights laws represent a start, but only a start, toward rectifying the problem.

DEFINING DISABILITY

When we try to define disability, we run into another paradox. Disability is a major factor in causing people to retire early, yet, despite the concept's importance, it resists definition.

Scholars admit that disability cannot be defined precisely. On the one hand, disability is something obvious—the inability to work. On the other, disability is something that can only be defined in abstract terms. We might think of a continuum that begins with illness or impairment and ends with disability. Most people recover from an incident of illness or from sustaining an impairment. In some cases, however, the transient illness or other medically defined condition leaves the person with a functional limitation—some lasting inability to perform "normal" physical or mental functions, such as the inability to climb stairs or to maintain amiable relations with coworkers. Some people may adapt themselves to the functional limitation with no loss of productivity and thus maintain their attachment to the labor force. Others may simply be unable to work because of their mental or physical conditions. Social scientists define such persons as disabled.[4]

In the real world, the definition of disability seldom conforms to this typology. With so many cases to process, the Social Security program follows rules that attempt to treat people in the same condition the same way, even though people respond so differently to illness or injury. The rules must withstand rigorous legal and political tests. The legal tests become manifest in the many levels of appeal through which lawyers may pursue a disability decision and challenge the Social Security Administration.[5] The political tests include the predilections of politicians to amend the definition to redress practices that their constituents reveal as unjust.

The application process demonstrates just how far an applicant may pursue a disability claim. Such a claim could be for either Social Security Disability Insurance or for Supplemental Security Income. Although the programs are quite different, the test for disability and the definition of disability are essentially the same for each. A person may call the Social Security Administration and arrange for an appointment at a local office. The local officer will assist the applicant with the request for disability benefits and check to see if the applicant has worked recently enough in covered employment to qualify for disability coverage. If not, an applicant may pursue a claim for Supplemental Security Income. That program has the additional burden of a means test that requires an applicant to prove his or her poverty but dispenses with the notion of "covered quarters." Then the officer will send the completed application to the state disability determination office. Officials in this office will review the medical and vocational evidence in the file to see if the applicant has an impairment "of such severity that he is not only unable to do his previous work but cannot considering his age, education, and work experience engage in any kind of substantial gainful work which exists in the national economy, regardless of whether such work exists in the immediate area in which he lives or whether a specific job vacancy exists for him or whether he would be hired if he applied for work."[6]

Let us assume that the state disability determination office rejects the claim. Then the applicant has the right to ask the state office to reconsider. If still denied, the applicant could bring his case before an administrative law judge, with full right of legal representation. If still declared ineligible for benefits, he and his lawyer could take the case to the Appeals Council of the Social Security Administration and finally to a federal district court, with full right of appeal through the courts.

Just as lawyers have pursued individual cases, so Congress has considered the entire system. The result has been special exceptions in the law to protect certain classes of individuals. A blind person, for example, qualifies for disability benefits under easier terms than any other individual. A blind person over 55 need only show he is unable to do his previous job; everyone else needs to demonstrate that they cannot do *any* job. Congress, in response to a public outcry over a "purge" of people on the rolls in the early 1980s, has also come to the protection of people who are on the disability rolls, providing them with legal protections that make it difficult to remove them. Finally, Congress has added special programs, outside Social Security, that protect people in particular occupations. Examples include coal miners, railroad employees, military personnel, and veterans.

As one might expect, the state disability determination offices use a standard process to assess the validity of disability claims. In effect, this process, a matter of regulation, defines disability in the Social Security program more definitively than does the formal definition of disability contained in the law itself.

In particular, the state agency follows a five-stage sequence that culminates in something called the grid. First, the state disability examiners ask if the applicant is engaging in "substantial gainful activity." In other words, they look to see how much money he is earning. If he earns over the set limit known as the SGA level,[7] he cannot get disability benefits. Second, the examiners ask whether the applicant has a severe impairment that significantly limits his physical or mental ability to work. If not, he cannot get disability benefits. Third, the examiners ask if the applicant's impairment "met or equalled" the medical conditions listed in the guidelines. These medical guidelines contain specific numerical values for clinical tests. If the applicant's impairment does meet or equal these guidelines, then the applicant receives benefits. Fourth, the examiners ask those whose impairments do not meet or equal the medical guidelines if the impairment nonetheless prevents the applicant from meeting the demands of past relevant work. If not, the applicant is denied benefits. Fifth, the examiners ask if the impairment prevents the applicant from doing other work. If it does, the applicant receives benefits.[8]

This fifth step is rather steep, forcing the examiners to make what appears to be a highly subjective decision. To bring a structure of rules to this decision, the examiners employ the grid. This grid uses "residual functional capacity" in combination with other variables to reach a decision. If, for example, a person's maximum sustained work capacity is limited to sedentary work and he is 50 to 54 years old, has less than a high school education, and no skilled work experience, then he is considered disabled. But if his previous employment experience includes skilled work, as defined in the regulations, then he is not disabled.

Although these rules may be definite, they do not transform disability determination into a science or conform to the social science concept of disability. It is not an easy matter to decide whether someone can only work in a sedentary job. Someone in a wheelchair might, for example, be able to do non-sedentary work. The system also allows people with severe impairments that meet or equal the medical listings, a record of sustained employment, and a spell of recent unemployment to collect disability benefits automatically. Yet few impairments are so severe as to knock a person out of work completely, particularly if that person has an extraordinary will to work and an employer willing to accommodate him.

Beyond the theoretical concerns of social scientists, any definition of disability contains an element of subjectivity. At the same time, effective social policy requires the nation to have a Disability Insurance program that, if it errs, must err on the side of compassion. We cannot base our policies on the expectation that people will act like Helen Keller or Franklin Roosevelt, individuals who were both extraordinary and privileged. All images of disability are deceptive, but it helps to keep in mind a picture of a 53-year-old man who has lower back pain and other ailments and faces an uncertain future with a declining firm in a declining industry. Such a man may well benefit from the early retirement program that we call Disability Insurance.

THE NUMBER OF PEOPLE WITH DISABILITIES

As matters stand, we do not even have an accurate count of the number of people with disabilities in the population. That is not surprising, if one realizes the extraordinary range of human experience that lies between Franklin Roosevelt and an unemployed steel worker with lower back pain. Factors such as age, education, personal motivation, alternative sources of income, physical barriers in the working environment, the attitude of employers toward the basic abilities of the handicapped, and the condition of the labor market all play a part in determining whether a particular person considers himself disabled.

Then, too, the data are old and possibly out-of-date, yet they are suggestive. The results of surveys conducted by the Social Security Administration in 1966, 1972, and 1978 show that about 17 percent of the adult population considered themselves as having some degree of work disability in both 1966 and 1978. Despite this agreement, the surveys report a substantial increase in the degree of severe work disability, defined as a person unable to work altogether or unable to work regularly, from 6 percent of the population in 1966 to 8.6 percent in 1978. In 1966, 19.2 percent of those in the severely disabled category reported themselves as being in the labor force; in 1978, this proportion had decreased to 13.6 percent.[9]

These and similar data, although fragmentary, have led many labor economists to believe that income transfers, such as Social Security Disability Insurance, have induced people who might previously have remained at work to drop out of the labor force. Indeed, the general trend is alarming. The non-participation rate of males, aged 45–54, reached a low of 3.5 percent in the early 1950s and then began to climb just as the SSDI program got under way. Using reasonably sophisticated econometric techniques, Jonathan Leonard, an economist at Berkeley, estimated that an increase of $180 in a yearly disability benefit had the effect of raising the proportion of SSDI beneficiaries in the population by a percentage point.[10] University of Wisconsin economist Robert Haveman and his collaborators have, however, disputed this finding. They estimate that a 20 percent increase in expected disability income would elicit a relatively small change in labor force participation among workers aged 45 to 62, roughly 0.64 to 1.04 percentage points.[11]

As always, these sorts of economic studies paint too clear a picture. It is not as though workers have a clear choice between becoming disabled or remaining in the labor force; for many, Disability Insurance represents the only income that is available to them. But there are people at the margins between work and retirement, and these are the people that should concern us.

It would seem that SSDI puts some impaired people on the margins of work and retirement in a trap. To remain adequate, benefit levels need to rise. As the benefit amount rises, however, more people are induced to join the rolls. Higher benefits imply larger disability rolls. Increasing adequacy, in the conventional Social Security sense of that term, means more retirement, less labor force participation, and, arguably, an increasingly inadequate disability policy. Can we do better, or must we accept work disincentives as the price of adequate benefits?

REHABILITATION

The most obvious escape from the trap involves the use of rehabilitation as a substitute for retirement pensions. In an ideal world, we would like those people contemplating early retirement through disability pensions to consider entering a course of rehabilitation instead. A successful rehabilitation would mean that the person would secure a permanent job, and a sense of satisfaction and self-reliance, rather than a retirement pension, and a sense of nagging doubt.

Over the course of the last fifty years, we have acquired a stock of social knowledge about the rehabilitation process. What we know does not lend itself to a sense of optimism. Rehabilitation, although an attractive abstract concept, is difficult to implement in practice. We realize that the rehabilitation of those receiving permanent monetary benefits, such as every single person on SSDI, represents a particularly difficult challenge. In fact, society has never met that challenge. The rehabilitation process does not function smoothly on a mass scale. If it did, it would be like ordering individual intensive therapy for millions of people and achieving a significant rate of "cure," in this case a job. Some people lack motivation; other people simply cannot find a job; other people might find a job if only the workplace were accessible to them.

Congress initiated a formal vocational rehabilitation program in 1920. Over the course of the last seventy years, this program achieved decidedly mixed results. The program operated on the state level and relied on vocational rehabilitation counselors, employed by the states but paid for in part by the federal government, to provide job counseling and other services to handicapped individuals. The idea was that a person with a disability would then get a job or, in the language of the program, be rehabilitated.

Shortly after the vocational rehabilitation program began, federal officials, who were in charge of administering the matching grants that the federal government made to the states, decided to study a group of 1,000 people rehabilitated between 1920 and 1924. They followed up this group in 1927 and again in 1931. When the economy was booming, as it was in 1927, the group appeared to be doing well. Although the people in the study had no earnings before rehabilitation in 69 percent of the cases, 80 percent of the group earned at least $15 dollars a week in 1927. When the economy was in depression, as it was in 1931, the group fared less well. In 1931 only 61 percent of the group made $15 dollars a week.[12] In other words, a successful rehabilitation was no guarantee against a downturn in the economy. The program counted someone with a job as rehabilitated, but these "rehabilitants" were often the first to be fired during a recession. People with disabilities had consistently higher unemployment rates than did the rest of the population.

The 1,000 people studied in 1927 and 1931, like most of the people who were rehabilitated by the program between 1920 and 1975, contained a much higher percentage of young, male, white, mildly impaired individuals than would the SSDI caseload. As late as 1948, the average age of someone successfully rehabilitated by the program was only 31; the median age of the SSDI caseload has never gone below 50. In other words, SSDI recipients could be expected to have even more trouble finding and holding a job than would the average person served by the vocational rehabilitation program.

Despite the mixed track record of the vocational rehabilitation program, Congress legislated the SSDI program in 1956 with the expectation that every applicant for SSDI would see a rehabilitation counselor. That was one of the reasons that Congress allowed disability determination services to be housed in state vocational rehabilitation departments. The rehabilitation link with SSDI failed to take hold, as the SSDI program attracted far more persons in advanced middle age with severe impairments than the state programs could possibly handle. Within three years, the Social Security Administration simply stopped referring severely disabled people to the state programs, and no one complained.

Undeterred by the obvious fact that few SSDI beneficiaries could be rehabilitated, Congress authorized the Beneficiary Rehabilitation Program (BRP) in 1965. This program, jointly run by the Social Security Administration and the Rehabilitation Services Administration, used trust fund money to reimburse 100 percent of the costs for rehabilitating Disability Insurance beneficiaries. In 1976 a gradual disenchantment with the BRP program began that culminated in the drastic alteration of the program in 1981.

Part of the disenchantment stemmed from the evaluations made by SSA to assess the efficiency of the Beneficiary Rehabilitation Program. Although initial evaluations produced ambiguous results, the SSA estimated the benefit-cost ratio as 1.60 in 1970 and 1.93 in 1972. These were not terrible returns on the investment of trust fund money; they meant that in 1970 each dollar invested in the program eventually returned a dollar and sixty cents. Independent evaluations soon began to cast doubts on these figures and on the program. The General Accounting Office examined a small sample of beneficiaries who had been terminated from the program after rehabilitation and found that 62 percent of the persons who left the benefit rolls would have left anyway without rehabilitation services. Other independent examinations found benefit-cost ratios only slightly over one.[13]

Because of the disillusionment with the program, possibly because of overblown expectations, it was discontinued. In its stead, Congress instituted a program under which the vocational rehabilitation agency would get reimbursed for its services plus a bonus only if the person left the benefit rolls and stayed off for a period of six months. Only modest use has been made of this program.

The relationship between rehabilitation and Social Security therefore comes bundled with a long and complicated history. The burden of this history suggests that Congress cannot simply mandate that people who apply for disability benefits should also receive rehabilitation and expect positive results. Someone who seeks disability benefits has, at the minimum, difficulty in holding a job, a belief in his infirmity and, for whatever reason, a desire to retire. For many the offer of rehabilitation seems unrealistic or punitive. "If I could get a job, I would have one. Here is one more punishment I must endure before I can get what is coming to me," an applicant might think. Even the most ardent rehabilitation fan would agree that rehabilitation works best for those who approach it with a sense of optimism.

CIVIL RIGHTS

If rehabilitation cannot get us out of the trap in which conditioning the receipt of benefits upon the state of retirement puts us, then maybe we should turn to the strategy of civil rights. This approach relies on changing the structure of the workplace to accommodate the needs of disabled persons, rather than changing the disabled persons to suit the needs of the labor market. As disability rights advocates use the term, "civil rights" means that employers should not use a person's handicap as a means of baring that person from a job. These advocates regard disability as something created by society, rather than as something that is inherent in the person with a disability. Simply put, a person with a disability is the victim of his differences from other people. What keeps a person with a disability from full participation in society is prejudice, not an inherent limitation in the person.

If that were true, then perhaps we should somehow force employers to overcome their sense of prejudice. If that were true, then maybe we could devise a means for employers to consider a person's abilities rather than his disabilities. If necessary, the employer could make what the lawyers call "reasonable accommodations," so that the employee could, for example, use the plant bathroom or get through the front door.

This idea has received a great deal of currency because of the 1990 passage of the Americans with Disabilities Act (ADA). This major piece of civil rights legislation brings civil rights protection for people with disabilities to the same level as that enjoyed by African Americans, other minorities, and women. It contains many features, such as the prohibition of discrimination against an individual with disability "in regard to any term, condition, or privilege of employment" or "in the full and equal enjoyment of the goods, services, facilities, privileges, advantages, and accommodations of any place of public accommodation operated by a private entity."[14] Passage of this legislation raises the question of whether it will become a vehicle for making the nation less dependent on retirement pensions.

If one traces the passage of the Americans with Disabilities Act, one discovers a completely different policymaking system than the one that governs Social Security. Continuity and stability govern policymaking for Social Security. The ADA creates a new area of government concern, for which no routines have been established.

To gain passage of the law, the proponents of this legislation made many promises. They sought to convince skeptics, many of whom represented business interests who believed they would bear the brunt of the new law, that the new civil rights for disabled persons would not be unduly costly to implement. They portrayed the law as an investment in America's future. At least part of the returns of the investment, proponents claimed, would come in the form of reduced expenditures for SSDI and SSI.

When Representative Tony Coehlo introduced the original version of ADA in the House, for example, he pointed to a Department of Transportation study that showed a link between accessible transportation, the entrance of people with disabilities into the labor force, and the reduction of welfare costs. He said the dividend would amount to $276 million in reduced Supplemental Security Income costs alone. He even indicated that a powerful multiplier applied. Ending discrimination against disabled people returned $3 for every dollar invested.[15] If one believed this formulation, the nation simply could not afford to pass up the investment. As the Senate Committee on Labor and Human Resources explained, "Discrimination denies people with disabilities the opportunity to compete on an equal basis and costs the United States, State, and local government, and the private sector billions of dollars in unnecessary expenses resulting from dependency and nonproductivity."[16]

Other advocates made similar points. Sandra Parrino of the National Council on Disability spoke of 36 million people placed in a "bondage of unjust, unwanted dependency" that cost billions of dollars a year.[17] Attorney General Dick Thornburgh, authorized to comment on the Bush administration's behalf, thought the law would put disabled people to work, increase their earnings, lessen dependency on the Social Security system, increase spending on consumer goods, and increase tax revenues.[18] "No longer does public policy need to focus exclusively on tickets out of the labor force," one of the present authors wrote in a statement for the Senate Committee on Labor and Human Resources. "Now we have the means to provide tickets into the labor force that will give people with disabilities the chance to participate in the nation's work force. This legislation, then, is a law in aid of the free market and not creature of the welfare state."[19]

This sort of rhetoric held particular appeal because the legislation would cost the federal government itself virtually nothing. The Congressional Budget Office estimated that the ADA would result in no direct spending by the federal government.[20] It was legislation on the cheap, mandating new responsibilities for private employers without offering any new financial assistance either to the employers or to the disabled persons themselves.

Through the entire legislative process, no one explicitly determined what the probable effect of the new law would be on Social Security Disability Insurance, the most important of the old laws. Instead, some advocates and experts made vague and unsubstantiated promises that the new law would indeed reduce the size of the disability rolls and save money. Congress never confronted the question directly because, in effect, a different Congress passed the ADA than the one that administered Disability Insurance. As Martha Derthick has argued, the very face of Congress changed when it moved from its role as initiator of new programs to its oversight role.[21] Furthermore, the Congress that legislated in the Social Security realm consisted of an entirely different set of committees than legislated other disability laws. Senator Edward Kennedy and the Senate Committee on Labor and Public Welfare worked on the ADA; Senator Lloyd Bentsen and the Finance Committee worked on SSDI.

CONCLUSION

Now comes the difficult process of drawing some conclusions that could serve as a guide to disability policy in the future. We have argued that

Disability Insurance may be a minor concern of Social Security policy but that it constitutes the most important component of disability policy. We have noted that, whatever the academics may think, disability is whatever the Social Security Disability Insurance program says it is. Further, the level of disability benefits itself influences the number of people who consider themselves disabled. We have argued that retirement alone may be an inadequate response to disability, that Social Security benefit computation procedures do not lead to equity of treatment among disabled persons, and that the bundling of retirement pensions and Medicare discourages many persons with disabilities from seeking employment.

At the same time, our examination of rehabilitation and civil rights, two alternatives to Disability Insurance, reveals that neither is a panacea for the problems of disability policy. In the case of rehabilitation, the concept looks better in the abstract than in reality. The historical evidence convinces us that people on the disability rolls cannot be rehabilitated. In the case of civil rights, the passage of the ADA has occurred too recently for us to evaluate the law's effectiveness. Still, the law appears to apply to people who remain in the labor force, not to people who are on the disability rolls. The ADA, in other words, may help to prevent people from going on the disability rolls, but it will do little for the people who are already on them.

Still, there is the possibility for the implementation of policies that create a synergism between civil rights and Social Security. One idea would be to have any person who meets or equals the medical listings for disability and who has a job offer to receive a special benefit. Such a benefit would consist of Medicare coverage and a special annual voucher that the person could use for disability-related expenditures, such as attendant care or the modification of his work station. This arrangement would assist employers who hired persons with disabilities, and it would assist the persons with disabilities themselves. It would, however, be costly, but surely the rhetoric of investment applies here. It would save money to have people with disabilities employed, rather than to pay them for not working. Use of the medical listing would be a powerful barrier to abuse, and the requirement of a job offer would give people with disabilities an incentive to seek and find work.

Such a program would do little for the people whom economist Richard Burkhauser calls the "doubly disabled."[22] These are people with little education and severe impairments who experience many difficulties finding and keeping jobs. The ADA also does little for such people. In a similar sense, SSDI does little for such people, unless they have managed to hold a job in the past or live in a family with a Social Security beneficiary. Some people, it would seem, need the protection of a strong and relatively flexible SSI program; other people need the protection that SSDI provides. Moreover, people who have worked and now find themselves with an impairment that keeps them from working should be allowed to retire with adequate compensation, grace, and dignity.

In this area of social policy, as in recent discussions of welfare reform, we must be content with the observation that one size does not fit all. No single program or policy can govern our response to disability. As welfare expert Richard Nathan puts it, different folks deserve different strokes. The trouble with the present policy is that it puts too much emphasis on the one stroke of retirement, rather than permitting a greater degree of flexibility. We think the nation can do better and are confident that striving for improvement in disability policy will be an important social policy objective in the years ahead.

Meeting and Financing
the Health Care Needs
of Older Americans

Whether we are concerned about the financial future of Medicare, the growing cost of health care, the availability of long-term care, health-related economic risks to elders, or ethical choices surrounding the allocation of health care, the large health policy issues affecting elderly persons can rarely be understood simply as "Medicare problems." Emerging in the context of a growing, diverse, elderly population and a large turbulent, health care environment, these issues transcend programmatic boundaries—though Medicare is often a central concern.

We begin this chapter, then, by describing the needs of the elderly for health care and the range of public and private mechanisms conditioning the elderly's access to health care. Then we review the major health policy issues affecting elderly persons, paying special attention to those that are closely tied to Medicare. More specifically, we discuss (1) the financial cost of health care for individuals, (2) quality of and access to acute, rehabilitation, and long-term care, (3) the growing financial cost to society of health care for elderly persons, and (4) ethical issues surrounding the allocation of health care resources.

THE HEALTH STATUS OF ELDERLY PERSONS

Old age is not what it used to be. More people reach age 65, and, once there, live longer. They often remain active and independent throughout most, if not all, of their old age. Yet increased life expectancy does not automatically translate into a healthier old age, either for individuals or cohorts. In fact, there is lively disagreement among experts about whether the older population as a whole is healthier and more able today than in the past. Some suggest that they are and can work longer.[1] Others, pointing to disability trends among older middle-aged and elderly persons and to the great diversity of health status among the old, suggest that we simply do not know.[2] In fact, there is reason to believe that some groups of elderly persons (e.g., higher socioeconomic status) may be experiencing a healthier and more active old age, while others live longer but more disabled old ages.

What we definitely know is that today's elderly population presents a heterogeneous picture with respect to its health status and health care needs. Asked about their health in 1989, almost 40 percent of non-institutionalized persons aged 65 and over interviewed as part of the 1989 National Health Interview Survey reported that it was very good or excellent, 32 percent that it was good, and 29 percent that it was fair or poor.[3] We also know that the likelihood of experiencing chronic health problems (e.g., arthritis, hearing deficits, Alzheimer's disease), along with substantial limitations in functional capacity, at some point in old age is very great. Old age does not, however, herald entrance to a slippery slope, from good to bad health. More likely, older people go through a variety of health transitions. Setbacks to independent living such as broken hips are often followed by improved functioning. Moreover, there is considerable evidence that lifestyle interventions, rehabilitation, and proper medical care can often help prevent, forestall, improve, or reverse functional incapacities. Also, it is important to recognize that many persons are able to function independently and continue to contribute to family and society in spite of significant limitations and little or no social service, health care, or family assistance. Many others, of course, cannot.

The need for institutionally- and/or community-based long-term care is often assessed by examining ability to perform activities of daily living, or ADLs, (e.g., eating, bathing, dressing, transferal to and from bed, using a toilet without help). It is also measured by examining the capacity to perform instrumental activities of daily living, IADLs, which involve basic household or social chores such as shopping, handling finances, preparing meals, taking medications, and housework. About two-thirds of the roughly 10.6 million U.S. residents with at least one ADL or IADL limitation in 1990 are 65 or older. Of these 7.1 million elderly persons, about 1.5 million are in nursing homes or other institutions—the remaining 5.6 million reside in community settings often with the assistance of family members.[4] While only 5 percent of the elderly live in nursing homes on any given day, long-term care experts Robert Kane and Rosalie Kane note that, on average, "persons aged 65 years have about a 40 percent chance of spending some time in a nursing home before they die."[5] Other survey data highlight how much greater the need for long-term care is among the very old. Researchers from the Agency for Health Care Policy and Research estimated that 19.5 percent of the non-institutionalized elderly aged 65 and over have difficulty performing at least one ADL or IADL. However, this includes only 9.9 percent of persons aged 65 to 69 and a startling 56.8 percent of those 85 and over.[6]

We also know that Medicare has greatly expanded access to acute care for the elderly as well as to institutionally-based post-hospitalization rehabilitative care and that the utilization of health care roughly doubles "with each decade after age 65." However, "there is still reason to be concerned with undertreatment," as many elderly persons choose not to seek care in spite of significant problems, and utilization of certain services such as dentistry and mental health does not increase with age.[7] And we know that most elders are not protected against catastrophic costs such as those that can arise from chronic ailments.

SOURCES OF HEALTH CARE AND RELATED SERVICES

Most older people are fairly well protected against the cost of acute care, but not so for long-term care. Fewer than one percent lack any coverage for acute care. About 95 percent are covered by Medicare, which funds roughly 45 percent of personal health care costs[8] for the elderly (see Figure 9.1). Medicare primarily funds hospital-based care, post-hospitalization rehabilitation in skilled nursing facilities, most physician services, hospice care, and limited home health services for homebound persons needing skilled care. Nearly three-quarters of elders covered by Medicare were also covered in 1989 by at least one private insurance plan and 6 percent by Medicaid, with only 17 percent lacking additional coverage.[9]

Next to Medicare, Medicaid is the most important public health care program for the elderly—paying for another 12 percent of their health care expenditures. In addition to providing low-income, low-asset elders with access to a substantial range of acute care benefits, Medicaid is the primary funder of nursing home care and also funds prescription drugs and a limited but growing share of community-based long-term care. Veterans Administration programs also provide substantial protection for both acute and long-term care needs to eligible veterans, and other publicly-funded health and long-term care benefits are funded through the Department of Defense, the Indian Health Service, and a variety of state, county, and local government programs.[10] Together, these other public programs fund 6 percent of the aggregate cost of health care for elders. Of growing importance, many community-based long-term care services are funded by the Older Americans Act, the Social Service Block grant, and state, county, and local governments. The range of available services often includes home health care, homemaker and home repair services, in home and congregate meals, respite care, adult day care, emergency alert systems, telephone reassurance, and congregate housing.[11] While many of these services can be found in most communities, their availability is generally limited relative to the numbers of elders requiring such support.

Almost 40 percent of the formal health care of older persons is privately funded, primarily by private insurance and out-of-pocket payments. The two major private insurance vehicles are individual "medigap" policies and

Figure 9.1
Who Pays for the Elderly's Health Care: 1987

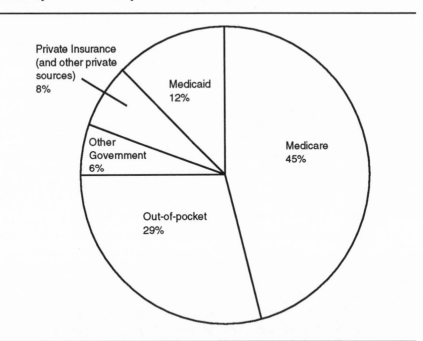

Private Insurance
(and other private
sources)
8%

Medicaid
12%

Other
Government
6%

Medicare
45%

Out-of-pocket
29%

Source: Daniel R. Waldo, Sally Sonnenfeld, David R. McKusick, and Ross H. Arnett III, "Health Expenditures by Age Group, 1977 and 1989," *Health Care Finance Review* 10, 4 (Summer 1989), and Daniel R. Waldo and Helen C. Lazenby, "Demographic Characteristics and Health Care Use and Expenditures by the Aged in the United States: 1977–1984," *Health Care Finance Review* 6, 1 (Fall 1984), as cited in AARP, the Federal Council on Aging, and the U.S. Administration on Aging, *Aging America: Trends and Projections: 1991 Edition* (Washington, D.C.: U.S. GPO, 1991), p. 135.

employer-provided insurance for retirees. About 70 percent of all elderly persons purchase medigap coverage, mostly to help cover acute care costs not protected under Medicare such as deductibles, copayments, and most drugs.[12] Unfortunately, though expensive, many gaps remain even with these policies, and they rarely provide more than incidental protection against long-term care costs. Private long-term care insurance is a growing area. The Health Insurance Association of America reports that 1.9 million policies were in effect in 1991 through 143 insurers. However, to limit their exposure, insurers generally design policies with such features as long waiting periods, limited period of coverage, restrictive eligibility requirements, large deductibles and copayments, and limited inflation protection. Moreover, they are expensive. According to the Health Insurance Association of America, "policies paying $80 a day for nursing care and $40 a day for home health care with inflation protection and a 20-day deductible period and a 4-year maximum coverage period had an average annual premium in 1990 of $1,335 when purchased at the age of 65 and $4,510 when purchased at the age of 79."[13] Thus, by itself, private long-term care insurance does not seem to be a likely vehicle for most elders to reduce substantially the financial risk posed by chronic illness.

Employer-provided health insurance for retirees covers about one-third of retired persons aged 55 and over, about 13 million people. These plans are often offered as part of an early retirement package as a way of continuing protections until Medicare eligibility at age 65. They are also provided as supplements to Medicare. Their growing cost is an increasing concern to employers, the overwhelming majority of whom are seeking to reduce protections or are expected to do so shortly by increasing retiree premium contributions, requiring deductible and coinsurance payments, tightening eligibility, and in some cases phasing out protections.[14]

Even with substantial health care coverage, elderly persons continue to pay almost one-third of their health care costs out-of-pocket, an estimated $1,540 of total per capita expenditures for elders of $5,360 in 1987. Prescription drugs and long-term care costs represent a large portion of these expenditures. Out-of-pocket expenditures would be even larger if the cost of premium payments for Medicare Part B were counted as such.

Though not officially counted as part of health care expenditures, much care is provided by family and friends to disabled elders, ranging from intensive, sometimes round-the-clock, personal care to running occasional errands. Bonds forged by years of marriage, child-rearing, and friendship and reciprocity result in the family being the major provider of care for disabled members. If this care had to be purchased, it would undoubtedly represent a huge national expenditure. Other expenditures, too, including those for domestic help or supportive living environments, such as continuing care retirement communities, could also arguably be counted as private health expenditures and considered part of the elder health care and social service system.

FINANCIAL RISKS OF ELDERS

Prior to the passage of Medicare in 1965, the risk to elders and their family of being bankrupted by hospital and other acute care costs was not dissimilar to the risks related to long-term care which are so prevalent today. Medicare has done much to protect family finances and open up access to acute care and other important health care services for elders (and, of course, the disabled). Other sources, private and public, add important dimensions of protection for many. Even so, individuals remain exposed to substantial risks. Out-of-pocket costs represent a growing portion of elderly households' spending, increasing from 7.8 percent of expenditures after taxes in 1972 to

12.5 percent by 1988. Since 1975 the share of beneficiaries' income going toward Medicare-funded health care has increased from 4.2 percent to 5.7 percent of per capita income in 1990.[15] Plainly these costs fall heaviest on moderate- and low-income households as well as on those experiencing catastrophic long-term care and acute care costs. This growing cost to elders is both a function of the general increase in health care costs as well as of specific increases such as those arising from Medicare beneficiary HI deductibles, copayments, and SMI premiums, which have roughly doubled after controlling for inflation since 1975. In 1993 Medicare beneficiaries must pay the first $676, $169 dollars per day after the 60th through 90th day of hospitalization and $338 per day if using lifetime reserve days. The SMI premium is $36.60 per month in 1993. Also, the costs of prescription drugs rank high as an added pressure on household finances. Little wonder that acute care costs still represent a potential burden for many elderly persons, especially those on limited income, and that many elders "are driven to purchase expensive private insurance policies in an almost desperate—and largely fruitless—effort to avoid exposure to potentially impoverishing financial burdens."[16]

Seeking to reduce the risk to elders for costs associated with long hospitalizations, prescription drugs, and other acute costs, the Medicare Catastrophic Coverage Act (MCCA) was enacted into law in 1988. Among its most central provisions, it placed a cap on yearly out-of-pocket costs for all Medicare services, covered substantial portions of the cost of prescription drugs, funded some short-term nursing home care and home care benefits,[17] and covered an unlimited number of hospital days. The legislation was to be funded primarily from a small increase in the SMI premium and a surcharge (up to $800 per person) on the income taxes paid by elderly persons. Since low- and moderate-income elders rarely pay income taxes, and since middle-income elders generally pay only small amounts of income taxes, if at all, the burden of the surcharge was designed to fall most heavily on higher-income elders. As Fernando Torres-Gil, Assistant HHS Secretary for Aging, pointed out, "Politically the tax hit the most vocal and articulate seniors while at the same time the poor and the middle income elderly were either not fully aware of the benefits or felt that they too would pay."[18] Also, many military and federal retirees already had full protection, and therefore received little or nothing in return for their increased payments. Further, the MCCA tax increases coincided with large increases in rates of most medigap policies. Consequently, the value added by MCCA was substantially obscured by jumps in medigap policy costs. Also, some considered this new tax a violation of social insurance principles since it was targeted narrowly on the group bearing the insured-against risk and not spread out over the entire workforce. Others considered it equitable policy since the burden was targeted mainly on higher-income elders. In the political firestorm that followed, Congress repealed most of the provisions of MCCA, a retreat that has reduced protection to some of the most vulnerable elderly while simultaneously fanning the flames of resentment against what is sometimes incorrectly perceived as unified opposition to the bill on the part of the elderly lobby. In truth, large groups like the AARP and the National Council of Senior Citizens actually supported the law.

Other ways of reducing the burden of acute care costs have been suggested. A report by a group of scholars, the Harvard Medicare Project, recommends decreasing deductibles and copayments while simultaneously raising premiums. Premiums are spread out across all beneficiaries, but the costs of deductibles and copayments are borne only by the sick, with those who are most ill bearing the greatest financial burden. Ironically, this 1988 report also suggested using a surtax to place greater financial burden on higher-income beneficiaries,[19] still a good idea perhaps but clearly one with significant limitations. To provide additional protection to elders and to further rationalize health care, the Harvard Project also recommends the development of a public supplementary health insurance plan that gives beneficiaries the opportunity to purchase an efficient alternative to medigap policies.

But even though acute care costs pose significant risks for elders, it is the cost of nursing home and community-based long-term care which looms as the major risk to the economic well-being of today's elderly. The aggregate costs to consumers are very large. Although Medicaid paid for 45 percent of the aggregate cost of nursing home care in 1988, payment for nearly all the rest (48 percent) came out-of-pocket—with the remainder coming from Medicare and other government programs (4 percent) and private insurance and private organizations (3 percent). In other words, consumers paid $20.8 billion of the $43.1 billion cost of nursing homes directly from their own resources. As for the nearly $10 billion in home care expenditures, consumers paid another $2.1 billion directly out of pocket in 1988, the rest coming from Medicare ($3.3 billion), Medicaid ($2.6 billion) and other public sources ($1.1 billion), and private insurance and organizations ($0.6 billion).[20]

The financial and personal toll exacted from elders and their family members of paying for such care is a growing concern. For some individuals (e.g., those who need "short-term" long-term care for rehabilitation), the costs are likely to be relatively manageable. But for others and their families, the need for expensive ongoing long-term care services could potentially overwhelm their finances. With the increased number of elders reaching advanced old age, it is not at all uncommon for families to have to spend the major portion of their resources to pay for long-term care, or, alternatively, to go without many services which could improve the quality of life for a disabled elder and their family. Today's 65-year-old has a roughly 20 percent chance of spending at least one year in a nursing home at roughly $30,000 a year. Moreover, as a report of the 1991 Advisory Committee on Social Security makes clear, "the group least able to afford high long-term care costs"—single and often widowed very old women—"is the same group which has the highest risks of incurring these costs."[21] While Medicaid provides funding for such care, eligibility requires depletion of resources—a process referred to as "spending-down." This has been mitigated somewhat by the retention of the "spousal-impoverishment" provision of MCCA, which enables the spouse of a person eligible for Medicaid nursing home benefits to keep half the combined liquid assets and to receive a monthly income of up to 150 percent of the poverty line. This provision, however, does not eliminate the possibility that elder spouses will be driven into financial want as a result of the long-term care needs of their husband or wife.

Another highly sensitive area concerns questions surrounding whether homes should be treated as assets, subject to Medicaid spend-down rules, or otherwise used to help fund nursing home care. On the one hand, home ownership and leaving an inheritance are valued goals of many and a source of dignity. It seems serendipitous to deny some elders the dignity of continued home ownership due to long-term illness while others of similar background are able to maintain this asset for their heirs. On the other hand, it seems unfair to ask low- and middle-class younger taxpayers to finance the long-term care of elders whose housing equity will shortly be passed on to their children, some of whom might be very well-off. Protecting the housing and financial assets of the comfortable and well-off elderly has become a growth industry for the legal profession. Ironically, today, Medicaid rules have encouraged many middle-income elderly persons to hire lawyers to protect their assets in the event that they need Medicaid to fund long-term care, what some might consider a form of "welfare cheating" and others simply a necessary adaptation to financial reality. Perhaps increased inheritance taxes earmarked to fund long-term care[22] would provide one incremental solution to this conundrum. This would spread the risk across a larger group and be more equitable from the point of view of those favoring progressive taxes.

What of the future? An expert panel on the Future of Income Security and Health Care Financing convened by the 1991 Advisory Committee on Social Security examined retirement income and health care expenditure projections from 1991 through 2020. With anticipated continued rises in the cost of acute health care and long-term care, and with out-of-pocket health care costs of the elderly expected roughly to double, the panel concluded that the anticipated real gains in the income of the elderly will likely be offset by health care expenditures.[23] Similarly, Maxwell School dean John Palmer points out that, even though the financial resources of future elders will generally increase, so too will costs arising from health care, most notably long-term care.[24] In fact, health and long-term care costs seem likely to pose the greatest economic threat for baby boomers when they retire.

QUALITY AND ACCESS TO ACUTE AND REHABILITATIVE CARE

For Americans who can afford health care, the quality of acute care in America and the availability of medical technology are outstanding.[25] For the most part, Medicare has succeeded admirably in providing elderly people and disabled people with access to hospital-based and other acute care services—that is, services requiring immediate but not long-term treatment. It also provides substantial "short term" long-term care, up to 100 days of rehabilitation and/or skilled nursing care following a hospitalization as well as limited home health services and rehabilitation equipment. As discussed, Medicare has also succeeded in usually (but not always) protecting against bankruptcy resulting from hospitalization. Without Medicare, beneficiaries would find the cost of comparable health insurance extremely high and many would be forced to go without it. And many middle-aged family members might be faced with such unpleasant choices as deciding whether to pay for their elderly parent's hospital stays or put money away for their children's educations.

The U.S. health care system, including Medicare and Medicaid, is oriented toward institutionally-based high tech care, with, until recently, very little emphasis on prevention, primary care, and "lower-tech" rehabilitation and services that help people with disabilities to function as independently as possible. New emphases on "wellness," the enrollment of growing numbers of elders in Health Maintenance Organizations (HMOs) which apply prevention and primary care strategies, greater reliance on rehabilitative facilities following implementation of Medicare's prospective payment system,[26] growing awareness of the importance of rehabilitation medicine for elderly persons, and the expansion of the community-based elder service networks, all have begun to move some care of elders out of in-patient hospital settings. Also the treatment of the elderly in ambulatory hospital settings has expanded rapidly, another response to the prospective payment system.

The health care system is directed toward "curing." Treatment of chronic illness presents physicians and other medical personnel with problems that are often seen as simultaneously less interesting and more frustrating, given the expectation that medical arts should lead to cures. There is some evidence that, once in the health care system, elderly persons receive less medical attention than they should and less physician time than younger patients, in part because of limited knowledge about geriatric care[27] and also because of negative attitudes toward the process of aging.

Recent changes in Medicare may encourage more primary care. A new physician payment system based on what is being called a "resource-based relative value scale" (RBRVS) is being phased in between 1992 and 1996. While payments to physicians for specific services are expected to decline, on average, by 3 percent, relative to what would have been, primary care physicians will generally benefit from this change while most specialists will not (excluding a few such as podiatrists, optometrists, and chiropractors).[28] Changing Medicare to cover routine physical exams without a copayment, eliminating the physician deductible, covering more preventive procedures, paying for primary health care to be brought to the homebound,[29] and adding reimbursement for dentures could further move the elder health care system away from potentially more expensive institutionally-based care. In terms of prevention, the 1991 Advisory Council on Social Security endorsed expanding public education and other efforts to promote healthy lifestyles through nutrition and exercise and by discouraging smoking and substance abuse, goals that are relevant to all age groups. Those concerned with strengthening primary care and adding preventive care benefits will observe that failure to do so may lead to unnecessary hospitalization or a poorer quality of life for beneficiaries. Those opposed to adding services to the Medicare program will note that even without the addition of new services, the program and the nation's health care system face enormous financing problems.

The health care system is enormously complex and the paperwork maddening. Standardizing claims forms offers one way to keep everyone's blood pressure down and further increase access to health care. To simplify the administration of Medicare, consideration is being given to eliminating the distinction between Medicare parts A and B. Another recommendation of the Harvard Medicare Project is to provide Medicare beneficiaries with access to information and assistance in negotiating the health care maze through the creation of a Medicare-funded ombudsman to be part of the national network of area agencies on aging.[30]

Efforts to control Medicare costs potentially have implications for quality of care and access. Such efforts have taken many forms, including professional review organizations to protect against unnecessary hospitalizations and surgical procedures. Legislation enacted in 1983 created a prospective payment system, which sets limits on reimbursement for hospital inpatient procedures by establishing a set amount to be paid for each diagnosis-related group (DRG). Each episode of illness requiring hospitalization, such as a hip replacement, falls into a particular DRG. Medicare-financed hospital admissions are now usually classified into DRGs, and a hospital is paid a set amount according to a patient's DRG. If providing care to the patient costs the hospital less than what Medicare pays for a particular DRG, the hospital makes a "profit." Alternatively, the hospital may experience a "loss" if, for instance, the patient stays in the hospital for more days than expected under a DRG.

Critics charge that the DRG system causes patients to be discharged "quicker" and "sicker," with possible adverse effects on their health and often without adequate rehabilitation or community-based services. Critics have also suggested that the system gives hospitals incentive to serve the most "profitable" cases, passing on less financially desirable cases to other settings. Also, some of the DRG savings are offset by the growth of Medicare expenditures for ambulatory care and rehabilitation. Proponents point out that DRGs have substantially reduced the average length of hospital stay, saving health care resources. Moreover, staying extra days in a hospital is not necessarily better for a patient. Others observe that the root of the problem concerns the limited discharge planning for hospitalized patients and the limited amount of community-based "short-term" care available for discharged patients. Thus, spouses and other family members who often care for recently discharged persons lack adequate support.[31]

LONG-TERM CARE

Families can and do provide the great bulk of care to the disabled elderly who are not in institutions, often at great emotional and financial cost. But family members need supportive services (some respite from the twenty-four-hour effort often required), and disabled elderly persons living alone have particular needs for services (transportation, chore services, home health services). Moreover, kinship supports are not always available, and, at times even when they are, expensive nursing home care may be more appropriate. Thus, for many reasons—including the growing number of very old people and a generally decreasing family size, which translates into relatively fewer family caregivers per disabled older person—the need for comprehensive and coordinated long-term care services is growing, both in the community and in institutions.

While many services are available in most communities, the long-term care system is riddled with problems. As Alice Rivlin, currently Deputy Director, Office of the Management of the Budget, and Joshua Weiner pointed out, "public costs are rising rapidly" and the burden of paying for long-term care "falls heavily on persons unlucky enough to need extensive long-term care and their families." Moreover, the strong institutional biases of the primary funding sources for long-term care result in far more funding being directed toward nursing home care as opposed to home care services. The involvement of many federal, state, and local agencies in the funding and delivery of services results in a complex and highly fragmented system, making access and coordination of services difficult. Those who can afford home-based and institutionally-based services have far better access to service, with private-paying patients generally receiving better care and better access to nursing homes.[32]

The problems of the existing system and the growing need to protect against the financial risk of long-term care raise many issues related to social insurance concerning the possible mix of public and private interventions that can best solve this problem. To what extent should the problem of long-term care remain one that is primarily the responsibility of families and individuals? Should government assist them? If so, what are the relative merits of interventions that would encourage individuals and private companies to purchase private insurance protecting against this risk, versus a social insurance approach or an approach that emphasizes protection through Medicaid? Are there combinations of social insurance, public assistance, and private approaches that could provide adequate protection for the population?

How much and what quality of long-term care should individuals have a right to receive? What private or public resources are available for additional protections?

One solution would be to encourage the development of private mechanisms to protect against the risk of long-term care, such as private long-term care insurance, continuing care retirement communities, and home equity conversion. In terms of private long-term care insurance, one question concerns whether a private product can be developed with low enough premiums to encourage individuals to protect themselves. Would, for instance, a 40-year-old be likely to save $50 each month to protect against a risk likely to occur only if he or she reaches age 85? Can a 75-year-old afford the high cost of starting such a policy? Other questions concern how companies can protect themselves against large financial risks and still offer products that provide adequate protection. To reduce their exposure to financial losses, companies often include high deductibles, exclude applicants likely to need long-term care, limit benefits, and provide little protection against inflation.[33] Even if attractive private products can be developed, large numbers of citizens—probably most—would not purchase this protection. Continuing care retirement communities make a commitment to provide, as needed, residents with a range of assisted living, long-term care, and nursing home options in exchange for a large initial fee plus monthly rent. While this option is useful for some elders who prefer and can afford this lifestyle, it is simply too expensive for most. Similarly, while many elders have accrued substantial equity in their homes, the use of home equity conversion mechanisms to free this equity to finance long-term care or other expenses faces many obstacles, which is why only a very few such agreements have been worked out nationally. These agreements generally involve banks giving loans to elder homeowners to be paid out monthly like many annuities in exchange for some or all of their home equity at death. Needless to say, this is a very emotionally sensitive area for most elders. Banks too have been reticent to enter into such agreements as they must bear the risk that an elder would live longer than expected.[34] By themselves, these and other private mechanisms may each be helpful for a small portion of elders. They are, however, unable to provide widespread protection and least likely to protect those at greatest financial or health risk.

By greatly liberalizing the assets and income tests and paying higher rates to providers of long-term care, the Medicaid program could be reformed to provide increased protection against long-term care costs. Here we need to ask whether a welfare-based solution is preferable to a social insurance solution. Can it provide adequate and dignified protection against the risks posed by long-term care? Can it provide for quality of care? Is it more efficient? Who will fall through the cracks? Advocates of incremental Medicaid reforms point out that they are well-targeted to those in greatest need. Moreover, they do not involve a major expansion in the role of government and are an efficient use of limited government resources. Noting existing problems of quality of long-term care, fragmentation of service, and restricted access which grow out of the current Medicaid program, those opposing this approach suggest that Medicaid does not provide an adequate model for financing long-term care.[35]

The creation of a social insurance program protecting the entire population from the risk of long-term care is being discussed today. Besides incremental expansions in Medicare (e.g., providing expanded home care benefits), there are three basic approaches: comprehensive social insurance models similar to Medicare, front-end nursing home coverage, and back-end nursing home coverage.

Comprehensive models would use the risk-pooling features of social insurance and earmarked taxes to cover a wide array of community- and institutionally based long-term care services.[36] As with today's medigap policies, private insurance might provide supplemental protection.

The front-end and back-end models rely more heavily on private insurance. Front-end proposals would provide social insurance protection for the first few months of nursing home care (e.g., three to six months), protecting the assets of the roughly one-quarter of persons admitted to nursing homes who later return to the community. This approach reduces the cost of private insurance to the consumer and makes it less risky for private insurers to offer protection.[37] However, while over 60 percent of persons admitted to nursing homes are "discharged" within six months, those staying six months or longer account for over 90 percent of all days used by "discharged" patients (includes discharge to home, to hospital, or by death).[38] Thus, the front-end approach leaves elders exposed to considerable risk, which must be protected against either by the purchase of private insurance that would still be quite expensive or through expanded Medicaid protection, if at all. Back-end approaches provide social insurance benefits after the first one or two years, leaving private mechanisms and/or Medicaid to pick up the initial cost.[39] These approaches would provide more protection than the front-end one, but the cost of private insurance would nonetheless be dear.

As the debate about what to do about the challenge of long-term care unfolds, a series of classic issues must be faced: Can we separate those in need of long-term care from the rest of the elderly and disabled populations? Ought we to insure only the elderly, or also include younger persons with disabilities and all others facing this risk? How would such a program be financed? In what sort of settings should long-term care be provided—homes or institutions? What is the proper public/private mix? Can we afford the cost of such a program? Alternatively, can we afford not to have such a program?

FINANCING HEALTH CARE FOR THE ELDERLY

Problems connected to financing the health care of the elderly population are joined to an even larger set of problems: the growing cost of health care in America. Yearly increases in the cost of most health care services have outstripped both inflation and increases in average wages of workers during almost every year since 1965. Thus, an increasingly large portion of the nation's gross national product is devoted to paying for health care—5.3 percent in 1960, 7.3 percent in 1970, 9.2 percent in 1980, and 12.2 percent in 1990. In non-inflation adjusted dollars, the nation's total health care expenditures grew from $27 billion in 1960 to $666 billion in 1990, or, as measured in constant 1990 dollars, from $120 billion to $666 billion.[40]

Roughly one-third of health care spending is directed at persons 65 and over. But, though seemingly counterintuitive, it appears that the growth of the elderly population explains only a modest portion of this astronomical growth. The 1990 Advisory Committee on Social Security reports that:

Over the last 20 years, personal spending for health care rose at an average annual rate of 11.6 percent. General inflation in the economy accounted for 52 percent of this growth, while another 11 percent resulted from increases in medical care prices above the inflation rate. Greater utilization and "intensity" of health care services contributed to another 28 percent to overall spending growth, and population increases accounted for the remaining 9 percent.[41]

Besides population aging, many factors contribute to the increased utilization and more intense application of medical technology, including consumer demand for and the proliferation of expensive technologies, reimbursement incentives that encourage increased services to patients, the practice of defensive medicine, physician training which emphasizes consideration of patient needs separate from cost considerations, and a medical education system that encourages specialization.[42] Cross-national experience also suggests that population aging is but one component of the growing cost of health care. Using the Organization for Economic Cooperation and Development (OECD) health data file, Thomas Getzen of Temple University's Center for Health Finance analyzes the cause of rising health care expenditures between 1960 and 1990 in twenty OECD countries.

During the period 1960 to 1988, average per capita income among OECD countries increased by 230 percent, and health expenditures increased by 460 percent. Inflation and rising GNP far outweigh all other causes as explanations of rising health care expenditure. Within this context of rapid economic growth, a 5–15 percent increase to population aging is easily obscured. There has been an error of emphasis; the dominant macroeconomic effects have not been highlighted. . . . If the population ages and there is no increase in GNP, governments cannot significantly raise health spending. Aging will increase the demand for health care, but adjustment to budgetary realities will limit that increase.[43]

What of the future? While it is simply not possible for health care costs to continue to grow at the same rate, the best estimates are that health care will consume a substantially larger portion of the nation's spending. The Health

Care Financing Administration has prepared four sets of projections about health care costs between 1990 and 2020, suggesting that under the worst case scenario 36 percent of GNP will be used for health care, 31.5 percent under their second projection, and 22.7 percent under their third and 13.7 percent under their best scenario.[44] We are not held hostage by demographic events or without options. Getzen's and others' findings suggest that we should not blame the elderly or other groups such as the poor for rising health care costs, but "recognize that 'the problem is us' and the system we have constructed."[45] Exactly how much of the nation's product will ultimately be devoted to health care will be substantially a function of the possibilities our economy allows and the political and administrative choices we, as a nation, make.

The health care financing problems of greatest concern to current elderly and perhaps of even greater importance to the elderly of the future concern the financing shortfalls projected in the Medicare Hospital Insurance (HI) trust fund and the growing cost of the Medicare Supplementary Insurance (SMI) program. For many reasons, including the politics surrounding the federal deficit, Medicare financing will be a major concern of Congress.

Barring congressional action, the Hospital Insurance (HI) Trust Fund, Medicare's larger trust fund, will be depleted shortly after the turn of the century, 2002 under the projection based on the intermediate set of assumptions.[46] Long-term, over seventy-five years, the program faces a large deficit under the projection based on the intermediate set of assumptions, requiring more than a doubling of HI's tax rate or a reduction of program outlays to less than one-half of what is currently anticipated. While there is no question that HI is heading toward exhaustion in the absence of corrective legislation, it is important for the reader to recognize that long-term projections of health care costs are far more uncertain than those for retirement pension costs. The reason: in addition to being based on assumptions about demographic and economic change, health care projections also incorporate numerous assumptions about health care utilization and service costs (e.g., lengths of stay, physician and hospital costs). Medical costs have been very volatile and are potentially subject to new regulation. Consequently, it is difficult to make very accurate estimates even a few years ahead, and the further out in time, the greater the overall uncertainty of the projections.

Because financing for Medicare's SMI trust fund is set so that income equals trust fund expenditures, SMI is actuarially sound, both in the short run and long run. About three-quarters of the program is funded from the general revenues of the federal government and the rest mainly through premium payments. However, program costs are growing rapidly. The trustees of the SMI program warn in their 1992 report that the cost of the program as a percent of gross domestic product is expected to increase fivefold by 2065 unless Congress acts to control "costs either through specific program legislation or as part of enacting more comprehensive health care reform."[47]

One way or another, these Medicare financing issues must be addressed during the 1990s. Within the context of reforms directed only at Medicare, consideration may be given to bringing more revenues into Medicare via such mechanisms as increasing payroll taxes, taxing alcoholic beverages and cigarettes, raising deductibles and other beneficiary charges, and taxing some of the currently tax-exempt fringe benefits. Levying larger premiums on middle- and upper-income beneficiaries is a proposal that some reject as a type of means-testing and others consider a fair way of distributing burdens. Alternatively, some have suggested treating a portion of the insurance value of being covered by Medicare as taxable income.

Given the rapidly growing reserves of the combined OASDI trust funds, reallocating a portion of the OASDI tax rate to Medicare's HI program (and possibly returning OASDI to a pay-as-you-go system) will likely be given very serious consideration. Certainly, the build-up of large reserves in the combined OASDI trust funds is well timed to the short-term financing needs of HI.

Consideration will also be given to benefit reductions (raising the age of eligibility for Medicare to 67) and to new ways of containing the cost of physician and other medical services. And as a strategy to achieve long-term savings (and to improve quality of life), consideration could also be given to investing further in biomedical research. In terms of the cost-saving goal, this area is tricky. The fruits of such research—new technologies and even disease reduction—do not always result in cost savings. But, when costly advances are made [both as individuals and as a nation], we often welcome them. And even with the necessary qualifications, seeking to delay the onset or to prevent diseases such as osteoporosis and Alzheimer's through research holds promise as a cost-savings strategy.

Each alternative likely to be considered has strengths and weaknesses, and a parallel set of proponents and opponents. For example, raising the age of eligibility for Medicare to 67 (as is currently scheduled for OASDI but not for Medicare) provides a seemingly logical way to reduce projected deficits (given increasing life expectancies at age 65 for successive cohorts). However, others would point out that it would place the cost of doing so primarily on those 65- and 66-year-olds with the highest medical costs. Increased payroll taxation is certainly possible, but of course it reduces the income that workers take home and the distributive effects are regressive, though this can be partially offset by increasing the earned income tax credit for low-income workers with dependent children. Reallocating a portion of OASDI payroll tax rates to HI would provide a quick shot in the arm to Medicare for roughly the next thirty years, but at a cost of moving away from partial advance funding of the baby boom generation's retirement and the benefits that some believe might follow from using Social Security to enhance national savings.[48] Containing costs is certainly desirable, but, depending on how it is done, it may shift costs onto other parties involved in the health care system (e.g., the family, private insurers, state governments) or result in poorer and/or inadequate care.

Because the Medicare financing issue is intertwined with larger health care cost and financing issues, a long-term solution will require more than simply increasing Medicare revenues (through tax increases and increased beneficiary payments) and/or decreasing expenditures (through benefit cuts and cost-containment measures). Ultimately, Medicare's financing problems as well as other problems, such as those surrounding the cost of Medicaid and long-term care, will need to be addressed in the context of broad reforms of the American health care system. But no matter how successful we are, we need to be aware that health care costs will increase and to plan for this increase. Even if inflation in hospital and other medical costs is brought under control, there is no doubt that the cost of publicly protecting the aged and disabled will remain high and will grow, given the anticipated growth of the elderly population and especially of the very old.

There is also no doubt that much needs to be done to stabilize Medicare's financing and that each option has some negatives. However, as analysts associated with the Harvard Medicare Project point out, "the support shown for the Medicare program over the years suggests a basic willingness to pay the costs of the benefits the public believes are necessary. The specific details of financing may in the end be less important than the perceived value of Medicare benefits."[49] In fact, a similar point could be made with respect to financing the full range of health and long-term care services that are needed by elders. No question it will be expensive, and no question major changes may need to be made in the organization and delivery of health care to elders and in the types of services we provide. But because we value the provision of health care for elderly persons, we will seek reasonable means to finance access within the confines of economic possibilities and the needs of other groups for private and public support.

ALLOCATING HEALTH CARE: ETHICAL CONCERNS

At many levels of economic, political, and organizational activity, decisions are made affecting how health care resources are allocated and ultimately who receives care. As the health care system is currently structured, the market economy substantially determines who can afford care, though many non-market mechanisms (Medicaid) also condition access. Those who have good health insurance coverage (usually a perquisite of a secure job) generally receive high-quality care, while the poor, the unemployed, and others who cannot afford care have access to a more limited quantity of care, which is often of lesser quality. Political decisions shape entitlements and the regulatory environment, expanding or contracting the types of services available and regulating such factors as nursing home beds, lengths of stay in hospitals, and private health insurance. At the level of patient care, every day, hospital administrators, physicians, nurses, and other health care providers decide whether patients receive treatment, what types of treatment they receive, who to send home, and the like.

Collectively, this could be considered a type of "rationing," though usually not the result of explicit decisions to give more care to some individuals and less to others. Increasingly, however, the need to address thorny allocation issues more directly than in the past is being thrust upon politicians, health care providers, citizens, and patients alike. Growing health care costs, a large portion of which go to the elderly, along with awareness of economic limits, population aging, limited access for many, and public dissatisfaction with the existing health care system are forcing a discussion about how health care resources should be used in the United States. The difficult questions for public debate concern such issues as (1) the fairness of existing allocations of resources across age and income groups, and (2) what criteria to apply when making difficult decisions about the allocation of scarce health care resources and the basis, if any, for rationing care to individuals.

The elderly have the distinction of being the only group of Americans with universal health insurance, Medicare. The rest of the population depends primarily on private insurance (usually provided through the place of employment), private savings, or sometimes Medicaid. In the course of the year, about 35 million Americans—many in families in which the head of the household works full time throughout the year and others in families struck by unemployment—lack any type of health insurance, private or public. Millions more who are covered do not have adequate protection. Medicaid, the welfare program designed to provide access to health care for the poor, provides benefits for less than one-half of the poor. And even coverage by health insurance is no guarantee against the financial hazards that can accompany catastrophic illness. This does not mean, of course, that the "uninsured" do not receive care; rather they usually have a less certain means of paying for it and often a lesser quality of care.

To some it seems unfair that elderly persons receive special protection and that such a large portion of health care resources are directed at older Americans. But others respond that the real inequity concerns the failure to protect all Americans against basic health care risks, not that protections have been extended to one relatively vulnerable group. They point out that the elderly have more need for health care protection, are less easily insured by private mechanisms, and that, even with Medicare, elders are rarely protected against the risk of long-term care or other catastrophic costs. Rather than focusing on the elderly having too much protection, more emphasis could be placed on making health care available to all.

How this goal might be accomplished is part of an ongoing national policy discussion. What form should additional insurance take? Should it be uniform and compulsory? Should it be mandated by government and hence required of all employers (who could use private insurers) such as envisioned by proposals which would require employers to provide health insurance to employees or make payroll tax contributions into a special health insurance fund? Or should it be modeled after a national health insurance program such as Canada's in which all citizens are entitled to basic health care and government controls costs by serving as the single payer? Or should it be based on proposals that would expand access to health care through the use of tax credits and seek to control competition through an expansion of managed care principles? Or does managed competition provide the best approach?

In the context of the growing costs of health care, population aging, and federal deficits, the expenditures on elders are increasingly isolated as a major cause of the nation's health care crisis. Some consider elder health care expenditures an inequitable and wasteful intergenerational transfer. Others, who do not necessarily oppose resource transfers for elderly persons, question whether there is a need to shift from age-based to needs-based entitlements or to scale-back benefits by, for instance, raising the age of eligibility for public benefits. Calling for a "caring" as opposed to "curative" orientation to the treatment of elderly persons, health ethicist Daniel Callahan advocates rationing health care by age; that is, withholding curative and life-prolonging care for elderly persons as a group after a certain age. Under his plan, persons who have lived out their normal years would no longer receive publicly supported acute health care but would still receive palliative treatments to make them more comfortable.[50] Callahan's ideas have sparked a major policy debate.

Responding to Callahan's call for age-based rationing, Harry R. Moody, another health ethicist, distinguishes between "rationing" as a decision to limit individuals' access to a scarce good, and "allocation" as "broad budgetary or policy priorities." He writes, "We can accept a social justice rationale for limiting the expenditure of health care resources without endorsing age-based rationing as the means of achieving this limitation."[51] Opposition to age-based rationing is not synonymous with opposition to making allocation choices that would encourage different patterns of utilization among the elderly and other groups. Moody suggests that the age-based rationing debate distracts attention from more important issues, such as how to control costs and "distribute the burden of paying for health care in an aging society."[52]

Others have criticized the idea of withholding some health care services on the basis of age as scapegoating the elderly for rising health care costs and falsely dichotomizing the distinction between curative and palliative care. It is also seen by them as unworkable in a litigious society, inequitable in a society that would retain a private health care sector, violating basic Judeo-Christian values of the sanctity of life, and as undermining the self-determination of elders.[53] At the very practical level of making patient care decisions, a panel of experts convened by the U.S. Congress Office of Technology Assessment found that for individual elderly patients, "chronological age is a poor predictor of the outcome of treatment with life-sustaining technologies." Most panel members concluded that "socioeconomic status should not be a barrier to access to health care, including life-sustaining interventions" and that decisions "regarding life-sustaining treatments must be based on an individual basis and should never be based on chronological age alone."[54]

CONCLUDING COMMENT ON HEALTH CARE

Shortly after the enactment of Medicare, Eveline Burns, a professor at the Columbia University School of Social Work, suggested that Medicare

has started us on a road from which there can be no turning back. Governmental involvement in the financing and organization of our health services is here to stay, and there is every indication that it will increase. Resolution of the policy issues at stake provides an agenda that will make the greatest demands on our ingenuity and resourcefulness for the rest of this century. It will also make great demands on our courage and our sense of public responsibility. Above all, it will be a crucial test of the strength of our conviction that all people should have the assurance of an equal opportunity to obtain a high quality of comprehensive health care under self-respecting conditions.[55]

Evidently, her words have withstood the test of time, though uncertainty and controversy continue to surround the question of whether health care is to become a right of citizenship.

Conclusion—An Invitation
to Shape the Future

The sheer amount of detail that surrounds Social Security and Medicare can often function like a high wall, shutting out people who have only a casual interest in these programs and fueling public misunderstanding. We have tried to work our way through some of the detail. What emerges from this examination is that Social Security and Medicare, our major social welfare commitments, are large programs that try to balance many important and often competing policy objectives. Consequently, while achieving many desired social goals, these complex programs embody compromises between sometimes conflicting policy objectives.

Because Social Security is so large, it must cover an almost impossibly wide range of situations. Social Security may be the sole source of income for a recently widowed woman and her children, but is one of several sources of support for those retirees who have private pension and other income-producing assets. It has to provide the basis for helping a 55-year-old steel worker, out of a job, who is suffering from debilitating lower back pain and is worried about not being able to help his children financially. If the program grants this person a retirement pension, that decision inevitably affects the way in which Social Security handles the application of a 32-year-old paraplegic whose pathway to work is blocked by a lack of attendant care and transportation. Discriminating among the various situations introduces further complexity into the program and raises the wall that keeps the public and others from understanding it.

Because Medicare is so large, it, like Social Security, influences a wide range of behaviors. Levels of reimbursement influence the willingness of physicians to treat elder and disabled beneficiaries. Decisions to cover selected services condition the ability of beneficiaries to seek treatment. Proposals for expansion of home care protections must be assessed against questions of whether new provisions will erode family supports. Likewise, cost-containment mechanisms such as the prospective payment system (DRGs) of reimbursement to hospitals must be measured against implications for patient care and the constraints placed on physician autonomy. Plainly, changes in one part of Medicare have implications for other parts of the health care system.

Because Social Security is so large, the program commands a lot of political attention, from both admirers and detractors. The admirers often make the argument that the program is the best we can do. They ask us to consider the realistic alternatives. What would happen if Social Security were voluntary? Would the well-being of society increase, or would the system come to an end and leave society worse off than before? The detractors often make the argument that there are untested approaches that, at least theoretically, would work better than Social Security. In a sense, both sides are right. One side settles for something less than perfect; the other side risks destroying a system that works fairly well in the pursuit of a possibly perfect system.

We tend to side with the faction that believes that we are better off muddling through with Social Security than we are trying to create something new—something that would have less political support and would be less certain than Social Security to reduce poverty. No doubt, were we to start anew, the system that would be designed might be very different from today's program. But with 41 million persons relying on the program for monthly benefits and with tens of millions more building their retirement plans around it, there is little wonder that powerful forces ally against radical change.

We would caution against those who claim that they have the big fix for Social Security, such as privatizing the program or trying to establish a minimum income program that is not funded by payroll taxes. We know that Social Security is an awkward and unwieldy institution. Any program that covers nearly everyone is bound to involve a great deal of money and to create many anomalies. Any program that has been before Congress so many times as has Social Security is bound to contain many questionable provisions, particularly when it comes to the fine details of, for example, allowing disability insurance beneficiaries to engage in trial work periods. Any program that has existed for such a long time is bound to show aspects of its age, particularly when it comes to such matters as making sure that women receive benefits that reflect contributions comparable to those of men. Any program that has enjoyed such success is bound to be burdened by problems that may be beyond its control, such as making adjustments in its financing during periods of slowed economic growth, encouraging people with disabilities to join the labor force or stemming the tide toward early retirement. And any program that brings in so much revenue is bound to be coveted by those who would like to use this revenue for other purposes.

Because the political process provides a vehicle for reconciling competing views and value preferences, we should not be surprised that Social Security and Medicare lack the perfection and elegance that some rational planners and some academics would impose. Nor should we be surprised that in seeking to achieve one goal such as poverty prevention, these programs may compromise other goals such as providing returns that are roughly proportional to contributions. Here we risk stumbling upon a cliché: this messiness is the price we pay for social policy in a democracy. Institutions subject to democratic control are bound to be messy, lumpy combinations of competing desires and plans.

Consequently, depending upon one's views, policy dilemmas and programmatic outcomes become subject to a variety of interpretations. The absence of health insurance for 35 million Americans, children and adults alike, is emphasized by some as a social injustice. Others, sometimes preferring less government intervention, find injustice and inequity in the fact that Medicare provides national health insurance for the elderly and for persons with severe disabilities while the nation's children lack such a guarantee. For the first group the inequity is the failure to protect all Americans. For the second group, inequity is found in the unequal protections afforded to different demographic groups. To some it is unfair that higher-income workers pay more payroll taxes than lower-income workers for the same Medicare protections. To others it is unfair that there are many elders who continue to lack adequate means to maintain their living standards during retirement.

We realize that concepts such as adequacy and equity are artificial constructs about which reasonable people can differ. That is why, throughout this book, we have often resorted to presenting both sides of particular questions. We realize also that policymakers and the public alike must make hard decisions, often necessitating trade-offs between desired goals such as poverty prevention, equity, and financial stability. That is why we have sought to make some of these trade-offs explicit. It has been our aim to explain some of the choices. It is up to the public, both experts and non-experts, to make these choices.

But, of course, this does not mean that we do not have our own views about the importance of Social Security and Medicare, about which issues should be primary for the Social Security and Medicare policy agendas, or about the policy interventions that should be considered. In this concluding section, then, we briefly review our thinking in a few areas.

CONCLUDING COMMENTS

As discussed in the opening chapter, we favor the social insurance approach to economic security that informs Social Security and Medicare. We think that, on balance, these programs have done much more good than harm, and that there is every reason to believe that this will be true in the future. We are, however, concerned that the public—including students and their professors, policymakers and their journalist chroniclers, employees and their employers—gain a better understanding of these programs. Poor information undermines public discourse and public confidence in democratic institutions. Myths and misinformation are the Achilles' heel of Social Security and Medicare. In the long run, vibrant social policy requires an informed public and an open political dialogue through which policymakers and experts help explicate choices.

We know that this view sounds naive. We know that it separates us from others who have commented on the program. Martha Derthick wrote in the late-1970s of how Social Security policymaking was restricted to a very limited number of participants in the executive branch and Congress. We admire her work and think many of her observations correct. Indeed, a very limited number of people have shaped Social Security policy agendas, though it should be noted that the substantive outcomes have been generally positive. Derthick argued that policymaking for Social Security should be opened up so that more people could participate.[1] Since then she has had some second thoughts. She has studied two examples of administrative failure—the initial implementation of the SSI program and the disability review of the early 1980s—and concluded that these failures were the fault of the American system.[2] In America, Congress and the president send contradictory messages to the executive agencies like the Social Security Administration. Little thought is given to the process of administration. Other experts have argued that it is not the constricted policy system that is the problem but rather the failure of Congress to heed the good advice of experts.

We believe that Social Security and Medicare are too important to leave to any one group, be they experts, academics, or journalists. We also think that we need expert and experienced administrators who are skilled at implementation and policymakers and experts who can help shape public discussions. We need a system that does not make impossible demands of social programs. And we need a system that makes an effort to anticipate future problems and does not leave every question to be decided according to the prevailing political whims.

As the final chapter of this book was being written, Americans elected Bill Clinton as their president. With a new administration, there is opportunity to take a fresh look at many issues. Whether this will happen remains to be seen. Certainly, as we have suggested, there is much that is right about these programs. Thus we believe an incremental approach to policy reform is generally preferable to radical reform. But incrementalism should not be used as an excuse to submerge new ideas or avoid making difficult decisions. One view is that Democrats, the traditional defenders of social programs, are least likely to consider departures from existing Social Security and Medicare policies. But, given the current context, the reverse may be true. Just as a Republican president, Richard Nixon, could take the political risk of opening the door to China, a Democratic president may be better positioned to consider policy reforms in Social Security and Medicare that were heretofore viewed as politically unacceptable.

In light of large federal deficits, we believe it almost certain that Medicare and Social Security beneficiaries will be called upon to share in deficit reduction efforts. We recognize that because Social Security is funded by an earmarked payroll tax and because it is running substantial surpluses, an argument could be made to exclude it from a budget reduction package. However, we believe that the political process will function to include it. In terms of Social Security, it is our belief that this pain will be best distributed by treating larger portions of Social Security as taxable income. If under the press of large deficits, decisions are made to reduce benefits by, for example, permanently delaying or skipping a cost-of-living adjustment, then we would hope that the *quid pro quo* would be substantial improvements in SSI such as those recently advocated in the report of the SSI modernization panel that was chaired by Dr. Arthur Flemming, secretary of Health, Education, and Welfare during the latter part of the Eisenhower administration. The panel recommended increasing SSI benefits to at least 100 percent of the poverty line, liberalizing the SSI assets tests to make it easier for persons with limited assets to qualify, increasing the program's staffing levels to allow for more personalized service delivery and more outreach, and allowing SSI beneficiaries to live in the homes of family members or friends without being penalized with a one-third benefits reduction.[3]

In spite of substantial improvements in the economic status of the elderly as a group and notwithstanding media stereotypes of "greedy geezers," there remain millions of elderly persons with poverty and near-poverty level incomes. They should not be forgotten, either in the context of celebrations over the successes of Social Security or budget deficit negotiations that ask the more financially able elders to do their fair share. A compassionate and just old-age policy requires that the needs of those who are at greatest risk remain paramount on the public policy agenda. It also requires that Social Security better reflect the value of the contributions to the care of family members that currently result in reduced benefits for many women, especially those who later divorce. And it requires maintaining the types of universal protections covered under Social Security and Medicare.

With respect to Medicare, it does not take a crystal ball to predict that its financing will soon be a major concern. Without substantial tax increases and/or benefit reductions, the Hospital Insurance portion of Medicare will go broke around the turn of the century. At a minimum, we would expect remedial legislation since Congress and the president are unlikely to let such important protection lapse. But, as nearly all agree, the Medicare financing problem cannot be dealt with effectively apart from the larger issues of health care financing and access. The rising cost of health care is undermining the entire health care system. Systemwide controls are needed for Medicare and the health care system, which teeter together on the brink of disaster. With the election of a new president, the window of opportunity for comprehensive reform of the health care system has widened. A meaningful national debate is needed about how best to control costs and how best to extend health care protections to all Americans. Decisions must be made about levels of care that all should minimally receive; about the future of the employer-based private health insurance system; about global budgeting; about insurance and claims for malpractice; about costly and wasteful paperwork generated by the existing system. In the absence of such decisions, little long-term progress can be made.

As for long-term care, it is not particularly courageous of us to predict the obvious, that it will grow in importance as an issue during the 1990s. Chronic and debilitating illness represents the primary risk to the economic well-being of today's and tomorrow's middle-income elders and their families. We believe an expansion of social insurance to cover substantial portions of this risk, making the remaining portions more amenable to private and in some cases welfare-based solutions, is desirable. One way or another, individuals, families, and government will pay for the costs of chronic illness, either through caregivers shouldering more than should reasonably be expected of family members, through the suffering of the chronically ill, through financial catastrophes which often accompany chronic illness, through depletion of private assets, through payments for private insurance, or through increased tax payments for social insurance and other public mechanisms. The social insurance approach can help spread the cost and the risk over the larger population, still allowing for supplementation by private insurance, assets, and other means.

Similarly, it does not require much political sophistication to know that disability will continue to pose hard policy questions. As we have noted, it is easier to frame these questions than to answer them. The challenges for disability policy are apparent: we need to learn how to provide reasonable compensation to persons with disabilities who cannot work while simultaneously providing pathways to work for those who can. The latter concern may require restructuring the incentives and benefits packages (transportation, attendant care, health benefits, and technical aids) of the disability program. Without a doubt, these concerns will grow in importance as the baby boom cohorts age and as Americans come to realize the implications of the civil rights guarantees in the Americans with Disabilities Act.

With respect to issues surrounding the retirement of the baby boom generation, we would caution that the "thirty-" going on "forty-something" stereotype of baby boomers—persons born from 1946 through 1964—creates a poor basis for planning retirement policy. It is important to recognize that baby boomers are a diverse group, varying by age, class, race, gender, economic status, and family status. Many, including those who have already accrued substantial equity and private pension protection, are heading toward an economically secure old age. The prospects for many others with low-wage histories, with very limited assets, and with limited educations are bleak, not only during retirement years but throughout the rest of their lives. There are many who fall between these two groups. While their current and future economic security is not assured, it seems probable. The youngest among the baby boomers are at greater risk since they will enter old age during the time that retirement and health care systems will be experiencing the greatest strains. Also at greater risk are the roughly 7 million single female baby boomers heading households with children and the roughly 8 million baby boomers with incomes below poverty.[4]

An old-age policy that seeks to address their needs and the cohorts that will follow them into old age must begin with a sound economy that creates employment, pension, and home ownership opportunities for more Americans. As the nation reassesses its Social Security, Medicare, and health care systems, the needs of those at greatest risk should be of foremost concern. As for the affluent among the baby boom and other age cohorts, there is probably relatively little that government can do to affect their economic security in retirement since well-being is already all but assured, with the possible exception that they too may be exposed to the risk of chronic and debilitating illness.

As for Social Security's financing, there is no cause for immediate alarm. The projected short-term deficits in the Disability Insurance Trust Fund can easily be handled by reallocating a small portion of the tax rate in the Old-Age and Survivors Insurance Trust Fund, which is projected to run huge surpluses for many years to come. Under the intermediate assumptions, sufficient funds exist to pay benefits through 2036. Even under the pessimistic assumptions, funds exist to make payments through 2019, and under the optimistic assumptions, the combined OASDI trust fund is scheduled to be solvent in perpetuity. Plainly these estimates are subject to revision based on economic and demographic change. Should future experience suggest that the shortfall will arrive sooner than expected, there is still much lead time to make necessary changes in payroll tax rates or benefits.[5] Should the economy perform better than expected or should policy changes that produce long-term savings, such as increased taxation of benefits (with the receipts going to social security) or a COLA delay be enacted, then the shortfall will occur later or possibly not at all.

Although Social Security is financially stable for many years to come, we are concerned that yearly reports of long-term deficits will likely erode public confidence in the program. If this occurs, it may then impel politicians to act sooner rather than later. Future gains in public confidence may be worth the political pain of instituting tax increases or benefit reductions sooner than may seem necessary from an analytic point of view. These changes could be structured to trigger in as the program's financing begins to decline. For example, instituting a floating tax rate to go into effect automatically after

2015 at the time that the combined OASDI trust fund ratio (of fund assets in relation to anticipated expenditures in a given year) drops below 150 percent might be one approach. Scheduling further increases in the age of eligibility for full benefits is another approach. It tends to be favored by those who believe benefit reductions are the most appropriate means of maintaining the program's long-term financing. Although we do not see the need for immediate action, we believe it important that political leaders maintain a flexible stance and take into account political variables such as changes in public confidence as well as the analytic concerns identified in financial projections.

Finally, we would like to comment on the disturbing tendency of recent years to scapegoat the elderly and misframe many important Social Security and Medicare policy questions as issues of generational equity. Too often, the rhetoric of concern for future generations has been used to undermine support for and justify reductions in Social Security and Medicare. It has not been used to assure the well-being of the young. The argument that is often advanced under this rubric suggests that spending on the elderly is responsible for federal deficits, the growing poverty among the nation's children, disinvestment in public education, and slowed economic growth. But imprudent tax cuts that mainly benefit higher-income persons and large increases in defense spending have caused the national debt to soar, not Social Security and Medicare. The social insurance programs largely pay their way through earmarked payroll taxes. Callous disregard of the needs of low-income children, disinvestment in their educations and health care, a stagnant economy, growing economic inequality, and loss of manufacturing jobs—not Social Security and Medicare and not the elderly—have created the crisis besetting low-income families. Deregulation that resulted in the collapse of savings and loans banks, imprudent corporate mergers, reductions in private and public investment—not Social Security and Medicare and not the elderly—are prime contributors to the nation's stagnating economy.

To begin to address the nation's economic problems, we must first define the problems properly. Confusing association with causation will not help. The improved economic status of the elderly is not a cause of the declining status of today's young any more than it is a cause of slowed economic growth. More powerful forces are operating and must be addressed. Moreover, all the elderly are not comfortable and all the young are not poor. There are millions of rich and poor among both groups.

To the extent that the rhetoric of generational equity highlights the risk that future generations cannot as easily achieve the American dream as in the past, it has a germ of truth. Again, we would emphasize that the real threat to the living standards of future generations—to our children—does not come from Social Security, Medicare, and today's or tomorrow's elderly. Ironically, although there is little that can be done to Social Security and Medicare that will affect the growth of the economy, the reverse is not true. In fact, the greatest threat to the future of Social Security and Medicare (or whatever health programs may follow) comes from the risk of economic decline. Should this occur, then undoubtedly protections would need to be drastically reduced.

As a nation we have done much that is right, but we have made serious mistakes in our approach to the economy and we also face a more competitive international environment. The solutions to current economic problems are found outside the Social Security and Medicare programs. The long-term health of the economy requires that we reduce consumption and invest more. Private and public investments are needed in research and development of new technologies, in new plants and equipment, in transportation and communications systems, in water and sewer systems necessary for community life, and in the development of today's and tomorrow's workers. Social investment is needed to provide educational opportunities and job advancement opportunities for all the young, to respond more effectively to the scourge of drugs affecting some among the young, to harness the talents of the unemployed, and to strengthen the nation's schools. These are the challenges that must be met to increase the prospects of young and old alike.

As the nation addresses these and other challenges, we submit that, once again, it may be time to think about "Social Security" less as a program and more as an ideal.[6] Today "Social Security" most often refers to the Old-Age, Survivors, and Disability Insurance program. But as originally conceived, the term "Social Security" referred to the vision of ensuring economic security for all Americans. As described in the report of the Committee on Economic Security in January 1935, Social Security incorporated the goal of assuring "an adequate income to each human being in childhood, youth, middle age, or old age—in sickness and in health." Though practical considerations dictated a piecemeal approach, the Committee recommended the eventual provision of "safeguards against all of the hazards leading to destitution and dependency" through stimulation of private employment and necessary public employment, and through a combination of social insurance, welfare, health, and social service measures.[7] Ultimately, only by thinking about the needs of the national community as a whole can the vision of Social Security be realized.

Finally, as the process of Social Security and Medicare policy reform unfolds, we would simply point to the effective way in which these policies have protected people against economic insecurity. We would praise the real ingenuity of the program administrators and analysts who have attempted to steer a course between equal and adequate treatment of beneficiaries. We would also ask that people not be fooled by the rhetoric of the moment to think that the future will somehow solve itself. The retirement of the baby boom age cohorts presents real, not artificial dilemmas.

We could also hope that people not be fooled by rhetoric that says the future is insolvable, nor allow themselves to be scared, as people bandy about large numbers when they talk about Social Security expenditures. Modest benefits paid to millions of people cost many millions of dollars, but they are modest benefits nonetheless. One must not be bullied by this tyranny of large numbers, nor by current academic discourse.

Instead, we believe that people should contemplate what sort of future it is that they want and then begin to bring about this future. We submit this policy primer as one place to start. We hope that this analysis helps some people to climb over the high wall of Social Security and Medicare detail.

Notes

Chapter 1

1. U.S. Bureau of the Census, *Measuring the Effect of Benefits and Taxes on Income and Poverty: 1986* (Washington, D.C.: U.S. GPO, 1988).

2. Theodore R. Marmor, Jerry L. Mashaw, and Philip L. Harvey, *America's Misunderstood Welfare State: Persistent Myths, Enduring Realities* (New York: Basic Books, 1990), p. 131.

3. William Haber and Wilbur J. Cohen, eds., *Readings in Social Security* (New York: Prentice Hall, 1948).

4. Robert M. Ball, *Social Security: Today and Tomorrow* (New York: Columbia University Press, 1978).

5. The most recent edition is Robert J. Myers, *Social Security* (Philadelphia: University of Pennsylvania Press, 1991).

6. Martha Derthick, *Policymaking for Social Security* (Washington, D.C.: Brookings Institution, 1979).

7. The best bibliographic guide to the Social Security program is W. Andrew Achenbaum, *Social Security: Visions and Revisions* (New York: Cambridge University Press, 1986). In *Social Security: The System That Works* (New York: Basic Books, 1988), Merton C. Bernstein and Joan Brodshaug Bernstein provide a useful guide to issues surrounding the future of Social Security and Medicare, including the financing problems of the early 1980s and policy issues surrounding the interaction of public and private pensions.

8. Congress did, however, reduce benefits payable in the long-run future, especially for covered workers without dependents.

9. The tax rates in the near future were actually lower than originally scheduled in the 1935 Act.

Chapter 2

1. Robert M. Ball, *Social Security: Today and Tomorrow* (New York: Columbia University Press, 1978), p. 4. See also Social Security Administration, "Social Security

Programs in the United States, 1987," *Social Security Bulletin* 50, 4 (April 1987), pp. 5–66.

2. Ann Kallman Bixby, "Overview of Public Welfare Expenditures, Fiscal Year 1988," *Social Security Bulletin* 52 (May 1991), p. 6.

3. Richard M. Titmuss, *Essays on the Welfare State* (Boston: Beacon Press, 1969), pp. 34–55.

4. See discussions in Mimi Abramowitz, "Everyone Is on Welfare: 'The Role of Redistribution in Social Policy' Revisited," *Social Work* (November/December 1983), pp. 440–45, and in Titmuss, *Essays on the Welfare State*, pp. 34–55.

5. "Tax expenditures" are defined as the decreases in "income tax liabilities that result from provisions in income tax laws and regulations that provide economic incentive" for certain activities and/or tax relief to certain types of taxpayers. See U.S. House of Representatives, Committee on Ways and Means, *Background Material and Data on Programs Within the Jurisdiction of the Committee on Ways and Means* (Washington, D.C.: U.S. GPO, 1991), p. 866.

6. U.S. House of Representatives, Committee on Ways and Means, *Background Material and Data on Programs Within the Jurisdiction of the Committee on Ways and Means* (Washington, D.C.: U.S. GPO, 1992), pp. 867–933.

7. House Committee, *Background Material and Data*, p. 927.

8. See Eric R. Kingson, Barbara A. Hirshorn, and John M. Cornman, *Ties That Bind: The Interdependence of Generations* (Cabin John, Md.: Seven Locks Press, 1986), pp. 51–68.

9. Thomas J. Espenshade, *Investing in Children: New Estimates of Parental Expenditures* (Washington, D.C.: Urban Institute Press, 1984), p. 3.

10. See Kingson, Hirshorn, and Cornman, *Ties That Bind*, pp. 51–68.

11. James N. Morgan, "The Redistribution of Income by Families and Institutions and Emergency Help Patterns," in Greg J. Duncan and James N. Morgan, eds., *Five Thousand American Families: Patterns of Economic Progress*, vol. 10, *Analysis of the First Thirteen Years of the Panel of Income Dynamics* (Ann Arbor, Michigan: Institute for Social Research, University of Michigan, 1983), pp. 2–16.

12. See Titmuss, *Essays on the Welfare State*, pp. 34–55.

13. Theodore R. Marmor, Jerry L. Mashaw, and Philip L. Harvey, *America's Misunderstood Welfare State: Persistent Myths, Enduring Realities* (New York: Basic Books, 1990), p. 227.

14. Marmor, Mashaw, and Harvey, *Misunderstood Welfare State*, p. 227.

15. Robert J. Myers, *Social Security*, 3rd ed. (Homewood, Ill.: Richard D. Irwin, Inc., 1985), p. 11.

16. Reinhard A. Hohaus, "Equity, Adequacy, and Related Factors in Old Age Security," in William Haber and Wilbur J. Cohen, eds., *Social Security Programs, Problems and Policies* (Homewood, Ill.: Richard D. Irwin, Inc., 1960), p. 62.

17. Social Security Administration, "Social Security Programs in the United States, 1987," *Social Security Bulletin* 50, 4 (April 1987), p. 11.

18. "Social Security Programs in the United States, 1987," p. 11; Kingson, Hirshorn, and Cornman, *Ties That Bind*, p. 71.

19. Lawrence H. Thompson, "The Social Security Reform Debate," *Journal of Economic Literature* 21 (December 1983), p. 1460.

20. J. Douglas Brown, *Essays on Social Security* (Princeton, N.J.: Princeton University Press, 1977), pp. 31–32.

21. Ball, *Social Security: Today and Tomorrow*, p. 5.

22. Wilbur J. Cohen, "The Social Security Act of 1935: Reflections, Fifty Years Later," in *50th Anniversary Edition: The Report of the Committee on Economic Security* (Washington, D.C.: National Conference on Social Welfare, 1985), p. 13.

23. The following is drawn from Wilbur Cohen to Joseph Califano, January 19, 1968, Cohen Papers, Madison, Wisconsin.

Chapter 3

1. Edward Berkowitz has written on these matters in greater detail in such publications as *Creating the Welfare State*, paperback edition (Lawrence: University of Kansas Press, 1992) and *America's Welfare State: From Roosevelt to Reagan* (Baltimore, Md., Johns Hopkins University Press, 1991).

2. For a good overview of the development of European social insurance programs, see Daniel Levine, *Poverty and Society: The Growth of the American Welfare State in International Comparison* (New Brunswick, N.J.: Rutgers University Press, 1989). We should stress that social insurance is not an inevitable response to industrialism and that it is heavily influenced by nation-specific cultural factors.

3. See Levine, *Poverty and Society*.

4. See the various papers in Margaret Weir, Ann Shola Orloff, and Theda Skocpol, eds., *The Politics of Social Policy in the United States* (Princeton: Princeton University Press, 1988).

5. These prohibitions are included in the Tenth and Fourteenth Amendments respectively.

6. The logistics of workers' compensation need not concern us here, but see Edward Berkowitz, *Disabled Policy: America's Programs for the Handicapped* (New York: Cambridge University Press, 1987), chapter 2.

7. For a good picture of the effects of the depression, see W. Andrew Achenbaum, *Social Security: Visions and Revisions* (New York: Cambridge University Press, 1986), p. 16, and Irving Bernstein, *A Caring Society* (Boston: Houghton Mifflin, 1985), p. 18.

8. Arthur Altmeyer, *The Formative Years of Social Security* (Madison: University of Wisconsin Press, 1966), pp. 7, ix.

9. Kelley Loe, *An Army of the Aged* (Caldwell, Ind.: Caxton Printers, 1936); Committee on Old-Age Security, *The Townsend Crusade* (New York: Twentieth Century Fund, 1936); Allen Brinkley, *Voices of Protest* (New York: Vintage, 1982).

10. Testimony of Dr. Francis Townsend before House Ways and Means Committee, in *Economic Security Act: Hearings Before the Committee on Ways and Means* (Washington, D.C.: GPO, 1935), p. 680 (hereafter *Hearings*).

11. Townsend testimony, *Hearings*, p. 680.

12. Testimony of Frances Perkins before House Ways and Means Committee, *Hearings*, p. 200.

13. Testimony of Edwin Witte before House Ways and Means Committee, *Hearings*, p. 6.

14. Witte testimony, *Hearings*, p. 83.

15. Witte testimony, *Hearings*, p. 6.

16. The master plan also included voluntary annuities intended, according to Witte, "to give self-employed people, housewives and so forth, the same opportunity

to make their own provisions for old-age that the employed persons are required to make" (Ibid., p. 6). These voluntary annuities met with early opposition in Congress and were quickly dropped from the legislation. In an executive (closed) session of the Ways and Means Committee, supporters of the administration agreed to eliminate the voluntary annuities in return for the committee's support for the compulsory old-age insurance program. The best source for the legislative history of the Act is Edwin E. Witte, *The Development of the Social Security Act* (Madison: University of Wisconsin Press, 1962).

17. See, for example, Barbara N. Armstrong to Murray Latimer, January 22, 1935, Murray Latimer Papers, George Washington University.

18. Congressman McGroaty in *Congressional Record*, 74th Congress, 1st session, 1935, pp. 5794–95.

19. Congressman Mott, ibid., p. 5457.

20. Witte, *Development of the Social Security Act*, pp. 78–79.

21. "Companies Known to Favor the Clark Amendment to the Social Security Act," in Rainard B. Robbins, "Confidential Material Collected on Social Security Act and Clark Amendment," July 11, 1935, Murray Latimer Papers. It is worth noting that the conference had to meet on two separate occasions to resolve the matter.

22. Senator Alben Barkley in *Congressional Record*, 74th Congress, 1st session, 1935, p. 9512.

23. Senator Thomas Connally, ibid.

24. Senator Bennett Champ Clark, ibid.

25. Paul Douglas, *Social Security in the United States* (New York: McGraw Hill, 1936), pp. 271–91.

26. See Rainard B. Robbins, "Supplementary Report on the Proposed Substitute for the Clark Amendment to the Committee on Social Security of the SSRC," May 27, 1936, Murray Latimer Papers.

27. "Cumulative Tax Collections, Benefit Payments, Net Excess of Tax Collections," (n.d.) and "Annual Appropriations, Benefit Payments, and Reserves," (n.d.), File 025, Chairman's Files, RG 47, National Archives.

28. "Text of Governor Landon's Milwaukee Address on Economic Security," *New York Times* (September 26, 1936), p. 31.

29. Edward Berkowitz, "The First Social Security Crisis," *Prologue* (Fall 1983), pp. 132–49.

30. This account of the 1939 amendments draws from Edward D. Berkowitz, "The First Advisory Council and the 1939 Amendments," in *Social Security After Fifty: Successes and Failures*, ed. Edward D. Berkowitz (Westport, Conn.: Greenwood Press, 1987), pp. 55–79.

31. See *Social Security Bulletin: Annual Statistical Supplement, 1981* (Washington, D.C.: Department of Health and Human Services, 1981), pp. 53, 54; Altmeyer, *Formative Years*, pp. 169–70; Mark H. Leff, "Historical Perspectives on Old-Age Insurance: The State of the Art on the Art of the State," in *Social Security After Fifty*, p. 42.

32. Quoted in *Readings in Social Security*, ed. William Haber and Wilbur J. Cohen (New York: Prentice Hall, 1948), p. 255.

33. Altmeyer, *Formative Years*, p. 185; Achenbaum, *Social Security*, p. 45.

34. See, for example, Elizabeth Wickenden, "Comments on Proposed Revised Policy Declaration by the United States Chamber of Commerce on Social Security for the Aged," December 9, 1952, Cohen Papers, Box 51.

35. Eisenhower to Edward F. Hutton, October 7, 1953, Central Files, Box 848, File 156-C, Eisenhower Library.

36. Edward Berkowitz discusses disability insurance at length in *Disabled Policy: America's Programs for the Handicapped* (New York: Cambridge University Press, 1987).

37. Actually, the outcome was more bizarre than that. Congress passed the Çdisability freeze but ruled that it should expire before applications could be taken.

38. See Monte M. Poen, *Harry S Truman Versus the Medical Lobby: The Genesis of Medicare* (Columbia: University of Missouri Press, 1979).

39. See Paul Starr, *The Social Transformation of American Medicine* (New York: Basic Books, 1982).

40. Wilbur Cohen to Ken Hechler, July 12, 1956, Cohen Papers.

41. Cohen to Dr. James K. Hall, August 19, 1961, Cohen Papers.

42. See Alice M. and Howard S. Hoffman eds., *The Cruikshank Chronicles* (Hamden, Conn.: Archon Books, 1989).

43. "Brief Summary of 'Hospital Insurance, Social Security, and Public Assistance Amendments of 1965,'" RG 235, General Counsel Records, Accession 71A-3497, Box 1 File Aw, December 31, 1964, Washington National Records Center, Suitland, Maryland.

44. Wilbur Cohen to the President, March 2, 1965, Cohen Papers.

45. Victor Christgau, "Fact Sheet No. 6—Reductions in Eligibility for Benefits for Men," in *Social Security Amendments of 1961* (Washington, D.C.: U.S. GPO, 1961).

46. Congressman Charles Vanik in *Congressional Record*, April 20, 1961, p. 6110.

47. See Mark H. Leff, "Speculating in Social Security Futures" (unpublished paper).

48. Paul Light, "The Politics of Assumptions" (unpublished paper). See also Paul Light, *Artful Work: The Politics of Social Security Reform* (New York: Random House, 1985), p. 50.

49. The story of the 1983 amendments is one that each of us has told elsewhere. We refer the reader to Edward Berkowitz, *America's Welfare State*, pp. 66–87, and to Eric Kingson, "Financing Social Security: Agenda-Setting and the Enactment of the 1983 Amendments to the Social Security Act," *Policy Studies Journal* 13 (September 1984), pp. 131–56. This chapter contains only some brief additional thoughts on the matter.

50. Quoted in Robert M. Ball, "The Original Understanding on Social Security: Implications for Later Developments," in *Social Security: Beyond the Rhetoric of Crisis*, ed. Theodore R. Marmor and Jerry L. Mashaw (Princeton: Princeton University Press, 1988).

51. Daniel Patrick Moynihan, "More Than Social Security Was at Stake," *Washington Post* (January 5, 1983), p. A-17.

Chapter 4

1. Social Security Administration, "Understanding Social Security," SSA Publication No. 05-10024 (Baltimore, Md.: Department of Health and Human Services, June 1992), p. 6.

2. United States General Accounting Office, *Social Security: Clients Still Rate Quality of Service High* (Gaithersburg, Md.: U.S. General Accounting Office, 1987), p. 2.

3. American Association of Retired Persons, *Toward a Just and Caring Society: The AARP Public Policy Agenda* (Washington, D.C.: American Association of Retired Persons, 1991), p. 56.

4. As discussed by the Social Security and Medicare Board of Trustees, *Status of the Social Security and Medicare Programs: A Summary of the 1992 Annual Reports* (Washington, D.C.: U.S. GPO, April 1992): "People who are self-employed are charged the equivalent of the combined employer and employee shares, but only on 92.35 percent of net earnings, and may deduct one-half of the combined tax from income subject to federal income tax."

5. Beginning in 1984, the self-employment tax rate became essentially the same as the combined payroll tax rate paid by workers and their employers. In 1989, a tax credit of 2.0 percent of net earnings from self-employment was provided against OASDI and HI contributions. After 1989 self-employed persons were allowed a federal income tax deduction equal to half of the combined OASDI and HI contributions they pay.

6. Social Security Administration, "Survivors," SSA Publication No. 05-10084 (Baltimore, Md.: Department of Health and Human Services, January 1991), p. 3.

7. Social Security Administration, "Survivors," p. 3.

8. U.S. House of Representatives, Committee on Ways and Means, *Background Material and Data on Programs Within the Jurisdiction of the Committee on Ways and Means* (Washington, D.C.: U.S. GPO, 1991), pp. 730–71.

9. Social Security Administration, "Medicare," SSA Publication No. 05-10043 (Baltimore, Md.: Department of Health and Human Services, January 1991), p. 15.

10. Social Security Administration, "Medicare," pp. 15–18, and U.S. House of Representatives, Committee on Ways and Means, *Background Material and Data on Programs Within the Jurisdiction of the Committee on Ways and Means* (Washington, D.C.: U.S. GPO, 1986).

Chapter 5

1. See Robert Atchley, *The Sociology of Retirement* (New York: Wiley/Schenkman, 1971). See also Juanita M. Kreps and Joseph J. Spengler, "The Leisure Component of Economic Growth," in National Commission on Technology, Automation, and Economic Progress, *Technology and the Economy*, appendix 2 (Washington, D.C.: U.S. GPO, 1966), and William Graebner, *A History of Retirement: The Meaning and Function of an American Institution, 1885–1978* (New Haven, Conn: Yale University Press, 1980).

2. James H. Schulz, *The Economics of Aging* (Westport, Conn: Auburn House, 1992), p. 18.

3. See Yung-Ping Chen, "Economic Status of the Aging," in *Handbook of Aging and the Social Sciences* (New York: Van Nostrand Reinhold, 1985), ed. Robert H. Binstock and Ethel Shanus. See also Robert L. Clark and David L. Baumer, "Income Maintenance Policies," ibid., and Schulz, *Economics of Aging*.

4. U.S. Senate Special Committee on Aging, in conjunction with the American Association of Retired Persons, the Federal Council on Aging, and the U.S. Administration on Aging, *Aging America: Trends and Projections: 1991 Edition* (Washington, D.C.: U.S. GPO, 1991), p. 60.

5. U.S. House of Representatives, Committee on Ways and Means, *Background Material and Data on Programs Within the Jurisdiction of the Committee on Ways and Means* (Washington, D.C.: U.S. GPO, 1991), p. 1102.

6. For those unfamiliar with the poverty measure, we provide a brief overview of some of the pros and cons of this methodology here. It is based on 1956 Consumer Expenditure Survey data showing that the typical American family spends about one-third of its income on food. Based on this and the Department of Agriculture's estimate of the cost of an emergency food plan, poverty thresholds were developed in 1966 for various types of families, with adjustment for family size, composition of family, age of head, and farm versus non-farm families. These thresholds are updated yearly for changes in the cost of living. Some consider the poverty measure to be unrealistically low, given that more recent survey data show that housing has become a more costly part of household budgets and food less so. Others have questioned establishing substantially lower poverty thresholds for elderly individuals and couples ($6,532 and $8,241, respectively, in 1991) as compared to individuals and couples under 65 ($7,086 and $9,165, respectively, in 1991). Others have suggested that the thresholds are too high because they do not take into account the value of in-kind benefits such as Medicare and Medicaid which are so important for the elderly. For our purposes, the poverty measure, though not flawless, is useful because it provides a good basis for charting the economic progress of the elderly over time and is one useful means of examining variation of economic status among the elderly. Further, it is a reasonable way of identifying those likely to be in difficult economic circumstances since, regardless of whether it is set high or low, few could argue that it represents a "plush" standard of living.

7. Joseph F. Quinn, "The Economic Status of the Elderly: Beware of the Mean," *The Review of Income and Wealth* 33 (March 1987), p. 64.

8. Bureau of the Census, "Money Income of Households, Families, and Persons in the United States: 1991," *Current Population Reports*, P-60, No. 180 (Washington, D.C.: U.S. GPO, August 1992), table 2, p. 5.

9. U.S. House of Representatives, Committee on Ways and Means, *Background Material and Data on Programs Within the Jurisdiction of the Committee on Ways and Means* (Washington, D.C.: U.S. GPO, 1992), pp. 1239, 1240 (hereafter House Committee, *Data 1992*), and Bureau of the Census, "Money Income and Poverty in the United States: 1990," *Current Population Reports*, P-60, No. 175 (Washington, D.C.: U.S. GPO, September 1991).

10. House Committee, *Data 1992*, table 14, pp. 1249–50.

11. Ibid.

12. Schulz, *Economics of Aging*, pp. 95–105.

13. Data from House Committee, *Data 1992*, p. 12. These data are based on the same assumptions about demographic economic change as are used to project Social Security's financing under alternative II, the most commonly accepted set of assumptions.

14. See Richard D. Lamm, *Mega-Traumas: America at the Year 2000* (Boston: Houghton Mifflin, 1985); Richard D. Lamm, "The Ten Commandments of an Aging Society (Denver, Colo.: Center for Public Policy and Contemporary Issues, 1987) in mimeo; Phillip Longman, "Justice Between Generations," *Atlantic Monthly* 256 (1985), pp. 73–81: Phillip Longman, *Born to Pay: The New Politics of Aging in America* (Boston: Houghton Mifflin, 1987); Peter G. Petersen and Neil Howe, *On Borrowed Time* (San Francisco: Institute for Contemporary Studies, 1988).

15. Eric R. Kingson, *The Diversity of the Baby Boom: Implications for Their Retirement Years* (Washington, D.C.: AARP Forecasting and Environmental Scanning Department, 1992), pp. 29–36.

16. U.S. House of Representatives, Committee on Ways and Means, *Retirement Income for An Aging Society* (Washington, D.C.: U.S. GPO, 1987), p. 354 (hereafter House Committee, *Retirement Income*).

17. Robert M. Ball, "Comment," in *Social Security and Private Pensions: Providing for Retirement in the Twenty-First Century*, ed. Susan M. Wachter (Lexington, Mass.: Lexington Books, 1988), pp. 104–5.

18. Emily S. Andrews and Deborah Chollet, "Future Sources of Retirement Income: Whither the Baby Boom," in *Social Security and Private Pensions*, pp. 91–92; House Committee, *Retirement Income*, p. 65.

19. Andrews and Chollet, "Future Sources of Retirement Income," pp. 91–92.

20. Kingson, *Diversity of the Baby Boom*, pp. 45–48.

21. William C. Apgar, Jr., Denise DiPasquale, Nancy McArdle, and Jennifer Olson, *The State of the Nation's Housing 1989* (Cambridge, Mass.: Harvard University Joint Center for Housing Studies, 1990), p. 20; John L. Palmer, "Financing Health Care and Retirement for the Aged," in Employee Benefit Research Institute, *Business, Work, and Benefits: Adjusting to Change* (Washington, D.C.: Employee Benefit Research Institute, 1989), p. 90.

22. Palmer, "Financing Health Care and Retirement for the Aged," pp. 89–90.

23. House Committee, *Retirement Income*, p. 354; and Andrews and Chollet, "Future Sources of Retirement Income," p. 72.

24. House Committee, *Retirement Income*, p. 354.

25. See, for instance, House Committee, *Retirement Income*, p. 353; and Michael D. Hurd, "Forecasting the Consumption and Wealth of the Elderly," in *Social Security and Private Pensions*, pp. 47–69.

26. Hurd, "Forecasting the Consumption and Wealth of the Elderly," p. 62.

27. House Committee, *Retirement Income*, pp. 65–66.

28. Elizabeth Wickenden, *Fact Sheet no. 13* (New York: Study Group on Social Security, 1984).

29. The reduction of 28½ percent of the PIA for those accepting benefits at age 60 will not change.

30. Frank Sammartino, "The Effect of Health on Retirement," *Social Security Bulletin* 50, 2 (February 1987), p. 41.

31. See Regina O'Grady-LeShane, Testimony before the Subcommittee on Retirement Income and Employment, U.S. House Committee on Aging, May 15, 1992.

32. Save Our Security, "Unfinished Business—Adequacy and Equity for Women in the Social Security System: Modified Earnings Sharing as an Approach" (Washington, DC: Save Our Security).

Chapter 6

1. Advisory Council on Social Security, *A Message from the American Public: A Report of a National Survey on Health and Social Security by the Advisory Council on Social Security* (Washington, D.C.: U.S. GPO, December 1991), pp. 20–24. Similar findings from a poll conducted in 1991 by the American Council on Life Insurance are

reported in this volume, indicating that 45 percent of the public report that they are not confident (50 percent are confident) "in the future of the Social Security system."

2. Board of Trustees, Federal Old-Age and Survivors Insurance and Disability Insurance Trust Funds, *1992 Annual Report of the Federal Old-Age and Survivors Insurance and Disability Insurance Trust Funds* (Washington, D.C.: U.S. GPO, 1992), p. 22 (hereafter Board of Trustees, OASDI, *1992 Annual Report*).

3. Board of Trustees, OASDI, *1992 Annual Report.*

4. Board of Trustees, OASDI, *1992 Annual Report.*

5. See, for example, the proposals put forth by Peter G. Petersen and Neil Howe in *On Borrowed Time* (San Francisco: Institute for Contemporary Studies, 1989).

6. Robert M. Ball, "Social Security Across the Generations," in John R. Gist, *Social Security and the Economic Well-Being Across Generations* (Washington, D.C.: Public Policy Institute of the American Association of Retired Persons, 1988), pp. 24–25.

7. Robert J. Myers, "Rebuttal to 'Why the Social Security Tax Rate Should Not Be Reduced,'" in *Social Insurance Update* (Washington, D.C.: National Academy of Social Insurance, June, 1990). See also Robert J. Myers, "Social Security's Health Is Robust," in *Generational Journal* 2, 1 (April 30, 1989), pp. 123–31.

8. See, for example, A. Haeworth Robertson, *The Coming Revolution in Social Security* (Reston, Va.: Reston Publishing Company, 1981), and A. Haeworth Robertson, *Social Security: What Every Taxpayer Should Know* (Washington, D.C.: Retirement Policy Institute, 1992).

9. Robertson, *Social Security: What Every Taxpayer Should Know*, p. 281.

10. Some funds are also invested in federally guaranteed securities and in securities issued by federally sponsored agencies. In actuality, however, almost all the trust fund investments are in special U.S. Treasury securities. See Board of Trustees, OASDI, *1992 Annual Report*, p. 8.

11. See Board of Trustees, OASDI, *1992 Annual Report*, p. 106.

12. See Board of Trustees, Federal Hospital Insurance Trust Fund, *1992 Annual Report of the Board of Trustees of the Federal Hospital Insurance Trust Fund* (Washington, D.C.: U.S. GPO, 1992), p. 8.

13. See Board of Trustees, *1992 Annual Report*, p. 18.

14. James H. Schulz, *The Economics of Aging* (Westport, Conn.: Auburn House, 1992), p. 161. In making this point, Schulz also cites Robert J. Myers, *Social Security* (Philadelphia: University of Pennsylvania Press, 1991).

15. Schulz, *Economics of Aging*, pp. 161–62.

16. Similar points are made by Theodore R. Marmor, Jerry L. Mashaw, and Philip L. Harvey in *America's Misunderstood Welfare State: Persistent Myths, Enduring Realities* (New York: Basic Books, 1990), pp. 216–19.

17. As defined in the Board of Trustees, OASDI, *1992 Annual Report*, the "real-wage difference is the difference between the percentage increases, before rounding, in (1) the annual average wage in covered employment, and (2) the average annual Consumer Price Index."

18. Board of Trustees, OASDI, *1992 Annual Report.*

19. Board of Trustees, Federal Old-Age and Survivors Insurance and Disability Trust Funds, *1988 Annual Report of the Federal Old-Age and Survivors Insurance and Disability Insurance Trust Funds* (Washington, D.C.: U.S. GPO, 1988).

20. David Koitz, "The Financial Outlook for Social Security and Medicare," *CRS Report for Congress* (November 26, 1991), p. 3.

21. A similar discussion and more expanded discussion of these two perspectives can be found in Eric R. Kingson, "The Greying of the Baby Boom in the United States: Framing the Policy Debate," *International Social Security Review* 44, 1–2, (1991), pp. 11–13. Similar points are made by Marmor, Mashaw, and Harvey in *Misunderstood Welfare State*, pp. 128–74.

22. Marmor, Mashaw, and Harvey in *Misunderstood Welfare State*, p. 136.

23. Petersen and Howe, *On Borrowed Time*.

24. Peter J. Ferrara, "The Prospect of Real Reform," *Cato Journal* 3, 2 (Fall 1983), pp. 609–21.

25. See, for example, the proposals put forth by Petersen and Howe in *On Borrowed Time*.

26. Gregory Spencer, "Projection of the Population of the United States, by Age, Sex, Race, and Hispanic Origin: 1992 to 2050," Bureau of the Census, *Current Population Reports*, P-25, no. 1092 (Washington, D.C.: U.S. GPO, November 1992), tables G and 2, pp. xiv–xv, 12.

27. Board of Trustees, OASDI, *1992 Annual Report*, p. 127. This trend can also be shown by comparing the change in number of beneficiaries per 100 covered workers. The number of beneficiaries (30 in 1991) for every 100 workers covered under Social Security has been quite stable since 1975. However, under the intermediate projections, this number is projected to increase to 37 beneficiaries per 100 workers in 2015, 49 per hundred in 2030, and 52 per hundred in 2050.

28. See William H. Crown, 'Some Thoughts on Reformulating the Dependency Ratio," *The Gerontologist* 24 (April 1985), pp. 166–71.

29. See Barbara Boyle Torrey, "Guns vs. Canes: The Fiscal Implications of an Aging Population," *AEA Papers and Proceedings* 72, 2 (n.d.).

30. Drawn from Eric R. Kingson, Barbara A. Hirshorn, and John M. Cornman, *Ties That Bind: The Interdependence of Generations* (Cabin John, Md.: Seven Locks Press, 1986), pp. 139–40. Supplemented by data from Spencer, "Population Projections of the United States," table 2, pp. 48–57.

31. Data from Board of Trustees, OASDI, *1992 Annual Report*, p. 87.

32. Board of Trustees, OASDI, *1992 Annual Report*, pp. 5, 130.

33. Koitz, "Financial Outlook for Social Security and Medicare," p. 2.

34. Kingson, "The Greying of the Baby Boom in the United States," p. 18.

35. Koitz, "Financial Outlook for Social Security and Medicare," p. 4.

36. See presentations by Henry Aaron, "We Are on the Right Track," Robert Myers, "Modifying Our Present Course," and Robert Ball, discussant, in *Conference Proceedings, Social Security Trust Funds: Issues for the 1990s and Beyond* (Washington, D.C.: Public Policy Institute, American Association of Retired Persons, February 23, 1989).

37. Many of the arguments presented in this paragraph can be found in Eduard A. Lopez, "Why Social Security Financing Should Be Reformed: A Response to Alice M. Rivlin," *Social Insurance Update* 21 (December 1991), and in Robert Myers, "Modifying Our Present Course," in *Conference Proceedings, Social Security Trust Funds*.

38. Schulz, *Economics of Aging*, p. 169.

39. Henry J. Aaron, Barry Bosworth, and Gary Burtless, *Can America Afford to Grow Old?* (Washington, D.C.: Brookings Institution, 1989), pp. 124–25.

40. Board of Trustees, OASDI, *1992 Annual Report*, p. 33.

41. Schulz, *Economics of Aging*, p. 182.

42. Schulz, *Economics of Aging*, p. 183.

43. These base amounts include adjusted gross income, plus one-half of Social Security income, plus certain non-taxable income such as interest from municipal bonds.

44. Board of Trustees, OASDI, *1992 Annual Report*, p. 106.

45. This would result in treating Social Security benefits in roughly the same manner as private pension and public pension benefits. The tax principle that is applied in these other pensions is that the individual's contribution should not be subject to taxation but that the portion of the benefit that exceeds that contribution should.

Chapter 7

1. Subrata N. Chakravarty and K. Weisman, "Consuming Our Children," *Forbes* (November 14, 1988), p. 225.

2. See Robert Pear, "U.S. Pension Funds Lift Many of Poor," *New York Times* (December 28, 1988), p. 1. See also U.S. House of Representatives, Committee on Ways and Means, *Overview of Entitlement Programs: 1992 Green Book* (Washington, D.C.: U.S. GPO, May 15, 1992), pp. 1301–14.

3. Advisory Council on Social Security, *Future Financial Resources of the Elderly: A View of Pensions, Savings, Social Security, and Earnings in the 21st Century* (Washington, D.C.: U.S. GPO, December 1991), p. 26.

4. Susan Grad, *Income of the Population 55 and Over, 1986*, prepared for the Social Security Administration (Washington, D.C.: U.S. GPO, June 1988), p. 83.

5. Theodore R. Marmor, Jerry L. Mashaw, and Philip L. Harvey, *America's Misunderstood Welfare State: Persistent Myths, Enduring Realities* (New York: Basic Books, 1990),
p. 223.

6. James H. Schulz, *The Economics of Aging* (Westport, Conn.: Auburn House), p. 145.

7. See U.S. House of Representatives, Committee on Ways and Means, *Background Material and Data on Programs Within the Jurisdiction of the Committee on Ways and Means* (Washington, D.C.: U.S. GPO, 1992), p. 1239 (hereafter House Committee, *Data 1992*).

8. Emily S. Andrews and Deborah Chollet, "Future Sources of Retirement Income: Whither the Baby Boom," in *Social Security and Private Pensions: Providing for Retirement in the Twenty-First Century*, ed. Susan M. Wachter (Lexington, Mass.: Lexington Books, 1988), pp. 91–92. See also Advisory Council on Social Security, *Social Security and the Future Financial Status of Women* (Washington, D.C.: U.S. GPO, December 1991), p. 5.

9. Regina O'Grady-LeShane, Testimony before the Subcommittee on Retirement Income and Employment, U.S. House Committee on Aging, May 15, 1992.

10. Arlene F. Saluter, "Changes in American Family Life," Bureau of the Census, *Current Population Reports*, P-23, no. 163 (Washington, D.C.: U.S. Bureau of the Census, August 1989), p. 7.

11. Laurel Beedon, "Women and Social Security: Challenges Facing the American System of Social Insurance," *Issue Brief* (Washington, D.C.: Public Policy Institute of the American Association of Retired Persons, February 1991), pp. 4–5.

12. These benefits were later extended to husbands as well, and today the program does not distinguish between husbands and wives (widows and widowers) with respect to benefit provision.

13. For discussion of women's earnings, see Diana M. DiNitto, *Social Welfare: Politics and Public Policy* (Englewood Cliffs, N.J.: Prentice Hall, 1991), p. 237.

14. O'Grady-LeShane testimony, May 15, 1992.

15. Saluter, "Changes in American Family Life," p. 7.

16. Beedon, "Women and Social Security," p. 8.

17. National Center for Health Statistics, "Life Tables," *Vital Statistics of the United States, 1987*, vol. 2, sect. 6 (February 1990) as cited in U.S. Senate, Special Committee on Aging, in conjunction with the American Association of Retired Persons, the Federal Council on Aging, and the U.S. Administration on Aging, *Aging America: Trends and Projections: 1991 Edition* (Washington, D.C.: U.S. GPO, 1991), p. 20. Interestingly, as reported on page 25 of this report, life expectancy for African Americans at age 80 is higher than it is for white Americans. However, in a personal communication (September 1992), Robert J. Myers cautions that this may well be due to faulty data and reporting.

18. Robert J. Myers, "Skewed Data Hurt *Times'* Social Security Editorial," letter to the editor, *Washington Times* (May 31, 1988).

19. These issues were discussed by the 1979 Advisory Council on Social Security, *Social Security Financing and Benefits* (Washington, D.C.: U.S. GPO, 1980), pp. 113–14.

20. Advisory Council on Social Security, *Social Security Financing and Benefits*, pp. 113–14.

21. Stephen Labaton, "Benefits Are Refused More Often to Disabled Blacks, Study Finds," *New York Times* (May 11, 1992), p. 1, A12.

22. General Accounting Office report, as cited by Labaton, "Benefits are Refused More Often to Disabled Blacks," p. 1, A12.

23. Paralleling these staff reductions and the related closing of some field offices is a growing emphasis on increased automation and on trying to get the public to do much more of their business (e.g., claims) via telephone. Those favoring further staff reductions point to faster processing times for claims and other improvements in efficiency. They argue that as automation proceeds it is reasonable to expect that the same level of public service can be provided by fewer people. Further, the increased ability to transact business with SSA via the telephone is often a convenience for the applicant, and survey results from a study conducted by the U.S. General Accounting Office in 1987 suggest that the public is generally satisfied with the service provided by SSA. See U.S. General Accounting Office, *Social Security: Clients Still Rate Quality of Service High* (Washington, D.C.: U.S. GPO, July 1987). It should also be noted that a related GAO study identifies serious management problems that "could interfere with SSA's ability to accomplish its mission effectively in the future." See GAO, *Social Security Administration: Stable Leadership and Better Management Needed to Improve Effectiveness* (Washington, D.C.: U.S. GPO, March 1987).

24. It is also probable that in some cases this works to the advantage of applicants since some claims may also be approved that would otherwise be denied if claims representatives had more time to devote to each application.

25. Eileen Sweeney, then with National Senior Citizen Law Center (now Children's Defense Fund), personal communication, December 30, 1988.

26. Social Security Administration, *Annual Report to Congress* (Baltimore, Md.: Social Security Administration, April 1992), p. 22.

27. These changes were recommended by the 1979 Advisory Council on Social Security, *Social Security Financing and Benefits* (Baltimore, Md.: Social Security Administration, 1979), p. 123.

28. Substantial portions of this discussion of the notch issue are drawn from Eric Kingson, Testimony before the Subcommittee on Social Security, Ways and Means Committee Subcommittee on Social Security, House of Representatives, July 23, 1992.

29. Schulz, *Economics of Aging*, p. 165.

30. From statement of the founding chairman of the National Committee to Preserve Social Security and Medicare. See James Roosevelt, *USA Today* (January 27, 1989).

31. Schulz, *Economics of Aging*, p. 165.

32. These proposals do more than simply lengthen the transition period. They also give partial windfalls.

33. See chapter 7 in U.S. General Accounting Office, *Social Security: The Notch Issue* (Washington, D.C.: U.S. GPO, March 1988), and see Joseph F. Defico, "Comments on the Social Security Notch Issue," director, Income Security Issues Human Resources Divisions, U.S. General Accounting Office, Testimony before the Subcommittee on Social Security, Ways and Means Committee, July 23, 1992.

34. National Academy of Social Insurance, *The Social Security Benefit Notch: A Study* (Washington, D.C.: National Academy of Social Insurance, November 1988), p. 5.

35. Chakravarty and Weisman, "Consuming Our Children," p. 225.

36. Laurence J. Kotlikoff, *Generational Accounting: Knowing Who Pays, and When, for What We Spend* (New York: Free Press, 1992), p. 36.

37. Anthony Pellechio and Gordon Goodfellow, "Individual Gains and Losses from Social Security Before and After the 1983 Amendments," *Cato Journal* 3, 2 (Fall 1983), pp. 440–42.

38. Geoffrey Kollman, "How Long Does It Take New Retirees to Recover the Value of Their Social Security Taxes?"CRS Report for Congress (January 15, 1992), pp. 1–2.

39. Eric R. Kingson, Barbara A. Hirshorn, and John M. Cornman, *Ties That Bind: The Interdependence of Generations* (Cabin John, Md.: Seven Locks Press, 1986), pp. 93–94.

40. Henry Aaron, *Economic Effects of Social Security* (Washington, D.C.: Brookings Institution, 1982), p. 78.

41. Robert M. Ball, "Social Security Across the Generations," in John R. Gist, *Social Security and the Economic Well-Being Across Generations* (Washington, D.C.: Public Policy Institute of the American Association of Retired Persons, 1988), p. 27.

42. Merton C. Bernstein and Joan Brodshaug Bernstein, *Social Security: The System That Works* (New York: Basic Books, 1988), p. 236.

43. Nelson Cruikshank (1987, in mimeo).

44. See House Committee, *Data 1992*, pp. 1142–44.

45. See House Committee, *Data 1992*, pp. 1116–17.

46. House Committee, *Data 1992*, p. 1079.

47. Bureau of the Census, "Poverty in the United States: 1991," *Current Population Reports*, P-60, No. 181 (Washington, DC: U.S. GPO, August 1992), table 3, pp. 4–5.

48. House Committee, *Data 1992*, pp. 1578–83.

49. Robert J. Myers, "Income of Social Security Beneficiaries as Affected by Earnings Test and Income Taxes on Benefits," *Journal of Risk and Insurance* (June 1985).

50. Congressional Budget Office estimate as reported in House Committee, *Data 1992*, p. 21.

51. Congressional Budget Office estimate as reported in House Committee, *Data 1992*, p. 22.

Chapter 8

1. This chapter provides only a brief introduction to disability policy. Edward Berkowitz has written many other books and articles on this subject, to which we direct the reader for more information. These include *Disabled Policy: America's Programs for the Handicapped—A Twentieth Century Fund Report* (New York: Cambridge University Press, 1987; paperback edition, 1989). He has also edited *Disability Programs and Government Policies* (New York: Praeger Press, 1979). Other articles and reports on particular aspects of disability policy include: "Emerging Issues in Disability Policy," in Special Committee on Aging, United States Senate, *Fifty Years of Social Security: Past Achievements and Future Challenges* (Washington, DC: U.S. GPO, August 1985); Testimony Prepared for the Senate Committee on Labor and Public Welfare in Consideration of the Americans with Disabilities Act, May 1989, reprinted in *Congressional Digest* 68 (December 1989), pp. 304–12 [with David Dean]; "One Comprehensive System? A Historical Perspective on Federal Disability Policy," *Journal of Disability Policy Studies* (Fall 1990), pp. 1–19 [with Richard Scotch]; "Rehabilitation in the Work Injury Program," *Rehabilitation Counseling Bulletin* 34 (March 1991), pp. 182–96 [with Monroe Berkowitz]; "Domestic Politics and International Expertise in the History of American Disability Policy," *Milbank Memorial Quarterly* 67, Supplement 2, Part 1 (1989), pp. 195–227; "Allocating Resources for Rehabilitation: A Historical and Ethical Framework," *Social Science Quarterly* (March 1989), pp. 40–52; "Incentives for Reducing the Costs of Disability," in Jack Meyer and Ken McLennan, eds., *Care and Cost: Current Issues in Health Policy* (Boulder, Colo.: Westview Press, 1989), pp. 203–26 [with Monroe Berkowitz]; "The Struggle for Compromise: Social Security Disability Insurance, 1935–1986," *Journal of Policy History* 1, 3 (1989), pp. 233–60 [with Daniel Fox]; "The Cost-Benefit Tradition in Vocational Rehabilitation," in *Measuring the Efficiency of Public Programs*, ed. Monroe Berkowitz (Philadelphia: Temple University Press, 1988), pp. 10–28; "Disability Insurance and the Social Security Tradition," in *Social Security: The First Half Century*, ed. Gerald D. Nash, Noel H. Pugach, and Richard F. Tomasson (Albuquerque: University of New Mexico Press, 1988), pp. 279–98; "Disability Insurance and the Limits of American History," *The Public Historian* (Spring 1986), pp. 65–82 [with Wendy Wolff].

2. Refers to the federal fiscal year.

3. Once on the Disability Insurance rolls, there is a trial work provision which allows beneficiaries to continue to receive Medicare benefits alone for a limited period of time.

4. We take this definition from the classic work of Saad Nagi, a sociologist

who has devoted considerable time and attention to defining and measuring disability.

5. Robert Myers observes that some lawyers have a bad effect on the disability program and the public by delaying the application and appeals process in order to charge their clients more and by coaching "people to give the 'right,' though fraudulent answers." Personal communication, September 1992.

6. Quoted in Berkowitz, *Disabled Policy*, p. 80, quoting a statement of congressional intent made in 1967.

7. In 1992 the substantial gainful activity level was set at $500 a month (net of impairment-related work expenses) for most workers with disabilities and $850 a month for those who are blind.

8. This description is drawn from Berkowitz, *Disabled Policy*, pp. 102–3.

9. John M. McNeil, "Labor Force Status and Other Characteristics of Persons with Work Disability: 1982," Bureau of the Census, *Current Population Reports*, Special Studies, P-23, no. 127 (Washington, D.C.: U.S. GPO, 1983).

10. Jonathan Leonard, "Social Security Disability Program and Labor Force Participation," Working Paper 392, National Bureau of Economic Research, Cambridge Mass.; Jonathan Leonard, "Labor Supply Incentives and Disincentives for Disabled Persons," in *Disability and the Labor Market*, ed. Monroe Berkowitz and M. Anne Hill (Ithaca, N.Y.: Industrial and Labor Relations Press, 1986), pp. 64–94.

11. Robert H. Haveman, Barbara L. Wolfe, and Jennifer L. Warlick, "Disability Transfer, Early Retirement, and Retrenchment," in *Retirement and Economic Behavior*, ed. Henry Aaron and Gary Burtless (Washington, D.C.: Brookings Institution, 1984), p. 77.

12. Edward Berkowitz, "The Cost-Benefit Tradition in Vocational Rehabilitation."

13. Monroe Berkowitz and others, "An Economic Evaluation of the Beneficiary Rehabilitation Program," in *Alternatives in Rehabilitating the Handicapped—A Policy Analysis*, ed. Jeffrey Rubin (New York: Human Services Press, 1982), pp. 1–87.

14. I take my sense of the bill from 101st Congress, 1st Session, *Senate Report 101-116*, "The Americans with Disabilities Act of 1989," August 30, 1989 (hereafter *Senate Report*); see especially p. 2.

15. Coehlo's remarks are quoted in Burgdorf to the National Council, July 28, 1988.

16. *Senate Report*, p. 6.

17. Quoted in *Senate Report*, p. 16.

18. *Senate Report*, p. 17.

19. Berkowitz and Dean, 1989, p. 308.

20. *Senate Report*, p. 90.

21. See Martha Derthick, *Agency Under Stress: The Social Security Administration in American Government* (Washington, D.C.: Brookings Institution, 1990).

22. Richard V. Burkhauser, "Beyond Stereotypes: Public Policy and the Doubly Disabled," *American Enterprise* 3, 5 (September/October 1992), pp. 60–69.

Chapter 9

1. James F. Fries, "The Workspan and the Compression of Morbidity," in *Proceedings of the Second Conference of the National Academy of Social Insurance* (Washington,

D.C.: National Academy of Social Insurance, 1991) (hereafter *Proceedings*), pp. 17–18.

2. See Robert Butler, Testimony before the National Commission of Social Security Reform (1982); Jacob J. Feldman, "Work Ability of the Aged Under Conditions of Improving Mortality," *Milbank Memorial Fund Quarterly/Health and Society* 61, 3 (1983), pp. 430–44; Jacob J. Feldman, "Has Increased Longevity Increased Potential Worklife?" in *Proceedings*; Lois M. Verbrugge, "Comment," in *Proceedings*.

3. U.S. Senate Special Committee on Aging, in conjunction with the American Association of Retired Persons, the Federal Council on Aging, and the U.S. Administration on Aging, *Aging America: Trends and Projections: 1991 Edition* (Washington, D.C.: U.S. GPO, 1991), pp. 108–9 (hereafter *Aging America*).

4. See U.S. House of Representatives, Committee on Ways and Means, *Background Material and Data on Programs Within the Jurisdiction of the Committee on Ways and Means* (Washington, DC: U.S. GPO, 1992), pp. 263–64 (hereafter House Committee, *Data 1992*).

5. Robert L. Kane and Rosalie A. Kane, "Health Care for Older People: Organizational and Policy Issues," in *Handbook of Aging and the Social Sciences*, ed. Robert H. Binstock and Ethel S. Shanas (New York: Academic Press, 1990), p. 423.

6. Data from Joel Leon and T. Liar, "Functional Status of the Noninstitutionalized Elderly: Estimates of ADL and IADL Difficulties," DHHS Pub. No. (PHS)90-3462 (June 1990), as cited in *Aging America*, p. 154.

7. Kane and Kane, "Health Care for Older People," p. 421.

8. "Custodial nursing home costs" are included in the calculation of "health care costs." If they were not, then Medicare would be considered as paying a higher proportion of health care costs.

9. *Aging America*, pp. 131–32, 137.

10. *Aging America*, pp. 138–41.

11. Kane and Kane, "Health Care for Older People," p. 424.

12. James H. Schulz, *The Economics of Aging*, (Westport, Conn.: Auburn House), p. 192.

13. See House Committee, *Data 1992*, pp. 284–85.

14. Milt Freudenheim, "Medical Insurance Is Being Cut Back for Many Retirees," *New York Times* (June 26, 1992), pp. 1, 20.

15. See House Committee, *Data 1992*, p. 255.

16. Mark Schlesinger and Terrie Wetle, "Medicare's Coverage of Health Services," in *Renewing the Promise: Medicare and Its Reform*, ed. David Blumenthal, Mark Schlesinger, and Pamela Brown Drumheller (New York: Oxford University Press, 1988), p. 66.

17. Schulz, *Economics of Aging*, p. 204.

18. Fernando Torres-Gil, "Seniors React to the Medicare Catastrophic Bill: Equity or Selfishness?" *Journal of Aging and Social Policy* 2, 1 (1990), pp. 1–2.

19. Harvard Medicare Project, "The Future of Medicare," in *Renewing the Promise: Medicare and Its Reform*, pp. 178–79.

20. House Committee, *Data 1992*, p. 280.

21. Advisory Council on Social Security, *The Financing and Delivery of Long-Term Care Services: A Review of Current Problems and Potential Reform Options* (Washington, D.C.: U.S. GPO, December 1991), pp. 12–13 (hereafter Advisory Council, *Financ-*

ing). See also Advisory Council on Social Security, *Commitment to Change: Foundations for Reform* (Washington, D.C.: U.S. GPO, December 1991), p. 51.

22. See discussion in Kane and Kane, "Health Care for Older People," p. 432.

23. Advisory Council on Social Security, *Income Security and Health Care: Economic Implications 1991–2020* (Washington, D.C.: U.S. GPO, December 1991), pp. 10, 133–35.

24. John L. Palmer, "Financing Health Care and Retirement for the Aged," in Employee Benefit Research Institute, *Business, Work, and Benefits: Adjusting to Change* (Washington, D.C.: Employee Benefit Research Institute, 1989), p. 91.

25. Advisory Council on Social Security, *Commitment to Change*, p. 41.

26. Kane and Kane, "Health Care for Older People," p. 427.

27. Kane and Kane, "Health Care for Older People," p. 426.

28. House Committee, *Data 1992*, p. 425.

29. Harvard Medicare Project, "The Future of Medicare," pp. 181–82.

30. Harvard Medicare Project, "The Future of Medicare," pp. 181–82. Except for the ombudsman, similar recommendations were made by the Advisory Council on Social Security, *Commitment to Change*, pp. 124–27.

31. Many of these points are also made by Schulz, *Economics of Aging*, pp. 200–202.

32. Alice M. Rivlin and Joshua M. Weiner, with Raymond J. Hanley and Denise A. Spence, *Caring for the Disabled Elderly: Who Will Pay?* (Washington, D.C.: Brookings Institution, 1988), pp. 8–9.

33. Rivlin, Weiner, Hanley, and Spence, *Caring for the Disabled Elderly*, p. 17.

34. Many of these points about continuing care retirement communities and home equity conversions are based on discussion found in Rivlin, Weiner, Hanley, and Spence, *Caring for the Disabled Elderly*, pp. 18–23.

35. Advisory Council, *Financing*, p. 39.

36. Advisory Council, *Financing*, pp. 39–40, and Rivlin, Weiner, Hanley, and Spence, *Caring for the Disabled Elderly*, p. 26.

37. Advisory Council, *Financing*, pp. 40–41.

38. See House Committee, *Data 1992*, pp. 274–75.

39. Advisory Council, *Financing*, p. 41.

40. See House Committee, *Data 1992*, pp. 286–88.

41. Advisory Council on Social Security, *Commitment to Change*, p. 55.

42. Advisory Council on Social Security, *Commitment to Change*, pp. 50–84.

43. Thomas E. Getzen, "Aging and the Growth of Health Care Expenditures," *Journal of Gerontology: Social Sciences* 47, 3 (May 1992), p. 103.

44. Advisory Council on Social Security, *Income Security and Health Care*, p. 8.

45. Getzen, "Aging and the Growth of Health Care Expenditures," p. 103.

46. Board of Trustees, Federal Hospital Insurance Trust Fund, *1992 Annual Report of the Board of Trustees of the Federal Hospital Insurance Trust Fund* (Washington, D.C.: U.S. GPO, 1992), p. 3. (Somewhat sooner under the intermediate assumptions used in the 1993 HI Trustees Report which was released as this book went to the printer.)

47. Board of Trustees, Federal Hospital Insurance Trust Fund, *1992 Annual Report*, p. 3.

48. Some of these points are also made by Nancy J. Altman, Alicia H. Munnell, and James M. Verdier, "Medicare Financing: The Government's Share," in *Renewing the Promise*, pp. 160–75.

49. Altman, Munnell, and Verdier, "Medicare Financing: The Government's Share," p. 174.

50. Daniel Callahan, *What Kind of Life: The Limits of Medical Progress* (New York: Simon and Schuster, 1990), p. 202. See also Daniel Callahan, *Setting Limits: The Medical Goals in an Aging Society* (New York: Simon and Schuster, 1987). See also discussions of Callahan's ideas by Robert L. Barry and Gerard V. Bradley, "Epilogue: Will the Real Daniel Callahan Stand up?" in *Set No Limits: A Rebuttal to Daniel Callahan's Proposal to Limit Health Care for the Elderly*, ed. Robert L. Barry and Gerard V. Bradley (Urbana: University of Illinois Press, 1991), pp. 117–18, and by Harry R. Moody, "Allocation, Yes; Age-based Rationing, No," in *Too Old for Health Care? Controversies in Medicine, Law, Economics, and Ethics*, ed. Robert H. Binstock and Stephen G. Post (Baltimore, Md.: Johns Hopkins University Press, 1991), p. 181.

51. Moody, "Allocation, Yes; Age-based Rationing, No," pp. 181, 188, and 192.

52. Moody, "Allocation, Yes; Age-based Rationing, No," p. 201.

53. See Robert H. Binstock and Stephen G. Post, "Old Age and the Rationing of Health Care," in *Too Old for Health Care?*, pp. 1–12 and other articles throughout the book.

54. Office of Technology Assessment, *Life-Sustaining Technologies and the Elderly* (Washington, D.C.: U.S. GPO, 1986), pp. 19, 23.

55. Eveline M. Burns, "Policy Decisions Facing the United States in Financing and Organizing Health Care," *Public Health Reports* 81, 8 (August 1966), p. 683.

Chapter 10

1. See Martha Derthick, *Policymaking for Social Security* (Washington, D.C.: Brookings Institution, 1979).

2. See Martha Derthick, *Agency Under Stress* (Washington, D.C.: Brookings Institution, 1990).

3. See SSI Modernization Project Experts, *Supplemental Security Income Modernization Project: Final Report of the Experts* (Baltimore, Md.: Social Security Administration, August 1992).

4. For further discussion of these issues, see Eric R. Kingson, *The Diversity of the Baby Boom: Implications for Their Retirement Years* (Washington, D.C.: AARP Forecasting and Environmental Scanning Department, 1992).

5. See Robert J. Myers, "Is the Social Security Sky Falling Again?" *Contingencies* (July/August 1992), pp. 53–54.

6. Similar points are made by W. Andrew Achenbaum in *Social Security: Visions and Revisions* (New York: Cambridge University Press, 1987).

7. Committee on Economic Security, *Report of the Committee on Economic Security* (Washington, D.C., January 15, 1935), p. 3, in National Conference on Social Welfare, *50th Anniversary Edition: The Report of the Committee on Economic Security of 1935* (Washington, D.C.: National Conference on Social Welfare, 1985).

Selected Bibliography

Aaron, Henry J. *Economic Effects of Social Security*. Washington, D.C.: Bookings Institution, 1982.

Aaron, Henry J., Barry Bosworth, and Gary Burtless. *Can America Afford to Grow Old?* Washington, D.C.: Brookings Institution, 1989.

Abramowitz, Mimi. "Everyone Is on Welfare: 'The Role of Redistribution in Social Policy' Revisited." *Social Work* (November/December 1983), pp. 440–445.

Achenbaum, W. Andrew. *Social Security: Visions and Revisions*. New York: Cambridge University Press, 1986.

Advisory Council on Social Security. *Commitment to Change: Foundations for Reform*. Washington, D.C.: U.S. GPO, December 1991.

Advisory Council on Social Security. *The Financing and Delivery of Long-Term Care Services: A Review of Current Problems and Potential Reform Options*. Washington, D.C.: U.S. GPO, December 1991.

Advisory Council on Social Security. *Future Financial Resources of the Elderly: A View of Pensions, Savings, Social Security, and Earnings in the 21st Century*. Washington, D.C.: U.S. GPO, December 1991.

Advisory Council on Social Security. *Income Security and Health Care: Economic Implications 1991–2020*. Washington, D.C.: U.S. GPO, December 1991.

Advisory Council on Social Security. *A Message from the American Public: A Report of a National Survey on Health and Social Security by the Advisory Council on Social Security*. Washington, D.C.: U.S. GPO, December 1991.

Advisory Council on Social Security. *Social Security and the Future Financial Status of Women*. Washington, D.C.: U.S. GPO, December 1991.

Advisory Council on Social Security. *Social Security Financing and Benefits*. Washington, D.C.: U.S. GPO, 1980.

Altman, Nancy J., Alicia H. Munnell, and James M. Verdier. "Medicare Financing: The Government's Share." In *Renewing the Promise: Medicare and Its Reform*, ed. David Blumenthal, Mark Schlesinger, and Pamela Brown Drumheller. New York: Oxford University Press, 1988, pp. 160–75.

Altmeyer, Arthur. *The Formative Years of Social Security.* Madison: University of Wisconsin Press, 1966.

American Association of Retired Persons. *Conference Proceedings, Social Security Trust Funds: Issues for the 1990s and Beyond.* Washington, D.C.: Public Policy Institute, American Association of Retired Persons, February 23, 1989.

Andrews, Emily S., and Deborah Chollet. "Future Sources of Retirement Income: Whither the Baby Boom." In *Social Security and Private Pensions: Providing for Retirement in the Twenty-First Century,* ed. Susan M. Wachter. Lexington, Mass.: Lexington Books, 1988.

Ball, Robert M. "The Original Understanding on Social Security: Implications for Later Developments." In *Social Security: Beyond the Rhetoric of Crisis,* ed. Theodore R. Marmor and Jerry L. Mashaw. Princeton: Princeton University Press, 1988, pp. 17–39.

Ball, Robert M. "Social Security Across the Generations." In John R. Gist, *Social Security and the Economic Well-Being Across Generations.* Washington, D.C.: Public Policy Institute, American Association of Retired Persons, 1988.

Ball, Robert M. *Social Security: Today and Tomorrow.* New York: Columbia University Press, 1978.

Barry, Robert L., and Gerard V. Bradley. "Epilogue: Will the Real Daniel Callahan Stand Up?" In *Set No Limits: A Rebuttal to Daniel Callahan's Proposal to Limit Health Care for the Elderly,* ed. Robert L. Barry and Gerard V. Bradley. Urbana: University of Illinois Press, 1991.

Beedon, Laurel. "Women and Social Security: Challenges Facing the American System of Social Insurance." In *Issue Brief.* Washington, D.C.: Public Policy Institute, American Association of Retired Persons, February 1991.

Berkowitz, Edward D. *America's Welfare State: From Roosevelt to Reagan.* Baltimore, Md.: Johns Hopkins University Press, 1991.

Berkowitz, Edward D. *Disabled Policy: America's Programs for the Handicapped.* New York: Cambridge University Press, 1987.

Berkowitz, Edward D. "The First Advisory Council and the 1939 Amendments." In *Social Security After Fifty: Successes and Failures,* ed. Edward D. Berkowitz. Westport, Conn.: Greenwood Press, 1987, pp. 55–79.

Berkowitz, Edward. "The First Social Security Crisis." *Prologue* (Fall 1983): 132–49.

Berkowitz, Edward D., ed. *Social Security After Fifty: Successes and Failures.* Westport, Conn.: Greenwood Press, 1987.

Berkowitz, Edward D., and Kim McQuaid. *Creating the Welfare State: The Political Economy of Twentieth Century Reform.* Lawrence: University of Kansas Press, 1992.

Berkowitz, Monroe, and others. "An Economic Evaluation of the Beneficiary Rehabilitation Program." In *Alternatives in Rehabilitating the Handicapped—A Policy Analysis,* ed. Jeffrey Rubin. New York: Human Services Press, 1982.

Bernstein, Merton C., and Joan Brodshaug Bernstein. *Social Security: The System That Works.* New York: Basic Books, 1988.

Binstock, Robert H., and Stephen G. Post. "Old Age and the Rationing of Health Care." In *Too Old for Health Care? Controversies in Medicine, Law, Economics, and Ethics,* ed. Robert H. Binstock and Stephen G. Post. Baltimore, Md.: Johns Hopkins University Press, 1991, pp. 1–12.

Binstock, Robert H., and Ethel Shanus, eds. *Handbook of Aging and the Social Sciences.* New York: Van Nostrand Reinhold, 1985.

Binstock, Robert H., and Stephen G. Post, eds. *Too Old for Health Care? Controversies in Medicine, Law, Economics, and Ethics.* Baltimore, Md.: Johns Hopkins University Press, 1991.

Bixby, Ann Kallman. "Overview of Public Welfare Expenditures, Fiscal Year 1988." *Social Security Bulletin 51* (May 1991).

Blumenthal, David, Mark Schlesinger, and Pamela Brown Drumheller, eds. *Renewing the Promise: Medicare and Its Reform.* New York: Oxford University Press, 1988.

Board of Trustees, Federal Hospital Insurance Trust Fund. *1992 Annual Report of the Board of Trustees of the Federal Hospital Insurance Trust Fund.* Washington, D.C.: U.S. GPO, 1992.

Board of Trustees, Federal Old-Age and Survivors Insurance and Disability Insurance Trust Funds. *1992 Annual Report of the Federal Old-Age and Survivors Insurance and Disability Insurance Trust Funds.* Washington, D.C.: U.S. GPO, 1992.

Board of Trustees, Federal Supplementary Medical Insurance Trust Fund. *1992 Annual Report of the Board of Trustees of the Federal Supplementary Medical Insurance Trust Fund.* Washington, D.C.: U.S. GPO, 1992.

Bureau of the Census. *Measuring the Effect of Benefits and Taxes on Income and Poverty: 1986.* Washington, D.C.: U.S. GPO, 1988.

Burns, Eveline M. "Policy Decisions Facing the United States in Financing and Organizing Health Care." *Public Health Reports* 81, 8 (August 1966).

Burtless, Gary, and Robert A. Moffitt. "The Effect of Social Security Benefits on the Labor Supply of the Aged." In *Retirement and Economic Behavior*, ed. Henry J. Aaron and Gary Burtless. Washington, D.C.: Brookings Institution, 1984, pp. 135–71.

Callahan, Daniel. *Setting Limits: The Medical Goals in an Aging Society.* New York: Simon and Schuster, 1987.

Callahan, Daniel. *What Kind of Life: The Limits of Medical Progress.* New York, Simon and Schuster, 1990.

Cates, Jerry. *Insuring Inequality.* Ann Arbor: University of Michigan Press, 1983.

Chakravarty, Subrata N., and K. Weisman. "Consuming Our Children." *Forbes* (November 14, 1988).

Chen, Yung-Ping. "Economic Status of the Aging." In *Handbook of Aging and the Social Sciences*, ed. Robert H. Binstock and Ethel Shanus. New York: Van Nostrand Reinhold, 1985.

Clark, Robert L., and David L. Baumer. "Income Maintenance Policies." In *Handbook of Aging and the Social Sciences*, ed. Robert H. Binstock and Ethel Shanus. New York: Van Nostrand Reinhold, 1985.

Cohen, Wilbur J. *Retirement Policies Under Social Security.* Berkeley and Los Angeles: University of California Press, 1958.

Committee on Economic Security. *Social Security in America.* Washington, D.C.: U.S. GPO, 1937.

Committee on Old-Age Security. *The Townsend Crusade.* New York: Twentieth Century Fund, 1936.

Crown, William H. "Some Thoughts on Reformulating the Dependency Ratio." *The Gerontologist* 24 (April 1985): 166–71.

Derthick, Martha. *Agency Under Stress: The Social Security Administration in American Government.* Washington, D.C.: Brookings Institution, 1990.

Derthick, Martha. *Policymaking for Social Security.* Washington, D.C.: Brookings Institution, 1979.

DiNitto, Diana M. *Social Welfare: Politics and Public Policy.* Englewood Cliffs, N.J.: Prentice Hall, 1991.

Feldman, Jacob J. "Has Increased Longevity Increased Potential Worklife?" In *Proceedings of the Second Conference of the National Academy of Social Insurance.* Washington, D.C.: National Academy of Social Insurance, 1991.

Feldman, Jacob J. "Work Ability of the Aged Under Conditions of Improving Mortality." *Milbank Memorial Fund Quarterly/Health and Society* 61, 3 (1983): 430–44.

Ferrara, Peter J. "The Prospect of Real Reform." *Cato Journal* 3, 2 (Fall 1983): 609–21.

Fox, Daniel. *Health Policies, Health Politics.* Princeton: Princeton University Press, 1987.

Fries, James F. "The Workspan and the Compression of Morbidity." In *Proceedings of the Second Conference of the National Academy of Social Insurance.* Washington, D.C.: National Academy of Social Insurance, 1991, pp. 17–28.

Gist, John R. *Social Security and the Economic Well-Being Across Generations.* Washington, D.C.: Public Policy Institute, American Association of Retired Persons, 1988.

Graebner, William. *A History of Retirement: The Meaning and Function of an American Institution, 1885–1978.* New Haven, Conn.: Yale University Press, 1980.

Haber, William, and Wilbur J. Cohen, eds. *Readings in Social Security.* New York: Prentice Hall, 1948.

Harvard Medicare Project. "The Future of Medicare." In *Renewing the Promise: Medicare and Its Reform,* ed. David Blumenthal, Mark Schlesinger, and Pamela Brown Drumheller. New York: Oxford University Press, 1988, pp. 176–192.

Hoffman, Alice M., and Howard S. Hoffman. *The Cruikshank Chronicles: Anecdotes, Stories, and Memoirs of a New Deal Liberal.* Hamden, Conn.: Archon, 1989.

Hohaus, Reinhard A. "Equity, Adequacy, and Related Factors in Old Age Security." In *Social Security Programs, Problems and Policies,* ed. William Haber and Wilbur J. Cohen. Homewood, Ill.: Richard D. Irwin, Inc., 1960.

Kane, Robert L., and Rosalie A Kane. "Health Care for Older People: Organizational and Policy Issues." In *Handbook of Aging and the Social Sciences,* ed. Robert H. Binstock and Ethel S. Shanas. New York, N.Y.: Academic Press, 1990.

Katz, Michael. *In the Shadow of the Poorhouse: A Social History of Welfare in America.* New York: Basic Books, 1986.

Kingson, Eric R. *The Diversity of the Baby Boom: Implications for Their Retirement Years.* Washington, D.C.: AARP Forecasting and Environmental Scanning Department, 1992.

Kingson, Eric R. "Financing Social Security: Agenda-Setting and the Enactment of the 1983 Amendments to the Social Security Act." *Policy Studies Journal* 13 (September 1984): 131–56.

Kingson, Eric R. "The Greying of the Baby Boom in the United States: Framing the Policy Debate." *International Social Security Review* 44, nos. 1–2 (1991): 243.

Kingson, Eric R., Barbara A. Hirshorn, and John M. Cornman. *Ties That Bind: The Interdependence of Generations.* Cabin John, Md.: Seven Locks Press, 1986.

Koitz, David. "The Financial Outlook for Social Security and Medicare." *CRS Report for Congress* (November 26, 1991): 2.

Kotlikoff, Laurence J. *Generational Accounting: Knowing Who Pays, and When, for What We Spend.* New York: Free Press, 1992.

Kreps, Juanita M., and Joseph J. Spengler. "The Leisure Component of Economic Growth." In National Commission on Technology, Automation, and Economic Progress, *Technology and the Economy,* appendix 2. Washington, D.C.: U.S. GPO, 1966.

Lamm, Richard D. *Mega-Traumas: America at the Year 2000.* Boston: Houghton Mifflin, 1985.

Leonard, Jonathan. "Labor Supply Incentives and Disincentives for Disabled Persons." In *Disability and the Labor Market,* ed. Monroe Berkowitz and M. Anne Hill. Ithaca, N.Y.: Industrial and Labor Relations Press, 1986, pp. 64–94.

Leonard, Jonathan. "Social Security Disability Program and Labor Force Participation," Working Paper 392. National Bureau of Economic Research, Cambridge, Mass.

Levine, Daniel. *Poverty and Society: The Growth of the American Welfare State in International Comparison.* New Brunswick, N.J.: Rutgers University Press, 1989.

Light, Paul. *Artful Work: The Politics of Social Security Reform.* New York: Random House, 1985.

Longman, Phillip. *Born to Pay: The New Politics of Aging in America.* Boston: Houghton Mifflin, 1987.

Longman, Phillip. "Justice Between Generations." *Atlantic Monthly* 256 (1985): 73–81.

Lubove, Roy. *Struggle for Social Security.* Cambridge, Mass.: Harvard University Press, 1968.

Marmor, Theodore R., Jerry L. Mashaw, and Philip L. Harvey. *America's Misunderstood Welfare State: Persistent Myths, Enduring Realities.* New York: Basic Books, 1990.

Moody, Harry R. "Allocation, Yes; Age-based Rationing, No." In *Too Old for Health Care? Controversies in Medicine, Law, Economics, and Ethics,* ed. Robert H. Binstock and Stephen G. Post. Baltimore, Md.: Johns Hopkins University Press, 1991.

Munell, Alicia H. *The Future of Social Security.* Washington, D.C.: Brookings Institution, 1977.

Myers, Robert J. "Income of Social Security Beneficiaries as Affected by Earnings Test and Income Taxes on Benefits." *Journal of Risk and Insurance* (June 1985).

Myers, Robert J. *Social Security.* Philadelphia: University of Pennsylvania Press, 1991.

Myers, Robert J. *Social Security,* 3rd ed. Homewood, Ill.: Richard D. Irwin, Inc., 1985.

National Academy of Social Insurance. *The Social Security Benefit Notch: A Study.* Washington, D.C.: National Academy of Social Insurance, November 1988.

National Conference on Social Welfare. *50th Anniversary Edition: The Report of the Committee on Economic Security of 1935.* Washington, D.C.: National Conference on Social Welfare, 1985.

Nelson, Daniel. *Unemployment Insurance: The American Experience, 1915–1935.* Madison: University of Wisconsin Press, 1969.

O'Grady-LeShane, Regina. Testimony before the Subcommittee on Retirement Income and Employment, May 15, 1992, U.S. House Committee on Aging.

Palmer, John L. "Financing Health Care and Retirement for the Aged." In Employee Benefit Research Institute, *Business, Work, and Benefits: Adjusting to Change.* Washington, D.C.: Employee Benefit Research Institute, 1989.

Patterson, James T. *America's Struggle Against Poverty.* Cambridge, Mass.: Harvard University Press, 1981.

Petersen, Peter G., and Neil Howe. *On Borrowed Time.* San Francisco: Institute for Contemporary Studies, 1989.

Poen, Monte M. *Harry S Truman Versus the Medical Lobby: The Genesis of Medicare.* Columbia: University of Missouri Press, 1979.

Quadagno, Jill S. *The Transformation of Old Age Security: Class and Politics in the American Welfare State.* Chicago: University of Chicago Press, 1968.

Quinn, Joseph F. "The Economic Status of the Elderly: Beware of the Mean." *The Review of Income and Wealth* 33, 1 (March 1987): 63–82.

Rivlin, Alice M., and Joshua M. Weiner, with Raymond J. Hanley and Denise A. Spence. *Caring for the Disabled Elderly: Who Will Pay?* Washington, D.C.: Brookings Institution, 1988.

Robertson, A. Haeworth. *The Coming Revolution in Social Security.* Reston, Va.: Reston Publishing Company, 1981.

Robertson, A. Haeworth. *Social Security: What Every Taxpayer Should Know.* Washington, D.C.: Retirement Policy Institute, 1992.

Rubin, Jeffrey, ed. *Alternatives in Rehabilitating the Handicapped—A Policy Analysis.* New York: Human Services Press, 1982.

Sammartino, Frank J. "The Effect of Health on Retirement." *Social Security Bulletin* 50, 2 (February 1987).

Schlesinger, Mark, and Terrie Wetle. "Medicare's Coverage of Health Services." In *Renewing the Promise: Medicare and Its Reform,* ed. David Blumenthal, Mark Schlesinger, and Pamela Brown Drumheller. New York: Oxford University Press, 1988, pp. 58–89.

Schulz, James H. *The Economics of Aging.* Westport, Conn.: Auburn House, 1992.

Social Security Administration. "Social Security Programs in the United States, 1987." *Social Security Bulletin* 50, 4 (April 1987).

SSI Modernization Project Experts. *Supplemental Security Income Modernization Project: Final Report of the Experts.* Baltimore, Md.: Social Security Administration, August 1992.

Starr, Paul. *The Social Transformation of American Medicine.* New York: Basic Books, 1962.

Stone, Deborah. *The Disabled State.* Philadelphia: Temple University Press, 1984.

Thompson, Lawrence H. "The Social Security Reform Debate." *Journal of Economic Literature* 21 (December 1983).

Titmuss, Richard M. *Essays on the Welfare State.* Boston: Beacon Press, 1969.

U.S. House of Representatives, Committee on Ways and Means. *Background Material and Data on Programs Within the Jurisdiction of the Committee on Ways and Means.* Washington, D.C.: U.S. GPO, 1992.

U.S. House of Representatives, Committee on Ways and Means. *Retirement Income for an Aging Society.* Washington, D.C.: U.S. GPO, 1987.

U.S. Senate, Special Committee on Aging, in conjunction with the American Association of Retired Persons, the Federal Council on Aging, and the U.S. Administration on Aging. *Aging America: Trends and Projections: 1991 Edition.* Washington, D.C.: U.S. GPO, 1991.

Wachter, Susan M., ed. *Social Security and Private Pensions: Providing for Retirement in the Twenty-First Century.* Lexington, Mass.: Lexington Books, 1988.

Weir, Margaret, Ann Shola Orloff, and Theda Skocpol, eds. *The Politics of Social Policy in the United States.* Princeton: Princeton University Press, 1988.

Wickenden, Elizabeth. "Comments on Proposed Revised Policy Declaration by the United States Chamber of Commerce on Social Security for the Aged." December 9, 1952, Cohen Papers, Box 51, Wisconsin State Historical Society, Madison.

Witte, Edwin E. *The Development of the Social Security Act.* Madison: University of Wisconsin Press, 1962.

Index

Aaron, Henry, 1, 110, 131
Advisory Committee on Social Security, 157, 158, 160, 164
Advisory Council on Social Security, 125
AFL-CIO, 45, 50
Agency for Health Care Policy and Research, 152
AIDS, 132
Aid to Families with Dependent Children (AFDC), 14–15, 82
Altmeyer, Arthur, 30, 38, 39
American Association of Retired Persons (AARP), 118, 157
American Medical Association, 44
Americans with Disabilities Act (ADA), 147–48, 149, 176
Andrews, Emily, 80

baby boom generation: diversity among, 176–77; fertility rates and, 102; financial risks for, 177; health care costs and, 158; history of Social Security and, 9; Hospital Insurance funding and, 166; notch babies and, 128; pay-as-you-go financing and, 109; retirement of, 50, 80, 87, 104, 106; Social Security surplus and, 50, 51; understanding Social Security and, 2

Baker, James, 50
Ball, Robert, 1, 4, 14, 23–24, 50, 80, 88, 131
Barkley, Alben, 36, 37
Beck, Robert, 50
Beedon, Laurel, 123–24
Beneficiary Rehabilitation Program (BRP), 146
Bentsen, Lloyd, 148
Bernstein, Joan, 131
Bernstein, Merton C., 131
Bismark, Otto von, 28
Blue Cross, 44, 46
Bosworth, Barry, 110
Bradley, Bill, 1
Brown, J. Douglas, 23
Burkhauser, Richard, 149
Burns, Eveline, 170
Burtless, Gary, 110
Bush administration, 148

Califano, Joseph, 138
California, 65
Callahan, Daniel, 169
Canada, 169
capitalism, 25
Carter, Jimmy, 49
Census Bureau, 2, 102
Chamber of Commerce, 42–43
children: cost of raising, 16; disability

About the Authors

ERIC R. KINGSON is Associate Professor in the Graduate School of Social Work at Boston College. He earlier taught at the University of Maryland at Baltimore. He was an adviser to the 1983 National Commission on Social Security Reform. Kingson currently serves on the editorial board of *The Gerontologist* and as a member of the board of the National Academy of Social Insurance. He is the author or co-author of *The Ties That Bind: The Interdependence of Generations* and *The Diversity of the Baby Boom Generation: Implications for Their Retirement Years.*

EDWARD D. BERKOWITZ is Professor of History and Public Policy and Chairman of the History Department at George Washington University. He has served as the Robert Wood Johnson Faculty Fellow in Health Care Finance at the Johns Hopkins Medical Institutions in 1987 and as the Visiting Scholar at the National Academy of Social Insurance in 1988. He serves on the editorial boards of the *Journal of Policy History* and the *Journal of Disability Policy Studies.* Dr. Berkowitz is author or co-author of *America's Welfare State: From Roosevelt to Reagan* (1991) and *Creating the Welfare State: The Political Economy of Twentieth Century Reform* (Praeger, 1988, 2nd ed., with Kim McQuaid). He is also editor of *Social Security after Fifty* (Greenwood Press, 1987).